Lecture Notes
in Business Information Processing   520

Series Editors

Wil van der Aalst⊙, *RWTH Aachen University, Aachen, Germany*
Sudha Ram⊙, *University of Arizona, Tucson, AZ, USA*
Michael Rosemann⊙, *Queensland University of Technology, Brisbane, QLD, Australia*
Clemens Szyperski, *Microsoft Research, Redmond, WA, USA*
Giancarlo Guizzardi⊙, *University of Twente, Enschede, The Netherlands*

LNBIP reports state-of-the-art results in areas related to business information systems and industrial application software development – timely, at a high level, and in both printed and electronic form.

The type of material published includes

- Proceedings (published in time for the respective event)
- Postproceedings (consisting of thoroughly revised and/or extended final papers)
- Other edited monographs (such as, for example, project reports or invited volumes)
- Tutorials (coherently integrated collections of lectures given at advanced courses, seminars, schools, etc.)
- Award-winning or exceptional theses

LNBIP is abstracted/indexed in DBLP, EI and Scopus. LNBIP volumes are also submitted for the inclusion in ISI Proceedings.

Shareeful Islam · Arnon Sturm
Editors

Intelligent
Information Systems

CAiSE Forum 2024
Limassol, Cyprus, June 3–7, 2024
Proceedings

Editors
Shareeful Islam Ⓘ
Anglia Ruskin University
Cambridge, UK

Arnon Sturm Ⓘ
Ben-Gurion University of the Negev
Beer-Sheva, Israel

ISSN 1865-1348   ISSN 1865-1356 (electronic)
Lecture Notes in Business Information Processing
ISBN 978-3-031-60999-2   ISBN 978-3-031-61000-4 (eBook)
https://doi.org/10.1007/978-3-031-61000-4

This Springer imprint is published by the registered company Springer Nature Switzerland AG
The registered company address is: Gewerbestrasse 11, 6330 Cham, Switzerland

If disposing of this product, please recycle the paper.

Preface

The CAiSE conference series provides a platform for exchanging experiences, preliminary research results, and ideas between academia and industry in the field of information systems engineering. The conference serves as the annual worldwide meeting point for the community of information system engineers. The 36th edition of the CAiSE conference was held in Limassol, Cyprus, June 3–7, 2024. This conference edition puts a special emphasis on Information Systems in the Age of Artificial Intelligence.

The Forum session facilitates the interaction, discussion, and exchange of ideas among presenters and participants. Similar to other recent Forum editions, two types of submissions were considered in 2024:

- *Visionary papers* that present innovative research projects which are still at a relatively early stage and do not necessarily include a full-scale validation.
- *Demo papers* describe innovative tools and prototypes that implement the results of research efforts.

The Forum received 31 submissions. Eight submissions were invited to the Forum from the CAiSE main research track, had already undergone the peer review process of the conference, and were also reviewed by two of the Forum Program Committee (PC) members. The other submissions were reviewed by three PC members. The submissions that achieved the highest consensus on novelty and rigor were accepted for presentation at the Forum. Out of the 23 regular submissions, 11 papers were accepted (48%). Altogether, 18 papers were accepted at the CAiSE 2024 Forum, which included ten vision papers and eight tool demonstrations.

We want to thank all the contributors to the success of the CAiSE 2024 Forum: the authors, the PC members, the Program Chairs of the main conference, the proceedings chair, and the General Chairs for their support in coordinating the Forum organization.

June 2024

Shareeful Islam
Arnon Sturm

Organization

Chairs

Shareeful Islam   Anglia Ruskin University, UK
Arnon Sturm   Ben Gurion University of the Negev, Israel

Program Committee

Abel Armas Cervantes	University of Melbourne, Australia
Agnes Koschmider	University of Bayreuth, Germany
Andrea Marrella	Sapienza University of Rome, Italy
Anna Zamansky	University of Haifa, Israel
Beatriz Marín	Universidad Politécnica de Valencia, Spain
Ben Roelens	Open Universiteit, Belgium
Christophe Feltus	Luxembourg Institute of Science and Technology, Luxembourg
Chung Lawrence	University of Texas at Dallas, USA
Corentin Burnay	University of Namur, Belgium
Drazen Brdjanin	University of Banja Luka, Bosnia and Herzegovina
Elena Kornyshova	CNAM, France
Evangelia Kavakli	University of the Aegean, Greece
Francisca Pérez	Universidad San Jorge, Spain
Genaina Rodrigues	University of Brasilia, Brazil
Georg Grossmann	University of South Australia, Australia
Giuseppe Berio	Université de Bretagne Sud and IRISA UMR 6074, France
Hans Weigand	Tilburg University, The Netherlands
Hans-Georg	Fill University of Fribourg, Switzerland
Henrik Leopold	Kühne Logistics University, Germany
Irene Vanderfeesten	KU Leuven, Belgium
Jānis Grabis	Riga Technical University, Latvia
Jānis Kampars	RTU, Latvia
Jennifer Horkoff	Chalmers University of Technology, Sweden
Johannes De Smedt	KU Leuven, Belgium
Jose Ignacio Panach	Navarrete Universitat de València, Spain
Manuel Resinas	University of Seville, Spain

Manuel Wimmer	Johannes Kepler University Linz, Austria
Marite Kirikova	Riga Technical University, Latvia
Marne de Vries	University of Pretoria, South Africa
Martin Henkel	Stockholm University, Sweden
Mattia Salnitri	Politecnico di Milano, Italy
Maya Daneva	University of Twente, The Netherlands
Michael Fellmann	University of Rostock, Germany
Oscar Pastor	Universidad Politécnica de Valencia, Spain
Pierluigi Plebani	Politecnico di Milano, Italy
Raimundas Matulevicius	University of Tartu, Estonia
Sergio de Cesare	University of Westminster, UK
Sergio Guerreiro	INESC-ID/Instituto Superior Técnico, Portugal
Stefan Strecker	University of Hagen, Germany
Steven Alter	University of San Francisco, USA
Suphamit Chittayasothorn	King Mongkut's Institute of Technology Ladkrabang, Thailand
Tong Li	Beijing University of Technology, China
Yves Wautelet	Katholieke Universiteit Leuven, Belgium

Additional Reviewers

Peter Ahn
Arvid Lepsien
Fabian Muff
Marcel Bühlman
Philip Winkler
Sven Christ
Yorck Zisgen

Contents

Demo Papers

Vision Papers

Event Data and Process Model Forecasting

Wenjun Zhou(✉)🆔, Artem Polyvyanyy🆔, and James Bailey

The University of Melbourne, Melbourne, VIC 3010, Australia
{wenjun.zhou,artem.polyvyanyy,baileyj}@unimelb.edu.au

Abstract. Process mining studies ways to use event data generated by information systems to understand and improve the business processes of organizations. One of the core problems in process mining is *process discovery*. A process discovery algorithm takes event data as input and constructs a process model that describes the processes the system that generated the data can execute. The discovered model, hence, aims to represent both historical processes with traces in the data and the yet unseen processes of the system (*total generalization*). In this paper, we introduce *process forecasting* as an alternative approach to process discovery. First, given historical event data, the corresponding future event data is forecasted for a requested period in the future (*event data forecasting*). Then, a process model is constructed from the forecasted data to describe the processes the system is anticipated to execute during the target future period (*process model forecasting*). The benefits of this alternative approach are at least twofold. Firstly, it divides the problem into two fundamentally different sub-problems that can be studied and mastered separately. Secondly, a forecasted model that describes the processes of the system from a given period rather than in general (*tailored generalization*) can help organizations plan future operations and process improvement initiatives.

Keywords: Process mining · Process forecasting · Process model forecasting · Event log forecasting

1 Introduction

Through studying the event log generated by organization information systems, *process mining* bridges the gap between data science and process science. Process mining can be used to identify process bottlenecks and noncompliance during the process execution to improve the process using its visual representations, such as Directly-Follows Graphs (DFGs), Petri Nets, and Process Trees [2]. These models are abstractions of the processes they represent, where event logs collected through a software system are used as the input for generating the models. This approach of transforming event logs into *process models* is also known as *process discovery*, a sub-field of process mining.

With the business demand for prediction of the future and the prospering of machine learning in recent years, researchers have started a trend of

© The Author(s), under exclusive license to Springer Nature Switzerland AG 2024
S. Islam and A. Sturm (Eds.): CAiSE 2024, LNBIP 520, pp. 3–10, 2024.
https://doi.org/10.1007/978-3-031-61000-4_1

predicting process elements. For example, Cardoso, J., and Lenič, M. [5] proposed an approach to business activity prediction. A line of research has focused on predicting time aspects in processes [3]. Existing techniques, however, focus on predicting case-level process elements, with the prerequisite that a process case has executed a few activities [22]. Very little research has focused on forecasting future process models. With the concept being proposed by Poll et al. [13], one technique has been devised to forecast future process models [15, 16].

A discovered process model aims to describe both the historical traces of the system found in the input event log and the unseen traces of the system that generated the data. Such *total generalization* of the discovered models helps to understand the system that generated the data. However, it is less useful for business planning, as it does not relate the described traces to the period when the system is expected to execute them. If one can get in possession of a process model or an event log that accurately describes the processes the system will execute in a given period in the future, they can use this knowledge to plan future operations or prepare for upcoming process drifts. In this paper, we introduce *process forecasting* as an alternative approach to process discovery that, given historical data, aims to construct event data or process models that describe future processes, hence implementing such a tailored generalization over the input data. Specifically, this paper makes these contributions:

- Definitions of event data and process model forecasting problems;
- Comparison of existing techniques for forecasting of process elements;
- Discussion of the challenges posed by process forecasting.

The next section presents the terms and background knowledge that supports the understanding of the subsequent sections. Section 3 discusses related work and compares the differences between process forecasting and other prediction techniques proposed by the Business Process Management (BPM) community. Section 4 presents event data forecasting and process model forecasting and discusses ideas for tackling these problems. Finally, Sect. 5 concludes the paper.

2   Preliminaries

Event Logs. In process mining, an *event log*, or a *log*, is a collection of events executed and recorded during the execution of multiple instances, or cases, of a business process. At least three compulsory attributes are recorded for each event: *activity*, *case identifier* (case ID), and *timestamp* [2]. Other common event attributes include *cost*, *duration*, and *resource*. The availability of these additional attributes depends on a particular dataset. The *activity* attribute refers to the executed activity that triggered the event. The *timestamp* attribute records the time of the occurrence of the event. Finally, all activities from the same business process instance share the same *case ID* attribute. In this paper, we use *trace* to refer to the sequence of *activities* that stem from the events with the same *case ID* ordered by the timestamps of these events.

Process Model. A *business process model*, or a *process model*, is an abstraction of a running business [17]. There are different levels of abstraction for constructing a process model. Process models at different levels of abstraction serve different purposes, such as understanding the true process compared to the designed ideal process and improving the process. A common way to construct a true process model is by using event logs collected from the running business software systems.

Process Discovery. Process discovery is a problem in process mining that studies ways to construct process models from historical traces recorded in an event log of a system [1]. A good discovered model should describe the traces in the event log (*good recall*), not describe traces not in the event log (*good precision*), be as *simple* as possible, and capture the traces the system can generate but are not in the event log (*good generalization*) [4]. By describing process traces of the system beyond those in the event log, the constructed process model encodes possible future traces of the system.

Process Simulation. Process simulation, especially business process simulation, involves creating a model that mimics the operations of a hypothetical business and analyzing its properties [14]. Process simulation can be used for various purposes, such as optimizing resource allocation, identifying bottlenecks, testing alternative scenarios, and assessing the impact of process variations. It is often used to evaluate and compare alternative process redesign solutions.

Process Drift Detection. Process drift in the business process context is a change in the operations of the business process, including sudden, reoccurring, incremental, and gradual changes [23]. These changes are identified using dedicated detection algorithms that incorporate the ability to predict future operations given the current data or identify the point of drift as soon as possible while minimizing false positives.

Predictive Process Monitoring. Predictive Process Monitoring (PPM) [12] focuses on case- or micro-level predictions; examples of the main use cases include outcome prediction, next activity prediction, and process duration prediction. PPM, as in all the listed examples, often operates within the scope of a single process case.

Process Forecasting. Process Forecasting is an umbrella term for predictions of process elements [13]. In this paper, the term *process forecasting* is used to refer to the problem of forecasting macro-level process elements, such as process models and event logs.

3   Related Work

In this section, we summarize works in process mining that tackle prediction tasks and discuss the differences between these existing works and our work.

Specifically, we review works in process discovery, process simulation, process drift detection, PPM [12], and process forecasting.

A discovered model encodes the historical event log as well as possible while also being simple and general to reflect the possible future traces. The benefits of process discovery are speed and diversity. It usually takes a relatively short time to construct a model from a large event log. In addition, many configuration parameters can be explored to discover models of different complexities and accuracies. The downsides are mainly two. First, process discovery is not specifically designed for prediction tasks. Second, there is no specific guideline for discovery to anticipate the future; in other words, how much generalization in discovered models is good enough is unclear.

Like process discovery, process simulation can be used for different purposes. It is often used in what-if analysis. For example, one may use process simulation to analyze "What is the extra cost and time if activity B is introduced between activities A and C." Process simulation can predict and evaluate the impact of changes, improvements, or disruptions without affecting the actual system. Nevertheless, the simulation system may depend on the quality of the discovered models, and hence, it inherits the downsides of the discovery algorithms.

Process drifts refer to changes in the way a business process is executed or in the environment in which it operates, leading to deviations from the expected or desired behavior [23]. Process drift analysis can inform process improvement initiatives, regulatory compliance efforts, and strategic decision-making. Identifying and addressing business process drift can improve operational efficiency, compliance with regulations, and customer satisfaction. It can also enable organizations to proactively respond to changing market conditions and emerging risks. One can use process drift detection techniques to analyze frequent drift patterns and predict the next drifts by projecting historical drifts into the future.

The vast majority of PPM techniques take historical event logs as input and learn models that encode possible process traces/cases. Then, the newly lodged process case is monitored, and the prefix of that case observed so far is used to generate predictions for that particular case. The benefit of PPM is that the prediction for a particular case can often be made in real-time, and the newly observed data can be used immediately to update the learned models to improve future predictions. PPM techniques are often deployed before they get used to allow sufficient training before the techniques get productive. The state-of-the-art PPM techniques often demonstrate high prediction accuracy [3,11,19,20] and are grounded in conventional statistical and process analysis techniques, while several existing works also explore deep learning approaches [6–8,19]. As mentioned in Sect. 2, PPM operates within the micro-, or case-, level. In contrast, Process Forecasting, including process model forecasting and event log forecasting, focuses on the model-, or macro-, level predictions.

Process Forecasting studies changes in process models over time. The concept was proposed in 2018; since then, only a few techniques have been proposed. The work by De Smedt et. al. [15,16], explores how statistical methods over time series help in forecasting the directly-follows relationships of real-life business

Table 1. Comparison of process prediction/forecasting techniques.

Techniques	Use cases	Pros	Cons
Process Discovery	Discover process models from event data	Simple, diverse, often fast	Unclear generalization level for prediction
Process Simulation	Evaluate business redesigns	Cost-effective	Prediction is scenario-based
Process Drift Detection	Detect process changes	Optimized for change detection	Limited to change detection
Predictive Process Monitoring	Predict case-level process elements	Prediction accuracy, diverse techniques, supports prediction of multiple process elements	Limited to case-level predictions
Process Forecasting	Predict macro-level process elements	Specialized for prediction	Can be complex

processes. The lesson learned from this work is that no method works well across all datasets. However, the quality of achieved forecasts can enable proactive business process planning, including process drift and change predictions.

Table 1 summarizes the advantages and disadvantages of the above-discussed approaches.

4 Process Forecasting

This section presents two problems in process forecasting: *event log forecasting* and *process model forecasting*. Figure 1 schematically shows the contexts of the two problems. Given an event log, process model forecasting (Fig. 1a) constructs process models that describe the processes the system that generated the input log will execute in a given period in the future, while event log forecasting (Fig. 1b) generates future event logs of the system for the requested period. For instance, process model forecasting can proceed in two steps. First, a process model can be discovered, or a future event log can be forecasted from the input event log. Then, the obtained artifacts can be used to induce a forecasted process model. Event log forecasting, in turn, aims to generate future event logs directly from the input log. One can then use a forecasted event log to construct a forecasted model, for instance, using process discovery techniques.

4.1 Process Model Forecasting

Given an event log of a system and a time period, the *process model forecasting* problem consists of constructing a process model that accurately describes the processes the system will generate in the given period. A solution to the process model forecasting problem can involve a process discovery from the log and then the use of the discovered model constructs to anticipate the constructs in the forecasted model. For example, one can break the event log into multiple time windows, discover process models for the different windows, and then project the trend in observed model constructs into the future. Smedt et al. [15] demonstrated that this approach could result in useful forecasted models. Depending on the employed abstraction level, one can operationalize this approach using time series forecasting.

4.2   Event Log Forecasting

Given an event log and a period in the future, the *event log forecasting* problem studies ways to generate an accurate log that the system that generated the input log will generate in the given period. If one succeeds in forecasting the genuine future log, they can prepare to support the corresponding process, for instance, by planning sufficient resources to ensure successful operations. As indicated in Fig. 1b, this approach deals with historical event logs directly. Given a forecasted event log, one can then construct multiple models that aim to represent this log. To this end, one can employ different discovery techniques. Such discovered models, if faithfully describing the forecasted log, can be accepted as forecasted process models. Event logs contain more information than process models, as they constitute the raw data, while models can be seen as aggregations of the data. Finally, if there are missing entries in the historical event log, the forecasts can be available for those fields for better process analysis and planning.

Despite the advantages described above, event log forecasting is associated with challenges. To generate an accurate forecasted event log, sophisticated techniques such as deep learning may be required, which may be costly in terms of resources and time required for training. Yet, there has been no successful demonstration that deep learning is indeed helpful for event log forecasting. Additional challenges include a lack of appropriate measurements for the forecasted results, as it may be insufficient to compare the forecasted log to ground truth on a trace-by-trace basis. In addition, if a forecasted log is aggregated as a forecasted model for evaluation, the effect of the discovery algorithm on the forecasting results may be unknown.

Figure 2 illustrates a hypothetical process forecasting pipeline and its relationship to process discovery. The upper branch describes an event log forecasting approach grounded in a deep learning technique, while the bottom branch captures the conventional process discovery steps. A potential benefit of using deep learning techniques for event log forecasting is that the problem can fit into the current deep learning architectures, such as Seq2Seq [18] and transformer [21].

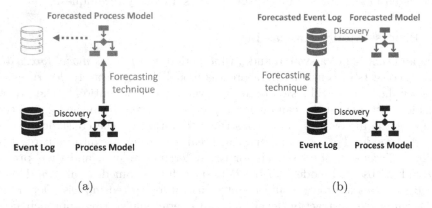

Fig. 1. Contexts of (a) process model forecasting and (b) event log forecasting.

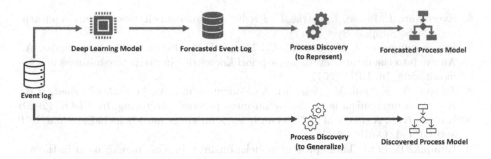

Fig. 2. Process forecasting and process discovery.

The success of Large Language Models (LLM) [9] has proved that the architecture is capable of handling sequence forecasting and generation tasks. Similar to LLM, the BPM community explores ways to build a Large Process Model (LPM) to solve forecasting problems [10]. However, such models are associated with challenges. Specifically, LLM suffers from long training time, and the training outcome is not guaranteed. In addition to that, it also consumes significant computing resources to build a model. Similar challenges will likely manifest if these models are used to solve the event log forecasting problem.

5 Conclusion

This paper presents and discusses problems of event data and process model forecasting, which are alternative approaches to process discovery studied in process mining that aim to construct artifacts that describe processes of the system for a specified period in the future. It is envisaged that accurate solutions to these problems will support organizations in planning their future operational processes. Several ideas for solving these new problems are discussed, pointing to deep learning models as a promising approach for tackling them.

References

1. van der Aalst, W.M.P.: Process discovery: capturing the invisible, pp. 28–41. IEEE Comput. Intell, Mag (2010)
2. van der Aalst, W.M.P.: Process Mining - Data science in action, Second Edition. Springer (2016) https://doi.org/10.1007/978-3-662-49851-4
3. van der Aalst, W.M.P., Schonenberg, M.H., Song, M.: Time prediction based on process mining. Inf. Syst. **36**(2), 450–475 (2011)
4. Buijs, J.C.A.M., van Dongen, B.F., van der Aalst, W.M.P.: Int. J. Cooperative Inf. Syst. Quality dimensions in process discovery: the importance of fitness, precision, generalization and simplicity **23**(01), 1440001 (2014)
5. Cardoso, J., Lenic, M.: Web process and workflow path mining using the multi-method approach. Int. J. Bus. Intell. Data Min **1**(3), 304–328 (2006)

6. Evermann, J., Rehse, J., Fettke, P.: Predicting process behaviour using deep learning. Decis, Support Syst (2017)
7. Francescomarino, C.D., Ghidini, C., Maggi, F.M., Petrucci, G., Yeshchenko, A.: An eye into the future: leveraging a-priori knowledge in predictive business process monitoring. In: BPM (2017)
8. Jalayer, A., Kahani, M., Beheshti, A., Pourmasoumi, A., Motahari-Nezhad, H.R.: Attention mechanism in predictive business process monitoring. In: EDOC (2020)
9. Kalyan, K.S.: A survey of GPT-3 family large language models including ChatGPT and GPT-4. CoRR (2023)
10. Kampik, T., et al.: Large process models: business process management in the age of generative AI. CoRR (2023)
11. Le, Mai, Gabrys, Bogdan, Nauck, Detlef: A hybrid model for business process event prediction. In: Bramer, Max, Petridis, Miltos (eds.) SGAI 2012, pp. 179–192. Springer, London (2012). https://doi.org/10.1007/978-1-4471-4739-8_13
12. Metzger, A., et al.: Comparing and combining predictive business process monitoring techniques. IEEE Trans. Syst. Man Cybern. Syst. **45**(2), 276–290 (2015)
13. Poll, R., Polyvyanyy, A., Rosemann, M., Röglinger, M., Rupprecht, L.: Process forecasting: towards proactive business process management, pp. 9–14. In: BPM (2018)
14. Robinson, W.N., Ding, Y.: A survey of customization support in agent-based business process simulation tools. ACM Trans. Model. Comput. Simul. **20**(3), 1–29 (2010)
15. Smedt, J.D., Yeshchenko, A., Polyvyanyy, A., Weerdt, J.D., Mendling, J.: Process model forecasting using time series analysis of event sequence data, pp. 47-61. Authors: In: ER (2021) Authors:In: ER (2021)
16. Smedt, J.D., Yeshchenko, A., Polyvyanyy, A., Weerdt, J.D., Mendling, J.: Process model forecasting and change exploration using time series analysis of event sequence data. Data Knowl. Eng. 145, 102145 (2023)
17. Smirnov, S., Reijers, H.A., Weske, M., Nugteren, T.: Business process model abstraction: a definition, catalog, and survey. Distrib. Parallel Databases. 30, 63–99 (2012)
18. Sutskever, I., Vinyals, O., Le, Q.V.: Sequence to sequence learning with neural networks. In: NIPS (2014)
19. Tax, N., Verenich, I., Rosa, M.L., Dumas, M.: Predictive business process monitoring with LSTM neural networks. In: CAiSE (2017)
20. Tschumitschew, K., Nauck, D.D., Klawonn, F.: A classification algorithm for process sequences based on markov chains and bayesian networks. In: KES (1) (2010)
21. Vaswani, A., et al.: Attention is all you need. In: NIPS (2017)
22. Verenich, I.: A general framework for predictive business process monitoring. In: CAiSE (Doctoral Consortium) (2016)
23. Yeshchenko, A., Ciccio, C.D., Mendling, J., Polyvyanyy, A.: Visual drift detection for event sequence data of business processes. IEEE Trans. Vis. Comput. Graph. **28**(8), 3050–3068 (2022)

Permission Analysis for Object-Centric Processes

Marius Breitmayer$^{(\boxtimes)}$ ⓘ, Lisa Arnold ⓘ, and Manfred Reichert ⓘ

Institute of Databases and Information Systems, Ulm University, Ulm, Germany
{marius.breitmayer,lisa.arnold,manfred.reichert}@uni-ulm.de

Abstract. The data-driven execution of object-centric processes in information systems requires powerful access control concepts that allow controlling, for example, which attributes of a business object a particular user (role) may read or write at a given point in time during process execution. In practice, it is crucial to be able to check whether the implementation of a fine-grained access control in an information system (i.e., the actual permissions) conforms with corporate requirements (e.g., compliance and security rules). If the execution of business processes is recorded in an event log, the actual access data can be compared with the specified permissions. Such a permission analysis includes the identification of both similarities and discrepancies between corporate requirements and actual implementation. This paper presents an approach for identifying, comparing, analyzing, evaluating, and classifying permissions in object-centric processes based on event logs.

Keywords: object-centric process mining · event log · process analysis · conformance checking · permission analysis · RBAC

1 Introduction

Many information systems (e.g., ERP systems) are object-centric business processes. The latter may be explicitly represented using process models or are implicitly implemented in the source code of the information system. In both cases, the efficient and secure execution of business processes requires effective access control mechanisms specifying which users (or user roles) may perform a particular action at a certain time during process execution [13]. In Role-based Access Control (RBAC) approaches, for example, permissions are granted to users based on their organizational roles [7]. The multitude of available roles, permissions, and process dependencies might result in gaps (i.e., forbidden access or unused permissions) between the required permissions and the actual access to object-centric processes as allowed by the respective information systems.

Due to continuous changes of roles and responsibilities and highly flexible business processes, the alignment of access control policies with the object-centric process implementation constitutes a non-trivial task. The effects of an unauthorized access might be severe, ranging from data breaches and privacy violations to compliance violations and operational disruptions.

© The Author(s), under exclusive license to Springer Nature Switzerland AG 2024
S. Islam and A. Sturm (Eds.): CAiSE 2024, LNBIP 520, pp. 11–19, 2024.
https://doi.org/10.1007/978-3-031-61000-4_2

To counter this problem, a systematic approach is required to evaluate pre-specified permissions (e.g., defined by a process model) with actual process execution (i.e., the access as reflected by an event log) to differentiate between correct permissions and deviations. Classifying deviations according to their relative frequency and severity is essential to realize suitable countermeasures.

The approach presented in this paper compares pre-specified permissions for object-centric processes with the actual access during process execution. In particular, it allows discovering deviations, deriving both the severity and relative frequency of each deviation, and classifying these deviations. This facilitates the discovery of differences as well as the prioritization of suitable countermeasures.

The paper is structured as follows: Sect. 2 introduces an object-centric process management system and its concepts for defining fine-grained permissions. Section 3 describes the approach for discovering, comparing, and prioritizing permissions. Section 4 evaluates the approach. In Sect. 5, we relate our work to existing approaches. Section 6 summarizes the paper and provides an outlook.

2 Backgrounds

2.1 PHILharmonicFlows

PHILharmonicFlows conceptualizes the way object-centric processes are commonly implemented in information systems. In particular, it allows specifying object-centric processes of different levels of granularity enriching the concept of data-driven process management with the concept of *objects*. Each object corresponds to a real-world business object that comprises data in terms of *attributes.*

An object lifecycle model describes the behavior of an object in terms of *states (e.g., Edit, Publish, Rate, and Rated* in Fig. 1) and *state transitions.* A state comprises *steps* (e.g., steps *Lecture, Name, Exam File, Max Points,* and *Solution* of state *Edit* in Fig. 1). The steps of a lifecycle process define which attributes are required before completing an object state.

At runtime, permissions are dynamically enabled based on the combination of state, role, and attribute [2]. An object-centric process involves multiple objects (e.g., *Submissions, Exercises*) with their corresponding lifecycles.

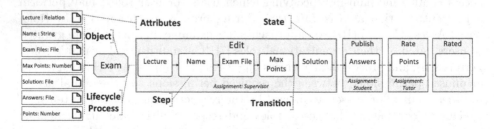

Fig. 1. (simplified) Lifecycle Process of Object Exam

2.2   Event Log

An object may be instantiated multiple times resulting in multiple *object instances* [3], which are executed concurrently. Their fine-grained execution is recorded in an event log containing data on a specific user, his role, the object type and instance, the object state, step or transition, the provided data value, and a timestamp (see Fig. 2). Row 5, for example, expresses that *User A* wrote attribute *Exam File* to object instance *Exam1* in state *Edit*.

1	User	Role	Object	Instance	State	Method	Parameter	Timestamp
2	User A	Supervisor	Exam	Exam1	Edit	InstatiateObject		1
3	User A	Supervisor	Exam	Exam1	Edit	GetForm		2
4	User A	Supervisor	Exam	Exam1	Edit	ChangeAttributeValue	Name	3
5	User A	Supervisor	Exam	Exam1	Edit	ChangeAttributeValue	Exam File	4
6	User A	Supervisor	Exam	Exam1	Edit	CommitTransition		5

Fig. 2. Event Log Example in CSV Format

2.3   Access Control in Object-Centric Processes

When implementing object-centric processes in information systems, fine-grained access control rules become necessary. To define which operations (e.g., to create object instances, to execute object states, to read, or to write object attributes, or to change object states) users may perform during process execution, various fine-grained permissions are granted to a role depending on the object, its state, and the object attribute or transition. For example, a write permission for role *Supervisor* on attribute *Exam File* of object *Exam* in State *Edit* allows users with role supervisor to provide the exam file accordingly.

In PHILharmonicFlows, fine-grained permissions are implemented according to the role-based access control (RBAC) principle (see Fig. 3) [2].

Users   Roles   Permissions   Operations   Objects

Fig. 3. Role-based Access Control Elements

3   Permission Comparison

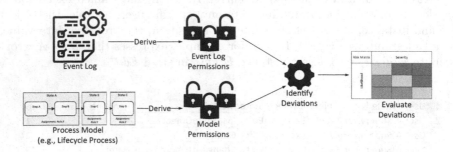

Fig. 4. Permission Comparison - General Idea

Figure. 4 depicts the general idea of the presented approach. On one hand, we consider the permissions as specified by any implementation artifact (i.e., process model). On the other, we consider the operations executed by users and recorded in an event log to derive required permissions respectively. We then compare pre-specified and actual permissions to obtain insights into the following scenarios:

1. A specified permission can be observed in the event log.
2. An access recorded in the event log is not covered by specified permissions.
3. A specified permission is not reflected by any event recorded in the log.

Our approach assesses deviations using a risk matrix [6]. Depending on the deviating permission (e.g., create object instance, execute state, read attribute, write attribute, or change state), its effects are derived and assessed regarding severity. For example, a non-authorized read access to an object might be less harmful than a non-authorized write access. We further consider the likelihood of deviations, allowing for a precise categorization and prioritization.

3.1   Permission Representation

In object-centric processes, permissions are defined with respect to objects, states, and attributes. We represent both specified permissions and the ones derived from the event log in terms of tables, enabling a smooth comparison. Columns of the table correspond to roles, rows to the combination of state and object attribute, and cells for the actual permission. Table 1 depicts an example representation for state *Publish* of object *Exam*, derived from the lifecycle process of object *Exam* (see Fig. 1). Table 2, in turn, was obtained by analyzing the event log for those events requiring permissions (see column *Method* in Fig. 2). For example, if a user with role *Supervisor* writes attribute *Exam File* in state *Edit* (see line 4 in Fig. 2), a write permission for this combination of object, state, and step must exist. In other words, we map the events recorded in the event log to the permissions required to execute them.

Table 1. Lifecycle Permissions of Object Exam in State Publish

Exam (Publish)	Supervisor	Student	Tutor
Step	State		
	Change	Execute	Execute
Lecture	Read	Read	Read
Name	Read	Read	Read
Exam File	Read	Read	Read
Answers	-	Write	-
Max Points	Read	Read	Read
Solution	Read	-	Read
Points	-	-	-

Table 2. Actual Access to Object Exam in State Publish according to Event Log

Exam (Publish)	Supervisor	Student	Tutor	Person
Step	State			
	Execute	Change	Execute	Execute
Lecture	-	Read	Read	-
Name	-	Read	Read	Read
Exam File	-	Write	Read	-
Answers	-	Write	-	-
Max Points	-	Read	Read	-
Solution	-	Read	Read	-
Points	-	-	-	-

3.2 Comparing Pre-specified with Actual Access

We compare the two representations (see Table 1 and Table 2) using an SQL full outer join syntax. The resulting *Null-values* enable the discovery of commonalities (i.e., no *Null-values* exist) and differences (i.e., *Null-values* exist) between the pre-specified permissions and the ones recorded in the event log. If *Null-values* exist in the event log part of the full outer join (see Table 3), we can identify permissions that have been specified, but are not used. If *Null-values* exist in the model part of the full outer join (see Table 4), we can identify access recorded for which no appropriate permissions exist.

Table 3. Comparison Tabs. 1 and 2: Permissions only in the model

Exam (Publish)	Supervisor	Student	Tutor
Step	State		
	Change	Execute	
Lecture	Read		
Name	Read		
Exam File	Read	Read	
Answers			
Max Points	Read		
Solution	Read		
Points			

Table 4. Comparison Tabs. 1 and 2: Permissions only in the event log

Exam (Publish)	Supervisor	Student	Tutor	Person
Step	State			
	Execute	Change		Execute
Lecture				
Name				Read
Exam File		Write		
Answers				
Max Points				
Solution		Read		
Points				

3.3 Permission Categories

Based on the comparison, we categorize each permission into one of three categories (see Table 5). First, there may be permissions that are specified in the model and for which the respective access can be observed in the event log (see

Both in Table. 5), and no action is required. Second, permissions may be specified, which cannot be observed in the event log (see Model-only in Table. 3). Permissions in this category might not be required and can be revoked. Third, permissions which are not specified may be observed in the event log (see Log-only in Table. 4). Log-only permissions constitute the most severe risk (i.e., violation) as they correspond to actions for which the required permission is missing.

Table 5. Permission Categories

Category	Both	Model-only	Log-only
Interpretation	Permission used	Permission not used	Permission not specified
Countermeasure	-	Revoke permission	Revoke / grant permission

3.4   Severity of Violations

To prioritize appropriate countermeasures, the severity of the respective violation needs to be assessed accordingly. Based on the respective category (i.e., model-only, or log-only) and the type of violated permission, we are able to identify the most severe deviations. In general, model-only permissions may be attributed a lower severity as no violation occurred. The severity of log-only permission violations should be assessed individually, based on domain knowledge and the respective context. The severity measures for log-only permissions described in Table. 6 only constitute a guideline in case no domain knowledge is available.

3.5   Risk Matrix Classification

We evaluate violated permissions using risk matrices which classify and prioritize risks by considering their likelihood in relation to their severity [6].

Table 6. Severity of Deviations based on violated Permission

Violated Permission	Model-only (Reason)	Log-only (Reason)
Instantiate Object	Low (not used)	Medium (can be undone)
Execute State	Low (not used)	Low (no change)
Read Attribute	Low (not used)	Low (no change)
Write Attribute	Low (not used)	High (change)
Change State	Low (not used)	Medium (can be undone)
New Role	Low (not used)	High (unclear purpose)

The likelihood is approximated by dividing the number of object instances for which the permission was violated by the total number of instances of that object in the event log. As a result, for each permission violation we obtain a value between 0 (i.e., no violation was identified) and 1 (i.e., each object instance faced the violation). Deriving the likelihood from the event log constitutes a major improvement compared to generic categories as estimated by domain experts.

The severity of a violation can be derived by analyzing the violated permissions (see Sect. 3.4). As the severity of a violation highly depends on the respective context, the guideline provided in Table. 6 may be adapted using domain knowledge or context information.

Figure 5 depicts the risk matrix derived for the running example. We adapted the severity of violations to better represent the context of the deviations and labeled the violations accordingly. The risk matrix can then be used to identify the most critical permission violations as well as to prioritize countermeasures.

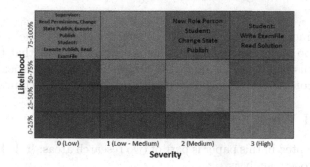

Fig. 5. Risk Matrix Running Example

4   Evaluation

To demonstrate the applicability of the approach for analyzing, assessing, and prioritizing the permissions of object-centric processes, we implemented a proof-of-concept prototype and applied it to an event log recorded from a large real-world deployment of PHILharmonicFlows in an e-learning scenario. Over one semester, the object-centric e-learning system was used for 133 users and ~40.000 event log entries (i.e., interactions) are recorded in the event log. The implementation, the event log, and generated risk matrices are publicly available[1].

Figure. 6 depicts the risk matrix for object *Submission*. A low severity, but high likelihood was observed for the *Execution* permission of role *Student* in states *Submit* and *Rated*, its *Change* permission in state *Submit,* and the *Execution* permission of role *Supervisor* in state *Publish*. Despite their frequent occurrence, these violations have a low severity, as read accesses to the attributes are permitted to role *Student* in both states in the process model. Due to the high likelihood, granting the permissions to the roles should be considered.

---

[1] https://cloudstore.uni-ulm.de/s/dBpJE2kqNGpqYFk.

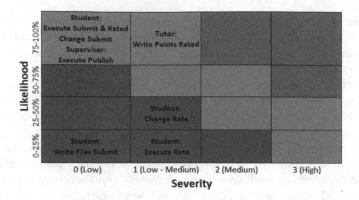

Fig. 6. Risk Matrix Object Submission

Despite a more severe consequence for some violations, the overall evaluation revealed no major risks. This real-life scenario indicates that the approach presented in this paper can be applied to large real-world scenarios and provide valid results, concrete recommendation, and prioritization of countermeasures.

5   Related Work

The work presented in this paper is part of two research areas: (role-based) access control and process analysis.

Role-based access control has been applied to a variety of scenarios, e.g., NoSQL databases [8] or process-aware information systems [10], and many RBAC variants (e.g., object-specific [11], or task-based [12]) exist.

In the context of process-aware information systems, role-based access control constitutes the most frequently adopted model to control access [10], and analysis approaches exist. The approach in [5] derives Linear Temporal Logic (LTL) statements from process-related models. These statements are checked against traces recorded in the event log. In [1], safety requirements are specified and verified by converting them to LTL expressions. [9] presents an approach for validating conformance between RBAC access control policies and corresponding implementations using an LTL transformation.

In [14], audit trails are used to identify anomalous process executions using specific workflow nets. An automated approach for deducing access control policies from event logs is introduced in [4]. The approach is capable of identifying unused and prohibited permissions.

In contrast, we represent permissions from object-centric processes as tables and prioritize deviations and countermeasures using risk matrices.

6   Summary and Outlook

This paper presented an approach to analyze permissions using event logs. Comparing specified permissions with the actual access recorded in the event log, permissions are categorized enabling the identification of permissions executed according to their specification, non-authorized access, and permissions that have not been used. Based on likelihood and severity, violated permissions are classified into risk matrices to prioritizing corresponding countermeasures. The event log is used to derive the likelihood, and the combination of deviation type (i.e., model-only, or log-only) and violated permission specifies the severity of a deviation. We evaluated the approach using a large real-world e-learning deployment.

In future work, we plan to apply the approach in additional scenarios which requires deriving permissions from other specifications such as ERP systems.

References

1. Ahmed, T., Tripathi, A.R.: Static verification of security requirements in role based CSCW systems. In: SACMAT, pp. 196–203. ACM, New York, USA (2003)
2. Andrews, K., Steinau, S., Reichert, M.: Enabling fine-grained access control in flexible distributed object-aware process management systems. In: IEEE 21st International Enterprise Distributed Object Computing Conference, pp. 143–152 (2017)
3. Andrews, K., Steinau, S., Reichert, M.: Enabling runtime flexibility in data-centric and data-driven process execution engines. Inf. Syst. **101** 101447 (2021)
4. Baumgrass, A.: Deriving current state RBAC models from event logs. In: 2011 Sixth ARES, pp. 667 – 672. IEEE Computer Society Press (2011)
5. Baumgrass, A., Baier, T., Mendling, J., Strembeck, M.: Conformance Checking of RBAC Policies in Process-aware Information Systems. In: Daniel, F., Barkaoui, K., Dustdar, S. (eds.) BPM 2011. LNBIP, vol. 100, pp. 435–446. Springer, Heidelberg (2012). https://doi.org/10.1007/978-3-642-28115-0_41
6. Duijm, N.J.: Recommendations on the use and design of risk matrices. Saf. Sci. **76**, 21–31 (2015)
7. Ferraiolo, D., Cugini, J., Kuhn, D.R.: Role-based access control (RBAC): features and motivations. In: Proceedings of 11th ACSAC, pp. 241–48 (1995)
8. Gupta, E., Sural, S., Vaidya, J., Atluri, V.: Enabling attribute-based access control in NoSQL databases. IEEE TETC **11**(1), 208–223 (2023)
9. Hansen, F., Oleshchuk, V.: Conformance checking of RBAC policy and its implementation. In: Deng, R.H., Bao, F., Pang, H.H., Zhou, J. (eds.) ISPEC 2005. LNCS, vol. 3439, pp. 144–155. Springer, Heidelberg (2005). https://doi.org/10.1007/978-3-540-31979-5_13
10. Leitner, M., Rinderle-Ma, S.: A systematic review on security in process-aware information systems - constitution, challenges, and future directions. Inf. Softw. Technol. **56**(3), 273–293 (2014)
11. Mundbrod, N., Reichert, M.: Object-specific role-based access control. Int. J. Cooperative Inf. Syst. **28**, 1950003:1–1950003:30 (2019)
12. Oh, S., Park, S.: Task-role-based access control model. Inf. Syst. **28**(6), 533–562 (2003)
13. Steinau, S., Marrella, A., Andrews, K., Leotta, F., Mecella, M., Reichert, M.: DALEC: a framework for the systematic evaluation of data-centric approaches to process management software. Softw. Syst. Model. **18**(4), 2679–2716 (2019)
14. van der Aalst, W., de Medeiros, A.: Process mining and security: detecting anomalous process executions and checking process conformance. Electron. Notes Theor. Comput. Sci. **121**, 3–21 (2005)

Incorporating Behavioral Recommendations Mined from Event Logs into AI Planning

Gyunam Park[1]([⊠])(iD), Majid Rafiei[1](iD), Hayyan Helal[2](iD),
Gerhard Lakemeyer[2](iD), and Wil M. P. van der Aalst[1](iD)

[1] Process and Data Science Group, RWTH Aachen University, Aachen, Germany
gnpark@pads.rwth-aachen.de
[2] Knowledge-Based Systems Group, RWTH Aachen University, Aachen, Germany

Abstract. AI planning plays a crucial role in the design and optimization of business processes, providing optimal plans, i.e., sequence of activities, based on manually crafted or formally documented rules. When these plans are executed in business processes, the supporting information systems record a wealth of event data. Analyzing such event data facilitates understanding implicit patterns and recommendations that have the potential to refine planning strategies significantly. In this paper, we introduce a systematic approach to mining these recommendations from event data and integrating them into AI planning, thus creating plans that are informed by both the regulatory hard rules and the flexibility of soft recommendations.

Keywords: AI Planning · Automated Planning · Process Mining · Behavioral Recommendations

1 Introduction

AI planning has been an essential tool in designing operational processes across various domains, primarily using rules derived from process models, regulations, and domain-specific knowledge [13]. In the domain of logistics, for instance, Fox et al. [7] have shown how planning algorithms can help optimize delivery routes and schedules, maximizing efficiency. The growing relevance of AI planning in healthcare has also been underlined. For example, Myers et al. [14] showcased how planning can be employed to design patient-specific treatment pathways. In the educational domain, AI planning has emerged as a tool for curricula design, helping in the sequencing of courses, lesson plans, and learning modules to adapt to students' varying capabilities and needs [5].

In real-life scenarios, rules used in AI planning can be broadly categorized into two distinct types: *hard rules* and *soft rules*. The former are non-negotiable regulations or immutable prerequisites, while the latter are more flexible, often shaped by historical trends and past experiences. Taking curricular designs in

S. Islam and A. Sturm (Eds.): CAiSE 2024, LNBIP 520, pp. 20–28, 2024.
https://doi.org/10.1007/978-3-031-61000-4_3

the education sector as an illustrative example, having "Data Structures" as a mandatory prerequisite for "Advanced Data Structures" exemplifies a hard rule. At the same time, the observation that students who first engage with "Algorithms" tend to excel more in "Advanced Data Structures" exemplifies a soft rule.

In dynamically changing domains such as education, logistics, etc., the efficiency of planning mechanisms can be significantly improved by integrating hard rules with soft rules. Such a fusion not only accommodates the structured requirements of planning but also allows for adjustments based on evolving insights and emergent patterns.

In this paper, we introduce a novel, two-phase approach to augment AI planning through behavioral recommendations as soft rules. The first phase aims to extract behavioral recommendations from event data that record the execution of plans. Using the *Declare* framework [15], we define pattern templates encompassing various behavioral attributes like precedence, response, and others. Subsequently, pattern candidates are instantiated for each template. By classifying cases that either align with or deviate from these patterns, we can statistically test the significance of observed behavioral patterns. Subsequently, the patterns that successfully meet this evaluation are suggested, whereas the remaining patterns are disregarded.

In the second phase, we incorporate these behavioral recommendations into the AI planning paradigm. Here, recommendation-based AI planning, also known as preference elicitation AI planning [4,12] emerges as a key technique. Classical AI planning focuses primarily on finding a plan that satisfies a set of hard constraints or goals. In contrast, preference-based planning recognizes that in many real-world scenarios, not all goals are equally preferred, thus introducing a notion of soft constraints or preferences. Regulations, in our context, act as these non-negotiable, hard constraints — they set the boundaries within which any plan must operate. In contrast, the recommendations derived from behavioral patterns function as soft guidelines or preferences. They guide the planning process towards solutions that have historically been beneficial but do not strictly bind the plan.

The remainder of this paper is organized as follows. Section 2 presents related work. Section 3 lays the foundational concepts necessary for understanding our approach, covering event data, the Declare framework, and the principles of AI planning. Section 4 details our proposed method for mining behavioral recommendations from event data. We then, in Sect. 5, describe the integration of these recommendations into AI planning, elaborating how they inform the generation of optimal plans. Finally, Sect. 6 concludes this paper.

2   Related Work

Classical AI planning typically involves formalizing a problem using states, actions, and goals, and then using algorithms to find a sequence of actions (plan) that achieves the specified goals. One of the classical algorithms is the STRIPS (Stanford Research Institute Problem Solver) planning formalism [6].

Preference-based AI planning has found extensive use in generating personalized recommendations and plans. One example of this is demonstrated in [18], where the authors combine Hierarchical Task Networks (HTNs) with user preferences to generate preferred plans. They extend the Planning Domain Definition Language (PDDL3) to allow for the specification of preferences over HTN constructs. Another instance of this approach can be seen in the work by Li et al. [11], where a temporal HTN planner is proposed to handle temporal constraints with preferences. This planner employs Simple Temporal Networks with Preferences (STNP) to represent temporal preferences and extends operators and methods for expressing temporal preferences within planning domain knowledge. Finally, Bienvenu et al. [2] provides a similar approach to ours, where classical AI planning with a bounded plan length is enhanced by temporal preferences in LTL_f.

However, specifying preferences in advance can be challenging and time-consuming, as user preferences may be complex, unknown, or incomplete. Consequently, preference elicitation (recommendation-based) frameworks for automated planning have gained increased attention. In [12], a preference elicitation framework for automated planning is presented. This framework facilitates user interaction through a restricted set of uncomplicated comparative queries, allowing for subsequent learning of a preference relation predictor based on the user's feedback.

In the broader context of data-driven approaches for study planning, which is the specific focus area of our work as an application of our approach, a systematic literature review in [20] highlights the prevalence of both "knowledge-base" and "machine-learning-based" methods for generating rules and recommendations in education. Various techniques have been proposed, including sequential pattern mining [1], statistical methods [16], and advanced machine learning techniques [3,9,19].

In the specific context of using event data to extract rules and recommendations for study planning, [17] represents a recent and highly relevant work. In this study, the authors extract a wide range of features from event data collected by a campus management system. They then employ decision tree models trained on these features to discover goal-based recommendations for study planning.

3   Preliminaries

AI Planning. AI planning is a fundamental domain within artificial intelligence that focuses on the automatic generation of sequences of actions to achieve specific goals, given a description of the initial state and a set of possible actions. Core concepts of AI Planning include the following.

- *State* (*s*) represents the configuration of the world at a given time point.
- *Action* (*a*) refers to an operation capable of transitioning the world from one state to another. In this work, we consider actions in planning and activities in events as analogous concepts: actions are entities that are planned, and their corresponding executions are recorded as events.

- *Preconditions* (Pre(a)) describe a set of states, at which an action is executable.
- *Effects* (Eff(a)) are results from executing an action, altering the state.
- *Plan* (π): An ordered sequence of actions $a_0, ..., a_k$, where, beginning from an initial state s_0, a_0 is executable at s_0 and results in s_1, a_1 is executable at s_1 and results in s_2, and so on, such that, a goal state s_g results from applying a_k to s_{k-1}.

Imagine designing a computer science curriculum while ensuring hard rules, i.e., prerequisites, are met.

- A *state* might represent the completion status of the "Data Structures" course.
- An *action* could be taking a course, such as "Advanced Data Structures".
- A course like "Advanced Data Structures" would have the *precondition* that "Data Structures" is already completed.
- The *effects* of introducing and completing "Data Structures" would be equipping students for more advanced courses.
- A *plan* in this scenario is a sequence of courses ensuring the prerequisites.

Given these concepts, AI planning can be formally presented as:

Definition 1 (AI Planning). *Let $\mathcal{S}$ be the universe of all possible states and $\mathcal{A}$ the universe of all possible actions. A planning domain $D = (A, S)$, where $A \subseteq \mathcal{A}$ is a set of actions and $S \subseteq \mathcal{S}$ is a set of states. A planning problem within domain D is denoted as $P_D = (s_0, G)$ where $s_0 \in S$ is an initial state and $G \subseteq S$ is a set of potential goal states. The objective of AI planning is to discover a plan π corresponding to problem P_D in domain D. This plan, when executed from s_0, should lead to a state s' such that $s' \in G$.*

Event Logs. If the plans are executed in operational processes, the executions are recorded as *event logs*. We use event logs to mine behavioral recommendations. Each event refers to an action (i.e., activity) in the plan that has occurred. Additionally, these events can possess diverse attributes such as a timestamp, a particular person as the activity performer, and associated costs. Table 1 represents an event log in an E-learning context. The event log contains two cases: student1 and student2. The first row represents an event, e1, belonging to student1, which describes student1' finishing Data Structure course on 2023-02-01 with a grade of 1.3.

The Declare Framework. In this work, we mine behavioral recommendations from event logs. The mined behavioral recommendations are formally represented using temporal pattern templates in *Declare* [15], a declarative language designed for process modeling and analysis. *Declare* is equipped with a set of temporal pattern templates that have been inspired by a catalog of temporal logic patterns used in model checking for a variety of dynamic systems from different application domains. Each temporal pattern template represents a distinct

Table 1. An Example of Event Logs in an Educational Context

Case ID	Event ID	Activity	Timestamp	Course Grade
student1	e1	Data Structures (DS)	2023-02-01	1.3
student1	e2	Advanced Data Structures (ADS)	2023-06-15	2.0
student1	e3	Algorithms (A)	2023-07-20	1.7
student2	e4	Data Structures (DS)	2023-02-01	2.6
student2	e5	Advanced Data Structures (ADS)	2023-06-15	3.2
student2	e6	Algorithms (A)	2023-07-20	2.9

temporal relationship, and temporal patterns are derivations of these templates corresponding to specific activities.

For the complete set of pattern templates in Declare, we refer readers to [15]. Frequent pattern templates in Declare include:

- **Response:** Upon the occurrence of activity a_i, activity a_j must eventually occur, denoted as Response(a_i, a_j).
- **Precedence:** Activity a_j can occur only if activity a_i has occurred beforehand, denoted as Precedence(a_i, a_j).
- **Exclusive Choice:** If activity a_i occurs, activity a_j must not occur, and vice versa, denoted as ExclusiveChoice(a_i, a_j).

4   Phase 1: Mining Behavioral Recommendations

Figure 1 provides an overview of mining behavioral recommendations from event data. Using the temporal pattern templates of the Declare framework, such as *precedence*, *response*, etc., we instantiate temporal pattern candidates. For each pattern candidate, we conduct *LTL checking* on all the cases of a given event log and classify them based on their alignment or deviation from the pattern. Next, we conduct *statistical testing* to ascertain the significant difference between the satisfied cases and violated cases, i.e., the validity of the temporal pattern. Only patterns that show a significant difference between satisfied cases and violated cases are recommended; the rest are discarded.

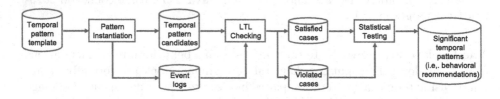

Fig. 1. Overview of Mining Behavioral Recommendations

Pattern Instantiation. First, the pattern instantiation function is designed to generate pattern candidates based on a template. For instance, given the *Precedence*
template and a set of activities, e.g., {Data Structures (DS), Advanced Data Structures (ADS), Algorithms (A)}, it would yield six pattern candidates such as {*Precedence*(DS, ADS), ...}.

LTL Checking. Next, the LTL (Linear Temporal Logic) checking function is essential for determining whether a specific event sequence (or trace) adheres to or violates a given pattern. For instance, for the student student1 in Table 1 with a course-taking sequence, i.e., $\langle$DS, ADS, A$\rangle$, this function could evaluate whether they followed the *Precedence*(DS, ADS) pattern.

The LTL checking function can be implemented in many ways [8,10]. Giannakopoulou and Lerda [8] translate LTL formulae into Büchi automata, which allows for the efficient checking of event logs against temporal properties. The automata-based checking leverages state exploration methods to systematically verify adherence or violation of LTL-specified patterns within event traces. For more detailed explanations of this technique and its application to the analysis of event logs, the reader is referred to [8].

Statistical Testing. Finally, the statistical testing function aims to assess the relative superiority of cases satisfying a specified pattern, i.e., $C_{satisfied}$, over those that violate it, i.e., $C_{violated}$. The distribution for each set, i.e., $C_{satisfied}$ and $C_{violated}$, is formed using a scoring function $score \in C_{satisfied} \cup C_{violated} \rightarrow \mathbb{R}$ that assigns values to individual cases based on particular characteristics or outcomes. This value could stem from various sources. One might consider the case's inherent attributes, such as the overall GPA of a student. Alternatively, one could focus on specific event attributes within a case, like a student's grade in the Advanced Data Structures course.

By comparing distributions derived from both sets of cases, the function determines the statistical significance of any observed differences. For instance, it can assess whether there is a significant difference in grades between students who adhere to and those who break from the *Precedence*(DS, ADS) pattern. Patterns securing a p-value below a predefined significance level (e.g., $p\_value < \alpha$) and satisfying the condition of the mean of $C_{satisfied}$ being at least a predefined difference level lower than $C_{violated}$ are recommended. Patterns that do not meet these criteria are considered not to have a significant or meaningful difference and are thus discarded.

5   Phase 2: Planning Based on Behavioral Recommendations

Figure 2 shows an overview of integrating behavioral recommendations into AI planning to generate optimal plans. Initially, conventional planning problems are taken and transformed by incorporating behavioral recommendations, which leads to the creation of *recommendation-based planning problems*. These enhancements include assigning weights to specific temporal patterns within the planning problems effectively prioritizing certain actions over others based on the provided recommendations. The process continues by merging these enhanced problems with defined planning domains, which include hard rules that the final plan must adhere to. Next, a recommendation-based AI planning system is employed to devise plans that are not only valid in terms of domain constraints but also optimized according to the incorporated recommendations. The final output is an optimal plan that maximizes the sum of the weights by respecting the recommended temporal patterns, ensuring that the plan is both feasible and closely aligned with the preferred behaviors identified by the recommendations.

Fig. 2. Overview of Planning Based on Behavioral Recommendations

Transformation. First, based on behavioral recommendations, we calibrate weights to align the planning domain with observed patterns. Action pairs resonating with these recommendations can be assigned higher weights (or lesser costs), elevating their likelihood in the optimal plan. For example, if data suggests that the `Algorithms` course preceding the `Advanced Data Structures` course leads to improved student performance in the `Advanced Data Structures` course, i.e., the precedence temporal pattern of this pair has a high weight, then a plan where `Algorithms` is planned before `Advanced Data Structures` is considered more optimal and recommended to students more than a plan where this does not hold.

Definition 2 (Recommendation-Based Planning Problem). *Let R be a set of siginificant temporal patterns, i.e., behavioral recommendations, mined from the the previous phase, and let $D = (A, S)$ be a planning domain. Let P_D be the set of all plans in this planning domain, a weight function $w_R : P_D \to \mathbb{R}^+$ maps plans to their weights and is calculated by:*

$$w_R(\pi) = \sum_{\substack{T(a,b) \in R \text{ s.t.} \\ T(a,b) \text{ holds in } \pi}} w_T(a, b)$$

where $w_T(a, b) \in [0, 1]$ is the weight of recommendation $T(a, b)$. For a planning problem $P_D = (s_0, G)$, a plan π is considered optimal if it is valid and maximizes the weight $w_R(\pi)$.

Recommendation-Based AI Planning. Solving a planning problem where actions can occur maximally once is in NP because the length of any valid plan is linear. Therefore, it can be modeled as an ILP feasibility problem. For any plan π where actions occur maximally once, there exists a unique tuple of relations $(e_\pi, <_\pi)$, where $e_\pi \subseteq A$, s.t. $a \in e_\pi$ iff. a occurs in π, and a total order $<_\pi \subset A^2$, s.t. $a <_\pi b$ iff. a occurs before b in π. An ILP feasibility problem searches for such tuples corresponding to valid plans.

Minimal length, minimal costs, or maximal rewards usually define optimality for such plans. In our setting, optimality is defined by the function $w_R(\pi)$. Thus, the ILP optimality problem:

$$\text{maximize } w_R(\pi) \text{ s.t. } \pi \text{ is a valid plan}$$

can solve any recommendation-based AI planning problem, where actions occur maximally once.

6   Conclusion

In this paper, we have presented a novel, two-phase approach that enhances traditional AI planning with behavioral recommendations derived from event data. By leveraging the Declare framework to define and instantiate pattern templates, we have successfully extracted meaningful behavioral patterns that serve as soft rules in the planning process. These soft rules complement the hard constraints typically used in AI planning, providing a more adaptable planning mechanism that reflects both the rigid requirements and the flexible preferences observed in real-world scenarios.

Acknowledgement. The authors gratefully acknowledge the financial support by the Federal Ministry of Education and Research (BMBF) for the joint project AIStudy-Buddy (grant no. 16DHBKI016).

References

1. Al-Twijri, M.I., Luna, J.M., Herrera, F., Ventura, S.: Course recommendation based on sequences: an evolutionary search of emerging sequential patterns. Cogn. Comput. **14**(4), 1474–1495 (2022)
2. Bienvenu, M., Fritz, C., McIlraith, S.A.: Planning Qual. temporal preferences. KR **6**, 134–144 (2006)
3. Britto, J., Prabhu, S., Gawali, A., Jadhav, Y.: A machine learning based approach for recommending courses at graduate level. In: ICSSIT, pp. 117–121 (2019)
4. Das, M., Odom, P., Islam, M.R., Doppa, J.R., Roth, D., Natarajan, S.: Preference-guided planning: an active elicitation approach. In: André, E., Koenig, S., Dastani, M., Sukthankar, G. (eds.) AAMAS 2018, pp. 1921–1923 (2018)
5. Desmarais, M.C., de Baker, R.S.J.: A review of recent advances in learner and skill modeling in intelligent learning environments. User Model. User Adapt. Interact. **22**(1–2), 9–38 (2012)

6. Fikes, R., Nilsson, N.J.: STRIPS: a new approach to the application of theorem proving to problem solving. Artif. Intell. **2**(3/4), 189–208 (1971)
7. Fox, M., Long, D., Magazzeni, D.: Explainable planning (2017)
8. Giannakopoulou, D., Lerda, F.: From states to transitions: improving translation of LTL formulae to Büchi automata. In: FORTE, pp. 308–326 (2002)
9. Jiang, W., Pardos, Z.A., Wei, Q.: Goal-based course recommendation. In: LAK, pp. 36–45 (2019)
10. de Leoni, M., Marrella, A.: Aligning real process executions and prescriptive process models through automated planning. Expert Syst. Appl. **82**, 162–183 (2017)
11. Li, M., Wang, H., Qi, C., Zhou, C.: Handling temporal constraints with preferences in HTN planning for emergency decision-making. J. Intell. Fuzzy Syst. **30**(4), 1881–1891 (2016)
12. Mantik, S., Li, M., Porteous, J.: A preference elicitation framework for automated planning. Expert Syst. Appl. **208**, 118014 (2022)
13. Marrella, A.: Automated planning for business process management. J. Data Semant. **8**(2), 79–98 (2019)
14. Myers, K.L., Jarvis, P., Tyson, M., Wolverton, M.: A mixed-initiative framework for robust plan sketching. In: Giunchiglia, E., Muscettola, N., Nau, D.S. (eds.) ICAPS, pp. 256–266 (2003)
15. Pesic, M., Schonenberg, H., van der Aalst, W.M.P.: DECLARE: full support for loosely-structured processes. In: EDOC, pp. 287–300 (2007)
16. Polyzou, A., Nikolakopoulos, A.N., Karypis, G.: Scholars walk: a Markov chain framework for course recommendation. In: Desmarais, M.C., Lynch, C.F., Merceron, A., Nkambou, R. (eds.) EDM (2019)
17. Rafiei, M., et al.: Extracting rules from event data for study planning. arXiv preprint arXiv:2310.02735 (2023)
18. Sohrabi, S., Baier, J.A., McIlraith, S.A.: HTN planning with preferences. In: Boutilier, C. (ed.) IJCAI, pp. 1790–1797 (2009)
19. Tan, J., Chang, L., Liu, T., Zhao, X.: Attentional autoencoder for course recommendation in MOOC with course relevance. In: CyberC, pp. 190–196 (2020)
20. Urdaneta-Ponte, M.C., Mendez-Zorrilla, A., Oleagordia-Ruiz, I.: Recommendation systems for education: systematic review. Electronics **10**(14), 1611 (2021)

Trustworthy Collaborative Business Intelligence Using Zero-Knowledge Proofs and Blockchains

Giovanni Quattrocchi(✉) and Pierluigi Plebani

Politecnico di Milano, Dipartimento di Elettronica, Informazione, Bioingegneria,
Milan, Italy
{giovanni.quattrocchi,pierluigi.plebani}@polimi.it

Abstract. In the era of data-driven decision-making, the ability to securely and reliably exchange analytical data among organizations (collaborative business intelligence) is becoming increasingly important. This paper envisions a novel framework for trustworthy data exchange, leveraging Zero-Knowledge Proofs (ZK-Proofs) to maintain data privacy and integrity, and the blockchain for reliable auditing. Our framework emphasizes enhancing business intelligence capabilities through non-operational analytics, particularly in the generation of aggregated insights for strategic decision-making among different organizations, without exposing the underlying raw data, thus preserving data sovereignty. We introduce a methodology to perform operations on data cubes using ZK-Proofs, allowing for the generation of more aggregated data cubes from initial raw data hypercubes. The framework exploits the Data-Fact Model to identify the available transformation paths on raw data.

Keywords: collaborative business intelligence · zero-knowledge proofs · data exchange · data warehouse · data sharing

1 Introduction

Collaborative business intelligence, that is, the integration of business intelligence across various organizations, plays a key role in exploiting collective insights and driving enhanced decision-making processes. By leveraging shared data and analytics, entities can uncover hidden opportunities, optimize operations, and foster innovation, ultimately leading to enhanced competitiveness and efficiency in the interconnected business landscape [2].

The pursuit of collaborative business intelligence brings to light a fundamental tension between data trustworthiness and sovereignty. On one hand, organizations seek to ensure the reliability and accuracy of shared data to make informed decisions. On the other hand, they must preserve control over their data, protecting its confidentiality and complying with regulatory requirements. Balancing these objectives is challenging, as increasing transparency to enhance

© The Author(s), under exclusive license to Springer Nature Switzerland AG 2024
S. Islam and A. Sturm (Eds.): CAiSE 2024, LNBIP 520, pp. 29–37, 2024.
https://doi.org/10.1007/978-3-031-61000-4_4

trustworthiness can inadvertently compromise data sovereignty, raising concerns about privacy, security, and competitive advantage [10].

The goal of this paper is to present an approach that combines Zero-Knowledge Proofs (ZK-Proofs) [5], a general purpose cryptographic protocol to verifying knowledge without revealing it, and blockchain to ensure data sovereignty and trustworthiness in sharing business intelligence information. Assuming the adoption of data-fact models to organize data for analytics, the ZK-Proofs are adopted to allow organizations to share the values of their relevant KPIs (Key Performance Indicators) without revealing the details of the data used to compute them. In this way, the sharing organization can maintain the full control on the internal data and, at the same time, the organizations with which the indicators are shared is sure that the indicators are trustworthy. In this context, a blockchain based platform is adopted to increase the level of trust by acting as a notarization element able to store claims which can be eventually verified by auditors in case of complaints.

The rest of the paper is structured as follows. Section 2 provides an overview of the related work, Sect. 3 describes our framework, and Sect. 4 concludes the paper.

2   Related Work

In recent times, especially within the European community, there has been a strong interest in the topic of data sharing. This interest largely stems from the goal of creating a Digital Single Market where companies and institutions can leverage platforms, models, and methods for sharing data. Indeed, with data now being considered an organizational asset, there is a growing emphasis on harnessing its value by sharing it with other organizations.

As highlighted in [7], the term "data sharing", given its generality, does not always convey all the aspects that need to be addressed for it to be realized. Therefore, it proposes a reference model that views data sharing as a process composed of five phases: preparation of a data set, data sharing agreement, data trading process planning, data exchange, and feedback. Data exchange, which is often confused with data sharing as a whole, actually represents the technical aspect that materializes the movement of data and must occur in compliance with the agreement established between the parties.

An additional, yet fundamental aspect in data sharing, is held by data agreement which revolves around the need to consider and mediate between the needs of those providing the data and those consuming it, and it could be summarized in two properties: data sovereignty [3] and data trustworthiness [9]. The former concerns the assurance that the data provided are as much as possible under the full control of those sharing it, whereas the latter is about ensuring that the acquired data is reliable in terms of quality. Only by considering the problem of data sharing from these two perspectives is it possible to overcome the barriers, especially organizational ones [4], that currently make it difficult to implement.

At the same time, it is also important to understand why data is exchanged. Is it to support operational processes or decision-making processes? In the former case, the granularity of the exchanged data will be very fine, and performance aspects will play an important role in defining the data sharing process. In the latter case, which is relevant in the context referred to in this work, it is crucial to ensure the correctness of the exchanged data. In this context, Collaborative Business Intelligence has been introduced as "where a company information assets are empowered thanks to cooperation and data sharing with other companies and organizations, so that the decision-making process is extended beyond the company boundaries" [8]. Here, three main approaches have been envisioned: (i) a centralized approach based on the existence of a single warehouse where all the analytics by the collaborating organizations are performed, (ii) a federated approach where a virtual integrated data warehouse is realized by distributing the analytics to the members of the federation, and (iii) a peer-to-peer approach where the global schema needed in case of federated approach is no longer required since object fusion and query reformulation techniques are adopted.

Building upon these foundations, this work aims to provide a solution that further increases the level of independence among various organizations. Indeed, in line with the principle of data sovereignty, each organization will make available the value of the KPIs, which will result from an agreement with those who will then use them. The user will then only need to request the data respecting the agreed-upon times and methods (e.g., format, type of call). Specifically, the work is based on the use of Zero Knowledge techniques coupled with the use of blockchain technologies. This will not only allow for the sharing of data but also ensure the truthfulness of the result without the need for the data provider to disclose the data that produced such a result.

Generally speaking, ZK-Proofs [5] are a cryptographic protocol that enables one party, the prover, to attest to the truth of a statement to another party, the verifier, without conveying any information beyond the veracity of the statement itself. In the context of data sharing, ZK-Proofs allow for validating computations over data (e.g., transformations, aggregations) without reveling the underlying data. In fact, by employing ZK-Proofs, an organization can conclusively prove, that specific operations have been correctly performed on an identifiable (e.g., using its hash) but unknown dataset by generating a cryptographic proof during the execution of the actual computation [1]. Such proof can used by the receiver of the operation output to verify the validity of the process.

Recently, notable work by Heiss et al. [6] has explored the use of ZK-Proofs in blockchain-based federated learning to enhance data sharing and computational integrity. Their approach leverages learning nodes as off-chain provers to submit ZK-Proofs, ensuring the computational correctness of learning parameters. This method offers a promising alternative to traditional incentive mechanisms, advancing the security and verifiability of blockchain-based federated learning systems.

3   Framework

In the pursuit of collaborative business intelligence, organizations often face the challenge of sharing valuable insights, such as KPIs, without compromising *data sovereignty*, that is the privacy and security of their underlying raw data. This challenge is particularly evident when dealing with data warehouses that aggregate vast amounts of sensitive information. On the other hand, the receiver of such data, typically another organization or department within the same organization, aims to be confident that the KPIs they are receiving are authentic and accurately reflect an actual transformation of valid raw data. This requirement creates a tension between preserving data sovereignty and ensuring the trustworthiness of shared insights.

Data sovereignty refers to the control and authority an organization has over its own data, particularly concerning privacy[1], compliance, and security. In the context of collaborative business intelligence, maintaining data sovereignty means ensuring that sensitive raw data remains confidential and is not exposed to unauthorized parties. However, traditional solutions to this challenge often fall short due to inherent trade-offs:

- *Sharing Raw Data to Prove Authenticity.* While sharing raw data with external parties would provide the most straightforward means of verifying the authenticity of derived KPIs, this approach directly contradicts the principle of data sovereignty. By exposing raw data, organizations risk compromising sensitive information, violating privacy regulations, and losing control over their proprietary data assets.
- *Simple KPIs Sharing.* Conversely, if an organization chooses only to share the KPIs without providing a means to verify their authenticity, it places a significant burden of trust on the data receiver. The receiver must trust that the KPIs have not been manipulated or falsified, which can be a significant concern in competitive or regulated environments where data accuracy is critical.

This dichotomy highlights the need for a solution that can bridge the gap between data sovereignty and data trustworthiness, enabling organizations to share actionable insights derived from their data while retaining full control over their raw datasets.

To this end, we propose a framework based on the integration of ZK-Proofs and blockchain. By allowing data providers to prove that their KPIs are derived from valid raw data without revealing the data itself, these technologies offer a way to maintain both data sovereignty and trustworthiness, fundamentally transforming the landscape of collaborative business intelligence. Figure 1 shows the overall approach that is detailed in the remaining of this section.

---

[1] It is worth noticing that, given the considered context, here personal data does not play any relevant role, thus the data sovereignty concerns the control over the business critical data.

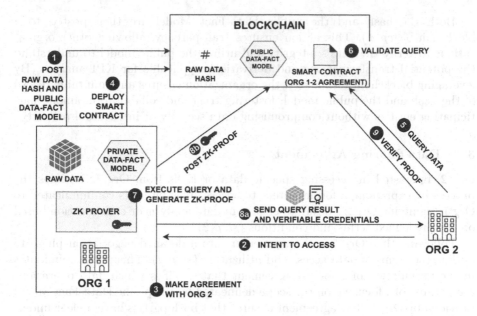

Fig. 1. The proposed framework.

3.1   Dataset Preparation

Consider a scenario in which an organization (Org 1 in the figure) seeks to share data with another organization (Org 2 in the figure) with the goal of enhancing business intelligence outcomes.

Org 1 holds raw data in the form of an hypercube managed by the in-house data warehouse. The associated Data-Fact Model serves as an abstract representation of the data structure and permissible operations on the data, such as aggregation or filtering, which are essential for deriving KPIs. However, the raw data and this Data-Fact Model, encompassing the full granularity and transformations of the raw data, are proprietary and sensitive, hence deemed private. Sharing them could inadvertently reveal underlying data patterns or business logic, threatening data sovereignty and the organization privacy and security.

To address this, Org 1 initiates the secure sharing process by computing a cryptographic hash of the raw data. This hash acts as a unique identifier, ensuring data integrity and enabling verification without revealing the data itself. The hash, inherently resistant to collisions and pre-image attacks, provides a secure fingerprint of the data.

Moreover, the organization crafts a public version of the Data-Fact Model. This sanitized model delineates a subset of operations and transformations that external parties can perform on the data, specifically tailored to derive the KPIs of interest. The public model is designed to provide necessary insights while safeguarding the raw data's confidentiality and the comprehensive transformations encapsulated in the private Data-Fact Model.

Both the hash and the public Data-Fact Model are then posted to a blockchain (*step 1*). This action ensures transparency, allowing other organizations to verify the data's integrity and utilize the public model to understand the potential transformations and derivations applicable for KPI analysis. By leveraging blockchain technology, the organization ensures an immutable record of the hash and the public model, fostering trust and collaboration among participating entities without compromising data security or intellectual property.

3.2 Data Sharing Agreement

Org 2, interested in accessing specific data or KPIs from Org 1, initiates the process by expressing a formal intent to access. This intent is communicated to Org 1, signifying Org 2's desire to engage in data analysis or collaboration based on the predefined terms and conditions (*step 2*).

Following this, Org 1 and Org 2 enter into a detailed negotiation phase to outline the terms of data access and utilization (*step 3*). This phase culminates in the formulation of a formal agreement that specifies which data operations are permissible, focusing on the scope delineated by the public Data-Fact Model provided by Org 1. The agreement ensures that both parties have a clear understanding of the data access boundaries, permissible transformations, and the intended use of the derived insights.

The agreed terms are then codified into a smart contract, which is deployed on the blockchain (*step 4*). This smart contract is intricately designed to regulate the data operations allowed within the boundaries set by the public Data-Fact Model. It incorporates mechanisms to access the Data-Fact Model stored on the blockchain, ensuring that all data operations initiated by Org 2 adhere to the agreed terms. Furthermore, the smart contract is endowed with the capability to verify ZK-Proofs, facilitating the validation of query results and data transformations without exposing the underlying raw data. The smart contract can reference the hash of the raw data, also stored on the blockchain, to validate the integrity and authenticity of the data being accessed and analyzed.

3.3 Query Execution

Org 2 encodes the desired operation, adhering to the constraints and capabilities defined in the public Data-Fact Model shared by Org 1. This operation is then packaged as an input and sent to the smart contract on the blockchain for validation (*step 5*). This step ensures that only permissible operations, as agreed upon in the smart contract, are executed on the data.

Upon receiving the request, the smart contract performs a validation process (*step 6*). It assesses the requested operation against the agreed-upon terms encapsulated within the contract and the public Data-Fact Model. The smart contract ensures that the operation is within the scope of allowed transformations and that it does not violate any data privacy or integrity rules set by Org 1. This automated validation by the smart contract serves to enforce the agreement's terms and to preserve the integrity of the data exchange.

Once the smart contract validates the operation, an event is emitted, notifying Org 1 of the approved request. Org 1 then initiates the execution of the requested transformation (*step 7*). This process is carried out through a dedicated Zero-Knowledge (ZK) circuit designed to perform the specific operation on the raw data. Importantly, the raw data remains undisclosed throughout this process, ensuring its confidentiality.

Alongside computing the result of the transformation, the ZK circuit also generates a ZK-Proof. This proof serves a dual purpose: it attests to the correct execution of the requested operation and confirms that the operation was performed on the raw data whose hash matches the one previously posted on the blockchain by Org 1. This ZK-Proof is crucial, as it allows Org 2 to verify the integrity and authenticity of the operation's result without exposing the underlying raw data.

3.4   Data Exchange

The ZK-Proof generated by Org 1 is then posted to the blockchain (*step 8a*). This action not only ensures the immutability and non-repudiation of the proof but also makes it publicly accessible for validation and auditing. The blockchain serves as a transparent ledger where all executed operations, verifiable through ZK-Proofs, are logged, providing a tamper-proof record of all data interactions.

The result of the transformation, a reduced hypercube of aggregated or transformed data, is transmitted to Org 2 (*step 8b*). Along with the result, Org 1 sends verifiable credentials. These credentials contain the transaction identifiers of both the original data operation request made by Org 2 and the transaction that recorded the corresponding ZK-Proof on the blockchain. This dual-reference mechanism ensures traceability and verifiability, linking the result directly to its provenance and the integrity of its computation.

Thanks to the received verifiable credentials, Org 2 engages the smart contract on the blockchain, specifically the ZK-Verifier function embedded within (*step 9*). This function allows Org 2 to validate the ZK-Proof against the stored hash of the raw data. The verification process confirms that the requested operation was indeed executed on the exact dataset represented by the hash on the blockchain, thereby ensuring data integrity and the validity of the transformation. This sophisticated interplay between ZK-Proofs, smart contracts, and blockchain technology ensures that Org 2 can confidently utilize the transformed data, knowing it is derived directly from Org 1's authentic raw data. Importantly, this entire process maintains the utmost data privacy, as the raw data itself is never exposed or transferred; only the proof of its correct transformation is shared. Moreover, the process upholds data integrity and verifiability, key components for trust in collaborative business environments.

In the event of disputes or verification needs by Org 2, an external auditor has the capability to i) access and trace the entire process on the blockchain, ensuring full traceability of the data interactions, and ii) validate that the published hash indeed corresponds to a real and authentic dataset. This level of oversight is made possible by the transparent and immutable nature of blockchain technology, which records each step of the process and the associated ZK-Proofs, ensuring that every operation can be audited and verified independently.

4 Conclusions

Collaborative business intelligence is key for leveraging collective insights across organizations, enhancing decision-making and operational efficiencies. However, in this distributed context many challenges exist such as the need for trust among parties and control over data. This paper investigated these issues and presents a framework based on ZK-Proofs and blockchain, that offers the means for data sharing across organizations upholding data sovereignty while ensuring the trustworthiness of shared insights.

Considering this work a first step which has the ambition of systematizing the elements necessary to respond to the need for data sharing in the business intelligence scenario, in this phase only a theoretical approach, albeit reasonable, was considered to validate the approach. For this reason, future work will focus on the development of a proof of concept and its deployment in a real-world use case to demonstrate the feasibility and practical applicability of the framework in addressing the challenges of collaborative business intelligence.

Acknowledgement. This work was partially funded by project MICS (3A-ITALY) CUP D43C22003120001 (grant PE00000004).

References

1. Ben-Sasson, E., Chiesa, A., Genkin, D., Tromer, E., Virza, M.: SNARKs for C: verifying program executions succinctly and in zero knowledge. In: Canetti, R., Garay, J.A. (eds.) Advances in Cryptology – CRYPTO 2013, pp. 90–108. Springer, Heidelberg (2013). https://doi.org/10.1007/978-3-642-40084-1_6
2. Elbashir, M.Z., et al.: Enhancing the business value of business intelligence: the role of shared knowledge and assimilation. J. Inf. Syst. **27**(2), 87–105 (2013)
3. Geisler, S., et al.: Knowledge-driven data ecosystems toward data transparency. J. Data Inf. Quality **14**(1), 1–12 (2021)
4. Gelhaar, J., Gürpinar, T., Henke, M., Otto, B.: Towards a taxonomy of incentive mechanisms for data sharing in data ecosystems. In: Pacific Asia Conference on Information Systems, p. 121 (2021)
5. Goldwasser, S., Micali, S., Rackoff, C.: The knowledge complexity of interactive proof-systems. In: Providing Sound Foundations for Cryptography, pp. 203–225 (2019)
6. Heiss, J., Grünewald, E., Tai, S., Haimerl, N., Schulte, S.: Advancing blockchain-based federated learning through verifiable off-chain computations. In: IEEE International Conference on Blockchain, pp. 194–201 (2022)
7. Jussen, I., Schweihoff, J., Dahms, V., Möller, F., Otto, B.: Data sharing fundamentals: characteristics and definition. In: Proceedings of the 56th Hawaii International Conference on System Sciences (2023)
8. Rizzi, S.: Collaborative business intelligence. In: Aufaure, M.-A., Zimányi, E. (eds.) Business Intelligence: First European Summer School, eBISS 2011, Paris, 3–8 July 2011, Tutorial Lectures, pp. 186–205. Springer, Heidelberg (2012). https://doi.org/10.1007/978-3-642-27358-2_9

9. Stalla-Bourdillon, S., Carmichael, L., Wintour, A.: Fostering trustworthy data sharing: establishing data foundations in practice. Data and Policy **3** (2021)

10. Weichbroth, P., Zurada, J.M., Olszak, C.M.: Exploring the benefits, challenges, and opportunities of collaborative business intelligence. In: Hawaii International Conference on System Sciences, pp. 278–287 (2024)

Towards Intelligent Systems to Improve IEC 62559 Use Cases and Smart Grid Architecture Models Quality

René Kuchenbuch[1]([✉])[iD], Laura Niemann[1][iD], Johann Schütz[1][iD], and Jürgen Sauer[2][iD]

[1] OFFIS e.V., Oldenburg 26121, Germany
`rene.kuchenbuch@offis.de`
[2] Carl von Ossietzky Universität Oldenburg, 26129 Oldenburg, Germany

Abstract. In the context of ICT-based Smart Grid components, the IEC 62559 Use Case Methodology and the Smart Grid Architecture Model Framework play a vital role in achieving a common understanding of the energy system during the modeling process. However, discrepancies in interpretations by heterogeneous stakeholders can lead to errors and costly consequences in subsequent project phases. With the aim to contribute to the development of AI systems capable of improving the quality of use case descriptions and models to avoid such costly consequences, this research gathers and presents functional requirements for the design of an intelligent system. An architecture will be developed to demonstrate its integration into the modeling process. A comprehensive requirement analysis is conducted, utilizing expertise from energy sector professionals, collected and evaluated using quantitative and qualitative research methods.

Keywords: Requirement Engineering · IEC 62559 Use Cases · Smart Grid Architecture Model · Smart Grid · Artificial Intelligence

1 Introduction

The modeling of ICT-based Smart Grid components relies on various methodologies, including the IEC 62559 Use Case Methodology managed by the IEC TC8 [5], and the Smart Grid Architecture Model (SGAM) Framework developed under the EU mandate M/490 [1]. These methodologies are commonly employed in national and European research and development projects to enhance a shared understanding of the joint objectives and requirements and, thus, to improve the interoperability [8]. The challenge lies in the necessity for collaboration among system owners, domain- and method experts, each with diverse backgrounds. This diversity carries the potential to result in errors within the IEC 62559 use cases descriptions and SGAM models [9]. Errors or deficiencies in those often result wrong assumptions and misunderstandings which can lead to malfunctions or other negative consequences for the joint mission capabilities; underscoring the need to improve their quality [4]. This research aims to support the development

S. Islam and A. Sturm (Eds.): CAiSE 2024, LNBIP 520, pp. 38–46, 2024.
https://doi.org/10.1007/978-3-031-61000-4_5

of intelligent systems to enhance the quality of IEC 62559 use case descriptions and SGAM models. The focus of this work lies on the requirement elicitation for such systems and the integration of these functional requirements into the modeling process of energy systems. To address these objectives, the following research questions are formulated: **RQ 1:** Which functional requirements can be identified for an intelligent system to improve the quality of IEC 62559 use case descriptions and SGAM models? **RQ 2:** How can the integration of these functional requirements into the creation process of IEC 62559 use cases and SGAM models be achieved to improve their quality?

The first research question aims to collect functional requirements for a potential AI-based system that aims to enhance the quality of IEC 62559 use case descriptions and SGAM models. The functional requirements gathered will be integrated into a concrete concept for the artifact named *Smart Grid Assistive AI in Requirement Engineering (SGAAIRE)*.

2 Background

This chapter outlines the foundational background of the study, focusing on the IEC 62559 Use Case Methodology for creating Use Case descriptions and the SGAM Framework for developing SGAM models. Both methodologies are interlinked and are referenced to each other in their original documents and are considered complementary [1,5].

IEC 62559 Use Case Methodology plays a crucial role in energy-related requirement engineering by providing a procedure for describing the static and dynamic aspects of the system-of-concern and its functions [10] within a given use case. From a static perspective, the actors within a system are described, while the dynamic perspective highlights the relationship between the actors and the system-of-interest. The IEC 62559-2 standardizes the structure of the template on which IEC 62559 use case descriptions are built [5].

Smart Grid Architecture Model (SGAM) is a reference model for technology-neutral analysis and visualization of Smart Grid-related use cases [1]. It serves as a framework for the structured analysis, visualization, and comparison of Smart Grid architectures, facilitating a common understanding among diverse stakeholders and usually created based on (IEC 62559) use case descriptions. The SGAM framework is based on three dimensions: *Interoperability Layers* (derived from the GWAC Stack: Component, Communication, Information, Function, and Business layers), *SGAM Domains* (acc. energy value chain into Generation, Transmission, Distribution, DERs, and Customer Premises), and *SGAM Zones* (acc. classification into Process, Field, Station, Operation, Enterprise, and Market zones). [1]

3 Methodology

The methodology (shown in Fig. 1) envisions an requirements analysis as well as prototyping the integration concept of a concrete system (SGAAIRE). The first

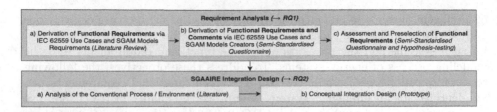

Fig. 1. Methodology of this study

task was to elicit functional requirements based on the requirements of IEC 62559 use cases and SGAM models from the literature that could be covered within intelligent systems. An online survey[1] involving participants from national and European projects like Redispatch 3.0 and int:net, experienced in IEC 62559 (n=21) and SGAM Framework (n=20), was conducted to evaluate the identified functional requirements and identify additional functional requirements by the participants. Therefore survey participants were required to possess experience with both the IEC 62559 use case and SGAM-based modeling in order to partake in the substantial question segment. The subjective assessment of quality is captured as quantitative data and analyzed through statistical data analysis and by hypothesis testing. The qualitative data was analyzed on the basis of a qualitative content analysis according to Kuckartz.

An integration concept for the SGAAIRE system was formulated based on selected requirements, involving a literature review analysis of the conventional process for creating IEC 62559 Use Case and SGAM Models descriptions within requirements management. This analysis aimed to identify how SGAAIRE could fit into the integration concept and explored the development of such a system using AI methodologies.

4   Requirement Analysis

Elaboration of the Proposed Functional Requirements: In a previous work [6], quality dimensions and metrics for model requirements were defined, derived from theoretical and empirical literature. Aspects of model comprehension and the Guidelines of Modeling were also taken into account. Due to the strong dependence between the SGAM framework and the IEC 62559 use case methodology, an SGAM model should exhibit consistency with its corresponding use case description. Furthermore, additional quality attributes derived from model comprehension, the Guidelines of Modeling, and the requirements form essential quality characteristics for the system.

The proposed functional requirements thus utilize the following quality dimensions acc. [6], which are used as a reference for the (subjective) evaluation of the model quality and could be used as metrics for evaluating an implemented

---

[1] Complete structure and characteristics can be seen on https://osf.io/x4cwg/?view_only=4f3ebe8af26f4c2682d1abea5e519fe3.

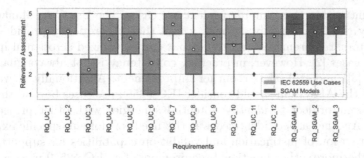

Fig. 2. Relevance assessment of functional requirements on IEC 62559 use cases and SGAM models on quality (n=18 for IEC 62559 UC and n=19 for SGAM models))

system: Correctness, Consistency, Relevance, Comprehensibility, Unambiguity and Reachability. Additionally to derive the proposed functional requirements, the requirements for IEC 62559 use cases and SGAM models mentioned in the cited reference [6] were considered in addition to the listed quality characteristics. Potential use cases for AI systems were identified that could contribute to the realization of the model requirements. Table 1 presents the proposed functional requirements and their sources.

Assessment of the Proposed Functional Requirements: In the survey outlined in the methodology section, an assessment of the domain as well as method experts resulted in determining the influence of functional requirements on the quality of IEC 62559 Use Cases as well as SGAM models. The participants could rate the individual requirements on a Likert scale from 1 (indicating very low relevance) to 5 (indicating very high relevance), with 3 representing a neutral rating. The outcomes of this assessment are depicted in the form of a boxplot, presented in Fig. 2. The alternative hypothesis $H_1^{RQ_i}$ was formulated that a proposed functional requirement RQ_i could have a positive impact on the quality dimensions according the user-base. Hypothesis tests employing the one-tailed one-sample t-test (with $\mu = 3$ and a significance level $\alpha = 0.05$) were utilized to substantiate the functional requirements in light of the research question. If the result of the statistical test yields a p-value less than or equal to α, the alternative hypothesis ($H_1^{RQ_i}$) is accepted. Conversely, if the p-value exceeds α, the null hypothesis ($H_0^{RQ_i}$) is accepted while $H_1^{RQ_i}$ is rejected. Table 1 presents the results in the form of the mean ratings provided by the experts and the corresponding hypothesis test.

Additional Functional Requirements, Comments and Perspectives arised from the Survey: Additional functional requirements ($n_{UC} = 3$ and $n_{SGAM} = 3$) emerged from the survey, as well as perspectives and comments that should be applied to the existing functional requirements. As **IEC 62559 use cases** can exhibit dependencies among each other, an unification of actors, terms, and dependencies across multiple use cases was sought. This unification is reflected in the requirements RQ_UC_1,2 and 7, and should be taken into account within these interdependent use cases. The Use Case Management Repository (UCMR) already presents a tool that theoretically provides assets such as actors, requirements, and terms that can be utilized across multiple IEC 62559 use cases [2]. However, in practice, consistency is not always guaranteed (see, e.g., [3]) and still offers room for improvement. Additionally, it was indicated that the AI system should consider IEC 62559 use cases beyond the scope of the current project to identify potential synergies with other projects and use cases. Another aspect identified was the need for domain-specific expertise, and the provision of justification and validation capabilities for supporting the need. Furthermore, other functional requirements for IEC 62559 use cases were

Table 1. Proposed functional requirements for an knowledgte-based system on the model requirements acc. [6]

Source acc. [6]	Functional requirement	Resonance ($\bar{x}$)	$H_1^{RQ_i}$ acceptance
UC_6,7,8, G_3,6	**RQ_UC_1:** The system should propose to add, remove, or change elements (e.g. Actors, Information Exchanges, Requirements, KPI, Keywords, etc.)	4,11	Accepted
UC_12, G_1,2	**RQ_UC_2:** The system should detect deviating and non-standard terms in free text fields	4,11	Accepted
UC_2, G_6	**RQ_UC_3:** The system should validate the title of use cases	2,22	Rejected
UC_3, G_3,4,6	**RQ_UC_4** The system should classify use cases into SGAM zones and domains	3,72	Accepted
UC_15, G_3	**RQ_UC_5:** The system should verify that all defined actors are listed in the complete description	3,77	Accepted
UC_1, G_4,6	**RQ_UC_6:** The system should suggest the Level of Detail from the use case (e.g. High Level, Low Level, ...)	2,55	Rejected
UC_10, G_1,2,6	**RQ_UC_7:** The system should point out inconsistencies in Actors, Information Exchanged, and Requirements that do not match the use cases type	4,47	Accepted
UC_16, G_3,5	**RQ_UC_8:** The system should check if the diagrams from the use case contain interactions	3,24	Rejected
UC_3, G_3,4,6	**RQ_UC_9:** The system should classify actors into SGAM zones and domains and list them in the Further Information field	3,76	Accepted
UC_9, G_1	**RQ_UC_10:** The system should suggest possible actor groups for simplification	3,44	Rejected
UC_13, G_3,6	**RQ_UC_11:** The system should propose Scenario Services in the step-by-step analysis	3,72	Accepted
UC_10, G_3,6	**RQ_UC_12:** The system should suggest actor types for actors by actor name and description	3,88	Accepted
All SGAM and G	**RQ_SGAM_1:** The system should generate work proposals for SGAM models based on IEC 62559 use cases description	4,11	Accepted
All SGAM and G	**RQ_SGAM_2:** The system should check SGAM models against a use case for completeness, redundancy, uniqueness, correctness, or understandability	4,10	Accepted
All SGAM and G	**RQ_SGAM_3:** The system should detect inconsistencies within SGAM models and show the propability	4,27	Accepted

also listed, such as the alignment of sequence diagrams using the step-by-step description or the generation of UML diagrams from this section.

On the **SGAM** side, the desire arose for classification proposals for components into zones and domain categorization, as well as protocol proposals for the Communication Layer. Additionally, a suggestion was made for identifying the necessary systems, actors, and dependencies from the IEC 62559 use case description, enabling the modeler to manually include them subsequently. Both aspects represent significant subsets in fulfilling the functional requirement RQ_SGAM_1. Furthermore, it was proposed that one possible functional requirement is for the AI system to comprehend, verify, or derive relationships between interoperability layers to raise protocols or more extensive requirements for the systems to be implemented. Another potential requirement could involve aligning the sequence diagrams of the IEC 62559 use cases with those of the SGAM model to determine whether the correct systems are communicating with each other. This requirement, in turn, forms a subset of the functional requirement RQ_SGAM_2.

5   SGAAIRE: Integration Conceptual Design

The artifact to be designed, *Smart Grid Assistive AI in Requirement Engineering (SGAAIRE)*, is part of a broader research work focusing on the identified functional requirements and aims to enhance quality and simplify modeling for IEC 62559 use cases and SGAM models. Based on SGAAIRE, a proposal for integrating an intelligent systems within the modeling workflows for creating use case descriptions and SGAM models is presented.

The conventional process for creating IEC 62559 use case descriptions and SGAM models involves collaboration among System Owners (represents System-of-Interest), Domain Experts (have comprensive understanding about the energy domain) and Method Experts (have profound knowledge on the IEC 62559 Use Case Methodology and the SGAM Framework) to accurately document the System-of-Interest for stakeholders [9]. The creation of artifacts is supported by context-specific resources like literature, manuals, standards, and existing use cases and SGAM models, alongside a toolchain comprising UCMR, SGAM Toolbox, and Word/PowerPoint templates for their creation and management. These elements are included in the integration concept (in Fig. 3).

This research extends the toolchain to include the AI system SGAAIRE, based on the acquired functional requirements (see Table 1) integrated into the UCMR to aid modelers during creation. Given the UCMR's widespread use in R&D projects for managing IEC 62559 use case descriptions, it's highly accessible to modelers. To give SGAM Support, the research proposes a SGAM Addon to provide a bi-directional interface for SGAM requirements. The entities as well as their relationships are displayed in Fig. 3.

The development of systems like SGAAIRE requires a robust data or knowledge base, particularly in AI domains such as Natural Language Processing (NLP), Machine Learning (ML), Deep Learning (DL) and Expert Systems (ES),

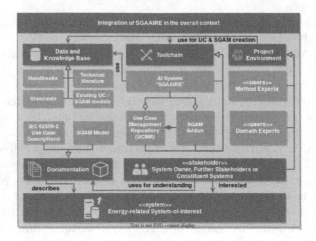

Fig. 3. Integration of SGAAIRE in the overall context

which underpin this research. These systems utilize data and expertise from domain and method experts. Identified data types are essential for implementing the system's functional requirements:

Existing Use Cases descriptions/SGAM models: AI use involves gathering rules and insights from diverse and sometimes inaccurate data in the application domain, including use cases and SGAM models. This data must be aggregated into a centralized dataset that meets legal requirements and is carefully prepared to support AI learning. *Standards, Manuals and Technical Literature:* With regard to Large Language Models (LLM), integrating energy domain standards, manuals, and technical literature is key to acquiring contextual knowledge. *Elaborated rules from further works:* In the energy context, various works have been conducted to identify overarching components and perform classifications, as well as to establish general frameworks, such as Smart Grid Standards Maps and environments, NIST Logical Reference Model, ENTSO-E Role Model and the IEC 62357-1 standard. These aspects provide potential rules that can be leveraged in Artificial Intelligence (AI), particularly concerning classification-related requirements.

6   Discussion

The collection of requirements for intelligent systems aims to facilitate the development of intelligent systems within the application domain of the IEC 62559 Use Case methodology and the SGAM Framework. In this contribution, SGAAIRE was introduced as a system designed to enhance the quality and consequently the modeling process. Currently, tools such as the UCMR [3], SGAM Toolbox [7], and NISTViz are available, which support the capture or creation of syntactically adequate IEC 62559 Use Cases and SGAM models. SGAAIRE is intended to provides semantic support, which can be integrated within the existing toolchain. In this context, requirements were collected and evaluated to improve quality and understand the desires of more experienced IEC 62559 Use Case and SGAM model creators. This initiative aims to stimulate research within these methodologies during the era of the LLMs/AI hype. A notable limitation of this study is the small number of participants involved in the survey. The expertise of our limited participant pool, with specialized knowledge in relevant methodologies, justifies this constraint, ensuring the insights' quality and relevance. Despite the small sample size, observable data distributions and strong tendencies emerged.

7   Conclusion and Further Work

Appropriate modeling of energy systems, especially with regard to the transition to smart grids and the convergence of IT systems, requires that all stakeholders have a common understanding of the system, the actors involved and the nature of information exchange. The concept for the intelligent system developed in this research endeavor serves as the preliminary step for an improved modeling of ICT solutions using the IEC 62559 use case methodology and the SGAM Framework. It also forms the basis for enhancing the quality of use case descriptions and architecture models. Functional requirements for such AI systems were gathered and evaluated through the input of domain and method experts from current research and innovation projects. Building upon the identified functional requirements, a concept for integrating SGAAIRE into the modeling process was devised. Based on the results of this study, the development in terms of the conception and implementation of SGAAIRE as intelligent system will take place in the further course, for improving model quality and interoperability efforts.

Acknowledgment. This research project was conducted as part of the int:net project (Funding Code No. 101070086) for supporting the development of interoperable solutions by enforcing energy-related knowledge base and standards [8].

References

1. CEN-CENELEC-ETSI: Smart Grid Reference Architecture (Nov 2012)
2. Gottschalk, M., Uslar, M., Delfs, C.: The Use Case and Smart Grid Architecture Model Approach. SE, Springer, Cham (2017). https://doi.org/10.1007/978-3-319-49229-2
3. Gottschalk, M., Sauer, J.: Towards identifying an approach for consistency checks to smart grid descriptions. In: 2015 International Symposium on Smart Electric Distribution Systems and Technologies (EDST), pp. 380–385. IEEE, Vienna, Austria (Sep 2015). https://doi.org/10.1109/SEDST.2015.7315238
4. Haskins, B., Stecklein, J., Dick, B., Moroney, G., Lovell, R., Dabney, J.: 8.4.2 Error cost escalation through the project life cycle. In: INCOSE International Symposium, vol. 14(1), pp. 1723–1737 (2004). https://doi.org/10.1002/j.2334-5837.2004.tb00608.x
5. IEC TC 8: Use case methodology - Part 2: Definition of the templates for use cases, actor list and requirements list. Standard IEC 62559-2:2015, International Organization for Standardization (2015)

6. Kuchenbuch, R., Schütz, J., Sauer, J.: Quality Properties of IEC 62559 Use Cases and SGAM Models. Energy Informatics (2023), in press
7. Neureiter, C., Engel, D., Trefke, J., Santodomingo, R., Rohjans, S., Uslar, M.: Towards consistent smart grid architecture tool support: from use cases to visualization. In: IEEE PES Innovative Smart Grid Technologies, Europe, pp. 1–6 (Oct 2014). https://doi.org/10.1109/ISGTEurope.2014.7028834, ISSN: 2165-4824
8. Reif, V., et al.: Towards an interoperability roadmap for the energy transition. e & i Elektrotechnik und Informationstechnik **140**(5), 478–487 (2023). https://doi.org/10.1007/s00502-023-01144-2
9. Schütz, J., Clausen, M., Uslar, M., Gómez, J.M.: IEC 62559-2 use case template-based smart grid architecture analytics. In: CIRED 2021 - The 26th International Conference and Exhibition on Electricity Distribution, vol. 2021, pp. 2935–2939 (Sep 2021). https://doi.org/10.1049/icp.2021.1909
10. Uslar, M., et al.: Applying the smart grid architecture model for designing and validating system-of-systems in the power and energy domain: a european perspective. Energies **12**(2), 258 (2019). https://doi.org/10.3390/en12020258

Pricing4SaaS: Towards a Pricing Model to Drive the Operation of SaaS

Alejandro García-Fernández(✉) ⓘ, José Antonio Parejo ⓘ,
and Antonio Ruiz-Cortés ⓘ

SCORE Lab, I3US Institute, Universidad de Sevilla, Sevilla, Spain
{agarcia29,japarejo,aruiz}@us.es

Abstract. The Software as a Service (SaaS) model is a distribution
and licensing model that leverages pricing structures and subscriptions
to profit. The utilization of such structures allows Information Systems
(IS) to meet a diverse range of client needs, while offering improved flexibility and scalability. However, they increase the complexity of variability
management, as pricings are influenced by business factors, like strategic decisions, market trends or technological advancements. In pursuit of
realizing the vision of pricing-driven IS engineering, this paper introduces
Pricing4SaaS as a first step, a generalized specification model for the
pricing structures of systems that apply the Software as a Service (SaaS)
licensing model. With its proven expressiveness, demonstrated through
the representation of 16 distinct popular SaaS systems, Pricing4SaaS
aims to become the cornerstone of pricing-driven IS engineering.

Keywords: Cloud-based IS engineering · Pricing · Software as a
Service

1 Introduction and Motivation

The Software as a Service (SaaS) model is a distribution and licensing model
wherein software is delivered as a service on a subscription basis. Instead of
purchasing and installing software locally on premises, users access the software
and its features through a web browser, or an Application Programming Interface
(API), over the cloud [3]. When an IS is provided as SaaS, it is also a service,
and as such "is a means of delivering value to customers by facilitating outcomes
customers want to achieve, without the ownership of specific costs and risks" [11].

The adoption of pricing plans (henceforth pricings), alongside subscription
models, has emerged as the predominant licensing mechanism within these systems, as they allow to meet a diverse range of client needs, providing a predictable
revenue stream for providers, and offering flexibility and scalability to users [13].
Such adoption has also been pivotal in the growth and sustainability of SaaS
development, representing a shift from traditional software licensing to a more
dynamic and user-centric approach.

Capacities collected in such structures are referred as "features", which we
define as "distinctive characteristics whose presence/absence may guide a user's

S. Islam and A. Sturm (Eds.): CAiSE 2024, LNBIP 520, pp. 47–54, 2024.
https://doi.org/10.1007/978-3-031-61000-4_6

decision towards a particular subscription". This notion provides a broader scope than the one given for Software Product Lines [2] or feature toggling [4,12,15]. In both cases, the concept tends to be fundamentally limited to increases in functionality [1], leaving out aspects such as capacity or quality of service.

Despite its advantages, anchoring the SaaS business model on dynamic pricing strategies means that market forces frequently shape the pricing structure (addition of features, alteration of usage limits, etc) [7]. In order to sustain competitiveness and ensure that pricing plans are effectively met, those changes must be timely implemented by the developers and properly supported by the architecture and deployment infrastructure of the system. This process -wherein business decisions influence pricing modifications, thereby initiating development efforts and changes on the architecture or deployment infrastructure- is coined as the *Pricing-driven development and operation of SaaS* [9].

Given this context, we consider that formalizing pricings is the foundational step towards offering support to these processes in a manner that is both cost-effective and efficient, laying a solid groundwork for the automating the analysis and management of the variability introduced by pricings within SaaS products. Although some researchers are already working on standardizing the definition of APIs' pricing [5] -a specific subset of SaaS- our primary goal is to design a general model that is able to represent the pricing of various SaaS types, thereby generalizing across all such systems.

From now on, after introducing our vision of *Pricing-driven development and operation of SaaS* and the main objective of the paper, the following contributions are made: i) Pricing4SaaS as an specification model to represent pricings of SaaS (Sect. 2), and ii) Yaml4SaaS, a syntax that turns Pricing4SaaS available to be used by the community (Sect. 2.3), and for which we provide a validation tool [8]. Finally we conclude the paper in Sect. 3 and propose future work within this research area.

2   Modeling the Pricing of SaaS

Although there is not yet a commonly accepted model that represents the pricing of SaaS, most providers share similar structures with multiple common elements. In this context, a pricing performs as a container of features, which relies on *plans* and *add-ons* to group them. The main difference between the latter two is that while users can only subscribe to one single plan, add-ons do not share such restriction, allowing users to subscribe to as many as they want. Within this model, a customer interacts with the SaaS by establishing *a subscription*, through which he commits to pay a periodic fee (aka usage tariff [14]) to gain the ability to access and leverage the functionality and information provided by the SaaS in the terms and limits set out by the chosen plan or/and set of add-ons.

To better explain the upcoming concepts, we will use Zoom as a running example, a cloud-based video conferencing service that enables users to virtually meet with others - either by video, audio-only or both, while conducting live chats - allowing users to record the sessions to view later. An adapted view of its pricing is represented in Fig. 1, and contains a subset of features from the original one.[1] In general, the pricing consists of three plans -which manage 10 features- and two add-ons -that manage one feature each-.

	BASIC FREE	PRO $15.99 per user/month	BUSINESS $21.99 per user/month
Max assistants per meeting	100	100	300
Max time per meeting	40 mins	30 hours	30 hours
Recordings cloud storage	-	5 GB	5 GB
Automated subtitles	✓	✓	✓
Reports		✓	✓
Voting in meetings		✓	✓
LTI integration			✓
Administrator portal			✓
End-to-end encryption	✓	✓	✓
Chat support		If more than $50 invoiced	✓

ADDITIONAL ADD-ONS

Huge meetings $50 per month	Translated captions $5 per month

Fig. 1. Partial view of Zoom's pricing

2.1 The Pricing4SaaS Model

Following an in-depth analysis of the pricing of thirteen real-world SaaS [7], we devised a common model that is able to represent any pricing of such systems in a unified way: **Pricing4SaaS** (see Fig. 2), generalizing solutions like Pricing4API [5].

Guided by the pricing model, within Pricing4SaaS, the user interacts with the pricing -encompassing plans, add-ons, or a combination thereof- through a subscription, which acts as a pivotal component in regulating the user's access to the IS functionalities according to the contract.

Both pricing components consist of **features**, which conform the minimum unit within the dissection of the structure. Depending on their contribution to the system, we have non-exhaustively devised up to eight different types, namely:

---

[1] Zoom's full pricing can be found here: https://zoom.us/pricing.

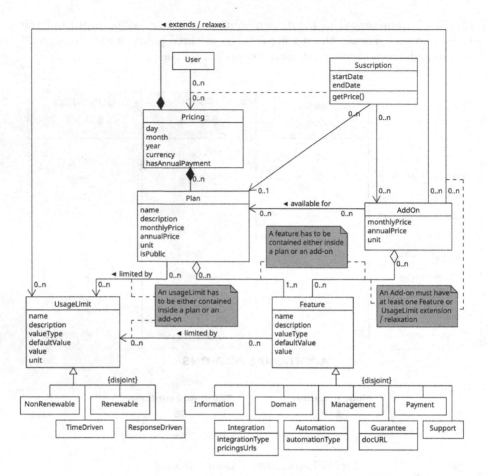

Fig. 2. Pricing4SaaS model

- **Domain:** provide functionality related to the domain of the system, allowing to perform new operations or using exclusive services; e.g. *voting in meetings*, which allows a meeting organizer to create single or multiple-choice survey questions within his meetings (Fig. 1). This type of feature is usually the most frequent within a pricing.
- **Integration:** permit users to interact with the system through its API, or to use functionalities from external third-party software within the system; e.g. *LTI Integration* on Zoom allows the addition of a meeting to any course activity created with a supported learning management system (LMS), such as Blackboard.
- **Automation:** they permit to configure the system in order to perform some actions autonomously or track thresholds and notify the user if anyone is exceeded. It also includes any task performed by a bot or AI, such as predictions, generative AI, etc; e.g. Zoom's *automated subtitles*.
- **Management:** are focused on team leaders and system administrators. They ease the supervision, organization and guidance of projects, and allow the

configuration of accounts and organization-based restrictions and rules; e.g Zoom's *Administrator portal*, which offers administrators a centralized tool to manage company's users for simplified billing and to declare advanced user management settings.
- **Information:** allow to see, use, visualize or extract additional data from the features described above; e.g. Zoom's *reports*, which provides owners and account managers with a variety of account, meetings and webinars statistics.
- **Guarantee:** technical commitments of the company that operates the system towards the users. For example, Zoom assures an *end-to-end encryption* for meetings.
- **Support:** expose the granularity of customer support offered within the plans; e.g. Zoom provides *chat support* for PRO and BUSINESS plans.
- **Payment:** specify payment conditions and possibilities.

The model also allows to determine a second-level classification for features, that will be considered as **common** or **specific** whether they provide the same functionality across all plans or not, e.g *automated subtitles* in Zoom is common. Such classification can be used to assess the level of privatization of a SaaS.

Finally, features, add-ons and plans can be limited by **usage limits**, which are also present in APIs [5]. Depending on the limitation they impose, we have classified them into four groups:

- **Renewable:** their limit is reset after a period of time, could be a day, week, month... For example, Zoom impose a *max assistants per meeting* limit on its *online meetings* feature.
- **Non-renewable:** define a static limit towards which the user approaches, and that will remain until the end of the subscription; e.g Zoom maximum *cloud storage capacity* for recordings.
- **Response-driven:** represent a limit where user consumes more or less of his quota depending on the computational cost of the SaaS associated with the request. As an illustration, the usage of OpenAI's Large Language Models (LLMs)[2] are constrained by the number of tokens acquired. The consumption of tokens varies depending on the length of the model's response to a prompt.
- **Time-driven:** with this type the quota is consumed by usage time, and is normally combined with a non-renewable limit; e.g Zoom's *max time per meeting*.

However, many SaaS offer add-ons to punctually extent these limits (similar to an API overage fee) [6]. For example, in Zoom, the maximum number of participants in a meeting can be extended by adding the *huge meetings* add-on to the subscription, which allows up to 1000 participants in a meeting.

As a final note, Pricing4SaaS distinguishes between public and private plans. On the one hand, we define a private plan as the one created after contacting the SaaS sales department to meet a client's specific needs, with negotiated costs (private), e.g Zoom Enterprise. On the other hand, public plans are available for every user, and have a fixed tariff.

---

[2] OpenAI LLMs pricing are available at: https://openai.com/pricing.

2.2 SaaS Pricing Validity Criteria

Defining a set of validation rules for pricings will complement Pricing4SaaS with additional benefits, e.g the automation of the validation process, which would allow the early detection of inconsistencies within the pricing before applying changes. This not only expedites the correction process but also prevents potential negative repercussions on customer experience and brand perception, economical losses, and so on. Furthermore, automated validation reduce the risk of human errors and facilitates the efficient management of variability. Thus, a valid pricing must verify the following conditions:

1. There are not two public plans with the same set of features and usage limits, as they must have differences among them by definition.
2. Every feature contained within a pricing must be included in, at least, one plan or add-on, i.e. there can be no published features that are inaccessible to users.
3. A pricing can have as many limits as required, but they must verify that: i) the duration covered by a limit must not surpass the contractual period of the subscription; ii) they must have an associated objective metric through which the user can monitor the use of a feature.

2.3 Yaml4SaaS: A Serialization of Pricing4SaaS

In order to demonstrate the applicability of Pricing4SaaS, we have designed a YAML-based syntax that describes a pricing with the directives of the model: **Yaml4SaaS**. This approach builds upon the accepted structure outlined in [10] and leverages the insights provided by Pricing4SaaS, enhancing the representation of pricing structures and establishing an unified and efficient way of capturing the intricacies of such pricing models (Fig. 3).[3] By using this syntax, we were able to model up to 16 commercial SaaS (results available in [8]).

We also created a command-line validation tool (available in [8]) that checks Yaml4SaaS and performs the validations in the previous section. It is a part of a library we are currently developing: *Pricing4Java*, a library built in Spring that offer a middleware component to intercepts the requests received by the back-end and evaluates the current state of the user subscription towards the pricing specification in Yaml4SaaS, stating which features are available under certain circumstances.

3 Conclusions and Future Work

In this paper, *Pricing-driven development and operation of SaaS* was presented as a conceptual framework that encapsulates the challenges and opportunities of managing SaaS systems whose pricing suffers frequent changes due to business

---

[3] A complete explanation of the syntax can be found in [7].

```
1   saasName: GitHub              28  plans:                    46  addOns:
2   day: 15                       29    FREE:                   47    extraGithubPackages:
3   month: 11                     30      description: ...      48      availableFor:
4   year: 2023                    31      monthlyPrice: 0       49        - FREE
5   currency: USD                 32      annualPrice: 0        50        - TEAM
6   hasAnnualPayment: true        33      unit: "user/month"    51      price: 0.5
7   features:                     34    TEAM:                   52      unit: GB/month
8     githubPackages:             35      description: ...      53      features: null
9       description: ...          36      monthlyPrice: 4       54      usageLimits: null
10      valueType: BOOLEAN        37      annualPrice: 3.67     55      usageLimitsExtensions:
11      defaultValue: true        38      unit: "user/month"    56        githubPackagesLimit:
12      type: DOMAIN              39      features:             57          value: 1
13    standardSupport:            40        standardSupport:    58    ...
14      description: ...          41          value: true
15      valueType: BOOLEAN        42      usageLimits:
16      defaultValue: false       43        githubPackagesLimit:
17      type: SUPPORT             44          value: 2
18    ...                         45    ...
19  usageLimits:
20    githubPackagesLimit:
21      description: ...
22      valueType: NUMERIC
23      unit: GB
24      defaultValue: 0.5
25      linkedFeatures:
26        - githubPackages
27  ...
```

Fig. 3. Yaml4SaaS syntax

factors. As an initial step towards developing automated tools that provide systems with self-adaptation to this changes, our research proposes Pricing4SaaS, a model designed to represent pricings of SaaS, and which generalizes the already presented Pricing4API model [5]. In addition, as a complement to this model, we have developed a YAML-based syntax, coined as Yaml4SaaS, whose applicability have been demonstrated towards real-life software products.

Several challenges remain for future work, but the main target is to design a framework that elevates pricing schemes to a first-class consideration in the implementation of IS, requiring the minimum human intervention to apply changes to the system derived from these structures, such as: addition/removal of features, usage limits thresholds modification, etc. As the access regulation to exclusive features presented in pricing plans results in either enabling or disabling elements from the user interface (UI), which can be automated with feature toggling techniques [4,12,15], we are developing a React library that automatically manages this type of toggling from a pricing serialized in Yaml4SaaS. On the other hand, we are focused in developing *Pricing4Java* as a novel approach to pricing management in back-end services.

Replicability and Verifiability

For the sake of replicability and verifiability, all the artifacts and datasets generated in this study are available in the laboratory package [7]. This material comprises of the companion technical report, which supports pricing frequent changes statements, our serialization of the pricing of each specific SaaS using Yaml4SaaS, jupyter notebook used to extract the statistical results.

Aknowledgement. Authors are thankful to Pedro Gonzalez Marcos for his support on the modeling of the pricings of SaaS. This work has been partially supported by grants PID2021-126227NB-C21 and PID2021-126227NB-C22 funded by MCIN/AEI/10.13039/501100011033/FEDER, UE, and grants TED2021-131023B-C21 and TED2021-131023B-C22 funded by MCIN/AEI/10.13039/501100011033 and by European Union "NextGenerationEU"/PRTR.

References

1. Benavides, D., Segura, S., Ruiz-Cortés, A.: Automated analysis of feature models 20 years later: a literature review. Inf. Syst. **35**(6), 615–636 (2010)
2. Benavides, D., Trinidad, P., Ruiz-Cortés, A.: Automated reasoning on feature models. In: Proceeding of the International Conference of Advanced Information Systems Engineering, (CAISE), pp. 491–503 (2005)
3. Cusumano, M.: Cloud computing and SaaS as new computing platforms. Commun. ACM **53**(4), 27–29 (2010)
4. Fowler, M.: Feature toggles (aka feature flags) (nd). https://martinfowler.com/articles/feature-toggles.html. Accessed Dec 2023
5. Fresno-Aranda, R., Fernández, P., Durán, A., Ruiz-Cortés, A.: Pricing4APIs: A rigorous model for RESTful API pricings. Submitted to Computer Standard and Interfaces (2023). https://doi.org/10.48550/arXiv.2311.12485
6. Gamez-Diaz, A., Fernandez, P., Ruiz-Cortes, A.: An analysis of RESTful APIs offerings in the industry. In: Proceedings of the International Conference on Service-Oriented Computing (ICSOC), pp. 589–604 (2017)
7. García-Fernández, A., Parejo, J.A., Ruiz-Cortés, A.: Pricing4SaaS - supplementary material (2023). https://doi.org/10.5281/zenodo.10292553
8. García-Fernández, A., Parejo, J.A., Ruiz-Cortés, A.: Yaml4SaaS syntax validation tool (2023). https://doi.org/10.5281/zenodo.10293191
9. García-Fernández, A., Parejo, J.A., Ruiz-Cortés, A.: Pricing-driven development and operation of SaaS: Challenges and opportunities. Accepted on JCIS (2024). https://doi.org/10.48550/arXiv.2403.14007
10. Gámez-Díaz, A., Fernandez, P., Ruiz-Cortés, A.: Automating SLA-Driven API development with SLA4OAI. In: Proceedings of the International Conference on Service-Oriented Computing (ICSOC), pp. 20–35 (10 2019)
11. What is it service management? https://www.axelos.com/certifications/itil-service-management/what-is-it-service-management ([nd]). Accessed 08 Dec 2023
12. Jézéquel, J.M., Kienzle, J., Acher, M.: From feature models to feature toggles in practice. In: Proceedings of the 26th ACM International Systems and Software Product Line Conference-Volume A, pp. 234–244 (2022)
13. Jiang, Z., Sun, W., Tang, K., Snowdon, J., Zhang, X.: A pattern-based design approach for subscription management of software as a service. Congress on Services-I, pp. 678–685 (2009)
14. Li, B., Kumar, S.: Managing software-as-a-service: Pricing and operations. Prod. Oper. Manage. **31**, 2588–2608 (6 2022)
15. Mahdavi-Hezaveh, R., Ajmeri, N., Williams, L.: Feature toggles as code: Heuristics and metrics for structuring feature toggles. Inform. Softw. Technol. **145**, 106813 (5 2022)

Validity at the Forefront: Investigating Threats in Green AI Research

Carles Farré[✉] and Xavier Franch

Universitat Politècnica de Catalunya, c/Jordi Girona 1-3, 08034 Barcelona, Catalonia, Spain
{carles.farre,xavier.franch}@upc.edu

Abstract. Green AI aims to make artificial intelligence energy-efficient and sustainable. Researchers have formulated new frameworks, methods, models and experiments aimed at the understanding and optimization of greenability in the AI arena. One of the emerging observations is that Green AI research has to cope with challenges, threats and limitations that are not always easy to overcome. In this paper, we investigate how validity threats (VTs) are reported in Green AI research. To this end, we address two research questions. RQ1 examines whether Green AI researchers identify VTs in their paper and what influences this practice. RQ2 categorizes the VTs mentioned in these papers, looking at their types and prevalence. We conclude with a list of takeaways and recommended actions aiming to enhance the understanding and management of VTs in the field.

Keywords: Green AI · Threats to Validity · Machine Learning

1 Introduction and Background

Most research in Artificial Intelligence (AI) in the last decade has sought to improve accuracy and related measures through the use of massive computational power at any price. Schwartz et al. [10] referred to this greedy approach as Red AI. In opposition, they introduced the concept of Green AI, an AI research approach that is more environmentally friendly and inclusive. Green AI is becoming popular and has originated a vibrant line of research [8], also in the field of Information Systems engineering [2].

Empirical studies in Green AI are conducted in particular environmental conditions, are restricted to particular models, and utilize particular datasets; thus, they are exposed to validity threats (VTs). The concept of a study's validity is tied to the credibility of its findings and the degree to which these findings are true and not influenced by the researchers' biases [12]. Consequently, VTs are deliberate design choices or uncontrollable external variables that potentially undermine the accuracy of the empirical results [3]. In the case of Green AI research, unmitigated VTs could lead to misguided efforts that fail to achieve meaningful emissions reductions or sustainable practices. Given the urgency of addressing climate change and the pivotal role AI can play, it is critical that Green AI research upholds the highest standards of rigor and validity to ensure its findings are reliable and impactful. It is justified then to investigate how Green AI studies identify, declare and mitigate VTs, and how the current state of affairs can be improved, if necessary. Towards this investigation, we use a dataset of 98 primary studies analysed in a recent systematic literature review on Green AI by Verdecchia et al. [11].

S. Islam and A. Sturm (Eds.): CAiSE 2024, LNBIP 520, pp. 55–63, 2024.
https://doi.org/10.1007/978-3-031-61000-4_7

2 Protocol

Goal. Using the *Goal-Query-Metric* template [4], we can state our goal as: *analyze* empirical research papers *for the purpose* of assessing their quality *with respect to* validity threats *from the viewpoint* of researchers *in the context of* Green AI. In this preliminary work, we decompose this goal into two research questions.

Research Questions. The first research question (**RQ1**) explores the awareness of the Green AI research community on the need to explicitly state the VTs related to their research, and investigates possible factors that may influence the response. We use scientific papers as a proxy of the Green AI research community activity.

Assuming that answer to RQ1 will show that a number of scientific papers do state VTs, the second research question (**RQ2**) explores their nature: which threats appear, which ones are more prevalent, and how they can be grouped into categories (Table 1).

Table 1. Research Questions

RQ1	Do scientific papers in Green AI research document VTs? Are there specific factors that influence their consideration?
RQ2	What VTs do scientific papers in Green AI research report? How can they be structured?

Population. We used the set of 98 scientific papers in Verdecchia et al. [11] as a starting point for our work. This selection is motivated by several factors: (1) it is a systematic review centered on Green AI; (2) it is contemporary (published in June 2023); (3) it follows a rigorous protocol; (4) it has very quickly gained popularity (43 citations according to Google Scholar); (5) it shares a replication package.

A closer look at this set reveals that some of the papers therein are not well suited for the purposes of our paper because they are not empirical and, thus, not exposed to VTs. Examples are the aforementioned Schwartz et al. paper [10] and Bender et al. discussion paper on the size of large language models [5]. As a result, we ended up with a data set of 83 papers to be considered in our study.

Data Extraction. We extracted and stored the data relevant to our study in a spreadsheet that is publicly available in zenodo [7]. The first sheet includes bibliometrics information of the initial set of 98 papers. The second sheet includes one row for each of these papers, recording whether they are excluded or not. For those papers that are not excluded, we include a number of columns towards providing additional details in answering RQ1 (more details in Sect. 3). The third sheet includes a row for every VT found in our set of papers; for each VT, we extracted: study id (Sxx), VT id (VTxx), its description as it is written in the paper modulo some rephrasing when needed, and the code derived while answering RQ2 (see below). The fourth sheet includes the classification and mapping we obtained for RQ2.

Data Analysis. RQ1 is addressed primarily through frequency analysis. For RQ2, we first applied content analysis to extract VT codes, followed by frequency analysis on the results. Since Green AI is an emerging field, we applied inductive coding [6], allowing codes to emerge from the papers without a predefined schema. Subsequently, we used a combination of inductive and deductive approaches to group the codes into categories, considering Wohlin's VT classification [12].

3 Results

3.1 RQ1

Out of the 83 papers that remain in the data set after applying the exclusion criterion described in Sect. 3.2, only one third (28 papers) explicitly identify VTs. Across these papers, we identified and documented 132 distinct VTs, with an average of 4.7 VTs per study, a median of 4, a mode of 3 (6 papers declaring 3 VTs), and a range of [1, 10].

Figure 1 (left) goes into more detail analysing how VTs are introduced in these 28 papers. We can see that only 7 of them introduce VTs in an independent section (in one case, subsection), which could arguably be considered the most appropriate reporting strategy. From the rest, 15 papers report VTs in the final part of the paper, mostly as part of the discussion, either integrated in a separate discussion section together with other discussion bits (8 papers), or integrated in sections that may combine to some extent discussion, conclusions or even future work. A small but still significant number of papers (5 papers) report VTs integrated in the core of the paper, either when presenting the experiment protocol or the results, making their identification difficult when reading the paper. A last paper discusses VTs in more than one place.

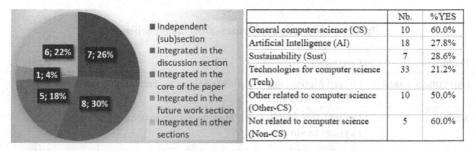

	Nb.	%YES
General computer science (CS)	10	60.0%
Artificial Intelligence (AI)	18	27.8%
Sustainability (Sust)	7	28.6%
Technologies for computer science (Tech)	33	21.2%
Other related to computer science (Other-CS)	10	50.0%
Not related to computer science (Non-CS)	5	60.0%

Pie chart legend: Independent (sub)section; Integrated in the discussion section; Integrated in the core of the paper; Integrated in the future work section; Integrated in other sections. Values: 6; 22% — 7; 26% — 1; 4% — 5; 18% — 8; 30%

Fig. 1. Placement of VTs in paper (left) and breakdown of papers stating VTs per area (right).

We have also reflected on the factors that may affect VT appearance. Specifically, we wanted to explore whether the area of the venue in which the paper has been published affects VT consideration by researchers. To this aim, we categorised the venues in which the 83 selected papers have been published into six different big areas, depending on the most dominant topic of the venue (see Fig. 1, right). We can see that AI and especially technological-oriented venues (e.g., on distributed systems, cloud computing, etc.) are less prone to analyse VTs than other categories. It is worth noting that all the three papers published in software engineering venues (included in the Other-CS category) do include VTs, two of them in a separate section, hinting that adhering to empirical guidelines is commonplace in this area [12].

We also wanted to explore to what extent the number of pages of the paper influences VT appearance. We normalised two-column papers into one column by multiplying their number of pages times 1.5 as to allow fair comparison. As representative observations (we do not show plot boxes for the sake of space), we can mention: (1) the average number of normalized pages for papers stating VTs is 19.9, compared to 15.2 for those that don't; (2) only 2 out of the 20 papers with lowest number of normalised pages, do declare VTs.

We also looked for content-related relationships among studies and VTs, i.e. whether the phase (training, fine-tuning, inference, …), the type of model (Convolutional Neural Network, Recurrent Neural Network, …), the problem domain (computer vision, natural language processing -NLP-, …) and similar factors had an influence on the analysis of VTs. However, we couldn't find any relationship to report. In fact, although some concrete instances of VTs were bound to one of these factors (e.g., threats related to the perplexity metric in NLP papers or to the internals of some Machine Learning (ML)-related operations such as matrix-matrix multiplications), the vast majority were related to the study protocol and execution itself; see next section for details.

3.2 RQ2

We analysed the 28 papers that declare at least one VT in order to respond RQ2. As a preliminary step, we summarized the VTs into a concise description, using paper authors' words as much as possible, but at the same time looking for a uniform style when looking at the complete set.

Table 2. Themes and categories of our coding schema.

Themes	Categories	#codes
Experimental Design	Overall Methodology, Variable Selection, Treatment Selection, Subject Selection, Treatment	59
Setting	Deployment Architecture, Hardware Infrastructure, Software, Physical Environment	22
Analysis	Statistical Analysis, Metric Selection, Conclusions	15
Measurement	Instrumented, Reported	14
Execution	Isolation, Workflow, Parameterization	10
ML Core	Algorithm, Model	6
Dataset	Characteristics, Manipulation	6

Then, we applied inductive coding to group the 132 VTs into 7 themes and 21 categories (see Table 2), each of them further subdivided into 1 to 5 subcategories, up to 39 subcategories in total. Some of the categories decompose into only one subcategory, but we still prefer to keep it to generate a balanced coding schema. Table 3 shows in detail the decomposition of one theme for illustration purposes (see our replication package [7] for the complete coding schema). Some observations follow:

- VTs related to experimental design are the most commonly reported (59 VTs, i.e. 45%). The most likely reason is that this kind of VTs are general and can be tailored to any domain, with a few adaptations (e.g., human subjects are not commonplace in Green AI papers, which tend to consider models as subjects). Because of this generality, they are well understood by the community and widespread textbooks (remarkably Wohlin et al.'s [12]) have analysed them thoroughly.
- VTs' abstraction level may be very diverse. We find in the papers VTs as different as "how history may affect the results" (S03, VT1) or "conclusions may be prone to subjective interpretations" (S11, VT5), compared to "some size multipliers are more efficient when it comes to matrix-matrix multiplication" (S08, VT09).
- More than half of subcategories (22) have been assigned to one or two VTs only. This is an indicator that VTs are quite distinct in nature. Still, there are three subcategories frequently mentioned: *Limitations of treatment* (15 VTs identified in 10 papers), *Inaccuracy of hardware implementation* (13 VTs identified in 11 papers) and *Reduced set of subjects* (13 VTs in 10 papers). This observation points out which are the kind of threats that the researchers are more concerned with.

Table 3. Example: *Execution* theme.

Category	Subcategory	Codes
Isolation	Interference	(S01, VT2) Interference of OS processes
		(S07, VT2) Unknown tasks in background
		(S12, VT3) Interference of many factors
Workflow	Sequence of runs	(S03, VT2) Sequence of runs in same object
		(S07, VT4) Influence of subsequent runs
	Order of execution	(S03, VT1) History of execution
		(S03, VT4) Worst performing on first input
Parameterization	Epoch	(S08, VT5) Fixed epoch count
		(S08, VT8) Relatively low epoch count
	Time budgets	(S12, VT4) Influence of time budgets

Moreover, we mapped the 39 subcategories to the VTs described in Wohlin et al.'s VT framework [12]. We refer to these latter VTs as WVTs to avoid confusion with the VTs identified in our analysis. The 33 WVTs are classified into four main WVT *Types*: Conclusion Validity (7 WVTs), Internal Validity (13 WVTs), Construct Validity (10 WVTs), and External Validity (3 WVTs). Table 4 shows a summary of this mapping, the details of which are also in our replication package [7]. Observations follow:

- 37 out of our 39 subcategories mapped into 15 WVTs, indicating that, even at this abstraction level, our classification is more fine-grained than Wholin et al.'s [12].

Regarding the remaining two categories: (i) *Representativeness of the model* was mapped into two WVTs (*Internal validity-selection* and *External validity-interaction of selection and treatment*); (ii) *Comparison in conclusion* was not mapped to any specific WVT (we were not able to find any correspondence), although it belongs to the *Conclusion Validity Type*.

- *Inadequate preoperational explication of constructs* (of type *Construct Validity*) is by far the most frequently mapped WVT: 7 subcategories comprising 34 VTs (26% of all the VTs) map into it.
- The fact that 65% of the VTs identified in our analysis refer to either Internal or Construct Validity suggests that Green AI researchers are mostly concerned with reliability of instruments, consideration of hardware and software influences, operationalization of theoretical constructs, and control over experimental conditions.
- Last, the high number of WVTs not addressed in our surveyed studies (18, i.e. 55%) is an indication that researchers on Green AI may be disregarding some important types of threats to validity.

Table 4. Mapping to WVTs.

WVT Type [12]	WVTs #mapped/total in Type	#Subcats	#VTs (% total)
Internal Validity	6/13	17	46 (35%)
Construct Validity	3/10	11	40 (30%)
Conclusion Validity	4/7	7	19 (14%)
External Validity	1/3	5	27 (20%)

4 Discussion and Vision

Our three most relevant observations from the study are as follows.

Observation 1: The Green AI Community Needs to Pay More Attention to VTs in Their Studies. The high percentage of papers that fail to mention VTs, coupled with the ad hoc description in most cases, highlights a lack of maturity in how Green AI research is reported. As stated earlier, Green AI needs to be properly contextualised to build useful theories that support the assessment of proposed solutions. To address this issue, sub-communities focusing solely on research results while disregarding practical considerations must gradually recognize the importance of critically analysing the implications of their work. A fundamental step in this direction would be for program committees and editorial boards to explicitly identify VT analysis as a criterion for evaluating papers, similar to the practice in the software engineering community [9].

Observation 2: There is a Lack of Guidance When Identifying and Classifying VTs. We have experienced a challenge when analysing and aligning the different VTs that appeared in the surveyed papers. Only four papers (S03, S07, S12 and S74) categorised VTs using the well-known classification by Wohlin et al. [12] into four types, but going further, only S03 explicitly made use of its finer-grained subclassification.

Observation 3: Description of VTs is Utterly Diverse Without any Specific Reason. In a somewhat similar vein, we have also observed how differently VTs can be described, for no obvious reasons, besides lack of space in the papers (which is, of course, an important impediment to elaborated VT reporting). As readers of the papers analysed in this study, we have experienced ourselves how important it is to include facts that help understand the reasons for, and consequences of, VTs.

To ameliorate these drawbacks, we envision two main actions.

Formulation of a Taxonomy of VTs for Green AI. We have tried to follow Wohlin et al.'s classification schema [12], which primarily focuses on experiments with human subjects. Consequently, certain subcategories, such as *Social threats to internal validity*, are irrelevant to Green AI studies. We believe that a comprehensive coding schema, potentially inspired by the preliminary proposal in this paper, would be valuable for Green AI authors. It could serve not only as a writing aid but, more importantly, as a checklist during the design of the experiment to identify threats that need to be addressed. Recent works by Ampatzoglou et al. [1] and Barón et al. [5] provide similar classifications in literature reviews and code comprehension fields, respectively.

Formulation of an Ontology for VT-Related Concepts. To clarify the theoretical framework for VTs, we propose defining an ontology compiling the most relevant concepts and their relationships. This ontology would pivot around the core concept of VT and would also introduce mitigation actions and rationale for explanations. Figure 2 exemplifies the role such an ontology could play. On the left, we show a VT from paper S03. The *instance-of* link connects this VT to the *Unbalanced classes* type introduced in our coding schema for RQ2. However, S03 argues this is not a VT, providing a justification based on a given fact. On the right, we show VT14 from S14, an instance of the *Fluctuation of energy measures* type. The VT is explained through an example (abbreviated in the figure). In this case, the authors applied a mitigation action.

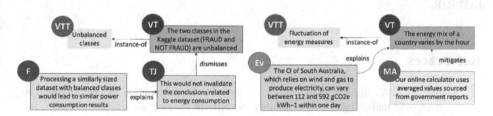

Fig. 2. Examples of ontology application: (S01, VT5) (left) and (S14, VT4) (right).

5 Validity Threats

Researcher Bias. The research method is highly qualitative, exposing it to researcher interpretation. To mitigate this threat, we split the 98 papers into three comparable subsets (P1 + P2 + P3). For P1, both researchers independently extracted data, proposed codes, and analyzed the papers in short iterations, consolidating their findings after each iteration. For P2 + P3, each researcher individually extracted VT-related data, cross-checking with the other researcher in case of doubt, and double-checking exclusions.

Under Representativeness of the Sample. This preliminary work uses the set of papers collected by Verdecchia et al. [11]. Given that the field is experiencing a steady increase of published works, this set may not be completely representative of the state of the art, both in terms of size and variety. However, it is worth noting that Verdecchia et al.'s paper: *(i)* applied a rigorous protocol for paper selection, and *(ii)* includes papers up to 2022, which minimizes the risk of obsolescence in our study.

Incomplete Identification of VTs. As explained in RQ1, most papers do not discuss VTs in a separate section. Therefore, we may have sidestepped some VT hidden in the middle of the text. To mitigate this threat, in addition to reading the paper, we systematically searched for strings such as "validity", "threat", "limitation", and the like.

Low Statistical Significance. We have not conducted any statistical analysis in this paper. The primary reason is that this work is an ongoing effort, and we do not intend to present conclusive findings at this stage.

6 Conclusions

This paper highlights the importance of validity threats in Green AI studies. We conducted a literature review on a representative set of papers and summarized the most relevant observations. Finally, we proposed two actions to improve the current situation. Our future work will elaborate on these actions through upcoming research.

Acknowledgments. This work is supported by the project TED2021-130923B-I00, funded by MCIN/AEI/https://doi.org/10.13039/501100011033 and the European Union Next Generation EU/PRTR.

References

1. Ampatzoglou, A., Bibi, S., Avgeriou, P., Verbeek, M., Chatzigeorgiou, A.: Identifying, categorizing and mitigating threats to validity in software engineering secondary studies. Inf. Softw. Technol. **106**, 201–230 (2019)
2. Anselmo, M., Vitali, M.: A data-centric approach for reducing carbon emissions in deep clearning. In: Indulska, M., Reinhartz-Berger, I., Cetina, C., Pastor, O. (eds.) Advanced Information Systems Engineering: 35th International Conference, CAiSE 2023, Zaragoza, Spain, June 12–16, 2023, Proceedings, pp. 123–138. Springer, Cham (2023). https://doi.org/10.1007/978-3-031-34560-9_8
3. Barón, M.M., Wyrich, M., Graziotin, D., Wagner, S.: Evidence Profiles for Validity Threats in Program Comprehension Experiments. ICSE 2023, pp. 1907–1919

4. Basili, V.R., Caldiera, G., Rombach, H.D.: The goal question metric approach. Encyclopedia Softw. Eng. (1994)
5. Bender, E.M., Gebru, T., McMillan-Major, A., Shmitchell, S.: On the Dangers of Stochastic Parrots: Can Language Models Be Too Big? FAccT 2021, pp. 610–623
6. Corbin, J., Strauss, A.: Basics of Qualitative Research. Techniques and Procedures for Developing Grounded Theory, 3rd edn. SAGE Publications (2008)
7. Farré, C., Franch, X.: Replication Package: Threats to Validity in Green AI Research (2024). https://doi.org/10.5281/zenodo.10607754
8. Martínez-Fernández, S., Franch, X., Duran, F.: Towards Green AI-based Software Systems: An Architecture-centric Approach (GAISSA). SEAA 2023, pp. 432–439
9. Ralph, P., et al. ACM SIGSOFT Empirical Standards. arXiv preprint arXiv:2010.03525 (2020)
10. Schwartz, R., Dodge, J., Smith, N.A., Etzioni, O.: Green AI. CACM **63**(12), 54–63 (2020)
11. Verdecchia, R., Sallou, J., Cruz, L.: A systematic review of green AI. WIREs Data Min. Knowl. Discov. **13**(4), e1507 (2023)
12. Wohlin, C., Runeson, P., Höst, M., Ohlsson, M.C., Regnell, B., Wesslén, A.: Experimentation in Software Engineering. Springer, Heidelberg (2012). https://doi.org/10.1007/978-3-642-29044-2

Requirement-Based Methodological Steps to Identify Ontologies for Reuse

Reham Alharbi[✉][iD], Valentina Tamma[iD], and Floriana Grasso[iD]

University of Liverpool, Liverpool, UK
{R.Alharbi,V.Tamma,floriana}@liverpool.ac.uk

Abstract. Ontology reuse is one of the fundamental activities of ontology development methodologies. By striving to reuse existing ontologies, developers align the new product with established models, an essential prerequisite for seamless communication and integration among systems. Although ontology reuse has been increasingly endorsed over the past twenty years, there remains a significant lack of practical solutions to assist developers in semi-automatically assessing the suitability of a candidate ontology for reuse, based on a new set of requirements. This paper advocates for an explicit phase to be incorporated into existing ontology development methodologies, involving a principled identification of candidate ontologies for reuse based on requirement similarity. The paper identifies the methodological steps that this phase should entail, and demonstrates these steps through a practical case study. It therefore offers concrete support to ontology engineers by providing an objective method to identify suitable candidate ontologies for reuse, and overall contributes to the ontology design endevour.

Keywords: Ontology Engineering · Ontology Reuse · Ontology Requirements

1 Introduction

Ontology reuse is a fundamental aspect of various ontology development methodologies aimed at reducing development time, leveraging validated fragments of knowledge, and achieving interoperability between systems [15,20]. However, numerous studies have confirmed that the practice of reusing ontologies is not widely adopted and lacks consolidation [7,11], even for mature domains like the biomedical one: indeed ontology reuse in Bioportal is surprisingly low (estimated at less than 5% [14]). This low uptake is not so much related to the practice of reuse itself, which has a set of well established tasks: it is the evaluation and selection of which ontologies to consider for reuse that remains a major challenge [3,7], as it relies heavily on the intuition of the engineers rather than effective decision-making mechanisms [3,7]. The lack of tools that can be used to facilitate reuse contrasts with disciplines like software engineering, where dedicated tools address a similar need for reusing artefacts [12], for instance using recommender systems as information filtering mechanisms [8]. Indeed, content-based

S. Islam and A. Sturm (Eds.): CAiSE 2024, LNBIP 520, pp. 64–72, 2024.
https://doi.org/10.1007/978-3-031-61000-4_8

recommender systems have proven effective in matching requirements [12] with those stored in historical databases of product releases.

Requirement similarity analysis in software engineering assumes that similar requirements identify similar software fragments [1], and despite reusing software differs inherently from reusing ontologies, we maintain that the identification of candidate ontologies should similarly be based on the requirements they model rather than simply the terms of interest (e.g. [2]). In other words, it is crucial to consider the scope of the ontology under development alongside the scope of the candidate ontologies, with the aim of assessing which aspects of a candidate ontology could fulfil the requirements of the ontology under construction.

One mechanism for representing requirements in ontology development is by means of Competency Questions (CQs) [10]. Therefore, by investigating whether an association exists between the similarity of requirements, expressed in the form of CQs, and the suitability of ontologies for reuse, we can determine if CQs can be used as proxy to recommend candidate ontologies.

This paper expands on previous work [4] and offers a two-fold contribution: (i) it provides developers with the methodological steps to carry out a "Reuse recommendation" phase of the ontology development life-cycle, and (ii) it establishes *requirement similarity* as an indicator of the reusability of ontologies or ontological fragments (independently validated through use).

The paper is organised as follows: Sect. 2 frames our research in the context of the state of the art. Section 3 presents the proposed methodological steps for reuse recommendation, and Sect. 4 introduces a case study which demonstrates a practical application of the approach. Finally, conclusions and future directions are presented in Sect. 5.

2   Background

Ontology reuse is an integral phase of several ontology development methodologies, and focuses mainly on the reuse of either terms in the ontology (i.e. classes, attributes, and relations) or patterns modelling some associated requirements. However, while determining *how* to reuse an ontology is an established task, determining *which* ontologies to reuse is often perceived as challenging and time-consuming [18]. This selection process heavily relies on the experience of ontology developers [3,7], primarily due to the lack of effective decision-making support [3,7]. Existing approaches focus mainly on ontology concepts, as particularly evident in certain domains such as in biomedicine, e.g., [14]. However, the reuse of ontology concepts is hindered by semantic heterogeneity [11].

Some approaches are starting to emerge to support the selection of ontologies to reuse which are requirement-based (notably [6] uses a Set-Theory based approach that selects ontologies that best satisfy certain semantic requirements), but these are still in their infancy. Neither there are many tools that provide at least semi-automatic reuse functionalities (one of such tools is ROBOT [13]). Recently, recommender systems have been used in the context of repositories, for instance, Ontology Recommender 2.0 [16] returns a list of ontologies whose terms match a given list. However, matches are specific to the repository and rely only on lexical features.

This is in contrast to software engineering, where code reuse is an established practice supported by different methodologies, editing and versioning tools (e.g. GitHub), and where Content-based recommender systems are used to facilitate the reuse of existing artefacts, dependencies, or traceability links [8]. Also, requirement retrieval assists in the retrieval of existing requirements on large industrial data sets [12]. For example, project OpenReq EU (https://openreq. eu/) released a service for similarity computation among requirements based on the *tf-idf* metrics [9]. The underlying hypothesis in these approaches is that artefacts associated to similar requirements are themselves similar and can be reused [1].

We maintain that much can be learnt from these approaches and transferred to ontology engineering, as the underlying hypothesis is fundamentally similar.

3   Assessing Requirements Similarity

In [4] we proposed to augment ontology development methodologies with a new explicit phase, *Reuse Recommendations*, immediately following the requirement specification. Input to the phase are (1) the ontology requirements, expressed as CQs, produced during the requirement specification phase of the ontology development process, and (2) a collection of requirements of existing ontologies, for instance a repository of CQs such as CORAL [10] and CQs dataset [22]. In what follows we will call (1) the Developer Requirements (DRs) and (2) the Existing Requirements (ERs). Output of the phase is a ranked list of recommended ontologies to reuse. Previously expressed as an informal workflow, we now formally identify four methodological steps that this new phase should entail (Fig. 1)[1]:

STEP 1. Similar Pair Identification: This step identifies pairs of similar requirements, expressed in terms of CQs, and includes the following tasks:

1. **Similarity Computation:** This task selects and computes the similarity method to use. Both lexical and semantic similarity are typically used for various requirement management tasks, and we assume the choice of semantic similarity measure is left to the ontology engineers, guided by constraints on the domain of application.
2. **Pair Choice:** This task chooses the most (semantically) similar pairs of requirements based on the similarity scores $\in [0,1]$ ranging from 0 (different) to 1 (identical), according to a threshold.

STEP 2. Term selection: This step determines requirements that are related when expressed in a vocabulary-agnostic pattern, as different CQs can have the same type and structure but different subjects, predicates or objects. Tasks are:

---

[1] In [4] we discussed at length Natural Language Processing (NLP) solutions which could be used to execute these tasks, we will not repeat this discussion here.

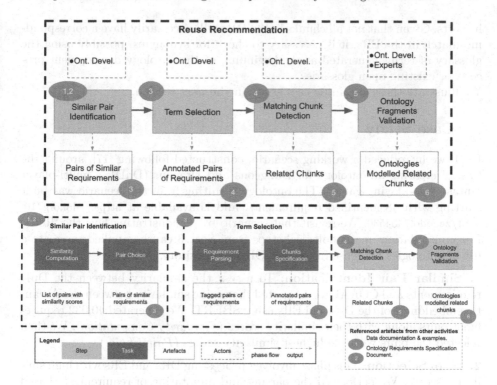

Fig. 1. Reuse recommendation phase: Methodological steps

1. **Requirement Parsing:** Tokenization, part-of-speech (POS) tagging, and dependency tree parsing are performed on each requirement, tagging each word accordingly. The tagged pairs of requirements are then passed onto the:

2. **Chunks Specification:** This task tags chunks in the requirements as entities and predicates, and then identifies the terms that are ontology-specific and compares them. Processes such as pattern detection [22] can be used to distinguish between *Entity Chunks (EC)*, i.e. noun or noun phrase, describing an object (entity) that is represented in the ontology as (class or individual), and *Predicate Chunks (PC)*, i.e. a verb or a phrasal verb that represents a relation between entities represented in the ontology.

STEP 3. Matching Chunk Detection: This step matches the chunks identified by assessing the semantic relationship between two chunks, considering both taxonomic and non-taxonomic (e.g., meronymy, antonymy, and cause-effect) knowledge. Knowledge bases like WordNet® https://wordnet.princeton.edu/ can be used to identify existing relationships, e.g. *synonymy, hyperonomy,* and *hyponymy,* and therefore to determine the chunks' relatedness.

STEP 4. Ontologies/Fragments Validation: Finally, this step selects the relevant ontologies or fragments for reuse. It may include extracting modules to match identified chunks, as suggested by [19]. Tools like ROBOT [13] can help automate the selection of relevant classes from external ontologies, avoiding full imports. Given that not all chunks in the DRs will necessarily have a corresponding match in the ERs, it is necessary to check for synonyms, possibly using the glossary of terms generated at the beginning of the ontology development process, or existing open glossaries.

We illustrate these steps in a case study in the next section.

4   Case Study

In [4] we introduced a working scenario, constructed following [17], around the task of creating an ontology for Dungeons and Dragons (DnD), a multi-player fantasy role-playing game[2]. The ontology resulting from the scenario was built starting with 48 identified requirements, and is available at https://doi.org/10. 5281/zenodo.7454530. We revisit that scenario by demonstrating how the 'Reuse Recommendation' methodological steps from Sect. 3 can be applied to create a list of ontologies for reuse from the CORAL repository.

1. Similar Pair Identification: To assess the similarity between the DnD requirements and CORAL we computed the cosine similarity between the semantic embeddings of the DRs and ERs using SBERT. We generated 40,032 requirement pairs along with their similarity scores (*Similarity Computation*). We then selected the pairs with the highest similarity scores (*Pair Choice*).

2. Term Selection: This phase involved processing DRs and ERs with high similarity scores. We performed the parsing and annotating of requirements based on Part-Of-Speech (POS) using SpaCy and the Penn Treebank system. This resulted in the identification of relevant nouns and verbs in each requirement. (*Requirement Parsing*). Then, a linguistic analysis was performed to determine classes and relationships from these requirements. (*Chunk Specification*) Chunks were categorised as Entity Chunks (ECs) or Predicate Chunks (PCs), with focus on ensuring the relevance and clarity of these chunks.

3. Matching Chunk Detection: The matching chunk detection phase identified 'related' requirements, defined by similar patterns and terms. The relationship between chunks relies on background knowledge and a 'relatedness' score, with WordNet® as the chosen knowledge base, organising words into synsets by synonymy and context. Table 1 presents examples of these matched chunks, their related synsets, definitions, and similarity scores.

4. Ontology Fragment Validation: With the support of the ontology engineer, we manually checked if the labels of the ontology elements matched the identified requirement chunks. For non corresponding chunks, we referred back to the initial glossary for synonyms. The step concluded with a ranked list of ontologies based on requirement matching rates.

Discussion. The *Reuse Recommendation* phase generated 38 validated pairs of requirements belonging to 5 out of the 14 ontologies in CORAL, covering 79.16% of 48 DnD requirements. The remaining 10 requirements did not

---

[2] https://dnd.wizards.com/what-is-dnd/basic-rules.

Table 1. Examples of matched chunks

Correspondence ID	4
DnD term	'skill.n.01'
Definition	an ability that has been acquired by training
CORAL term	'role.n.04'
Definition	normal/customary activity of a person in a particular social setting
Similarity Score	0.561538462
Correspondence ID	7
DnD term	'player.n.01'
Definition	a person who participates in or is skilled at some game
CORAL term	'friend.n.01'
Definition	a person you know well and regard with affection and trust
Similarity Score	0.705882353

match any requirement in the expert benchmark (available at https://doi.org/
10.5281/zenodo.7454530). We categorised them, with the support of an external
DnD expert, into four classes (1) *matched* to the benchmark; (2) *new* to the
benchmark *and acceptable*; (3) *unmatched* to the benchmark *but acceptable*; and
(4) *unmatched* to the benchmark *and unacceptable*. Table 2 lists the candidate
ontologies for reuse, detailing their number of requirements and the number of
requirements in the four identified classes (columns A, B, C, and D respectively).
The *matched* class consists of the retrieved pairs of requirements that match the
benchmark (a total of 20 pairs across the candidate ontologies). From a further analysis of the remaining matches, we identified a total of 10 pairs that
are not in the benchmark (*new and acceptable* class). Additionally, we identified a total of 10 pairs in the (*unmatched but acceptable* class): these differ from
the assigned matches in the benchmark, but convey the same meaning as the
assigned pairs, when considered by the DnD expert. This reiterates the issue
that requirements, being expressed in natural language, could in fact result in a
plurality of representations. For instance, dnd_34: Which are the adventure
locations in a map? was matched with req32: Which are the places of
interest in a town? whereas the assigned pair in the benchmark was req35:
which places of interest are in a province?. The last class, *unmatched
and unacceptable*, comprises a total of 8 pairs that are considered *True Nega-
tives* as they neither matched the benchmark nor were accepted by the expert in
the confirmation exercise. Ultimately, we were able to assign matches to 40 out
of the 48 DnD requirements (83.33%) before proceeding to the final validation
fragment phase. This was performed manually, by verifying whether the labels
of the ontology elements matched the chunks identified in the requirements.

These results support the findings from two different studies [3,7] that argue
that the choice of an ontology for reuse is predominantly a subjective decision

Table 2. Candidate ontologies for reuse detailing their number of requirements (#Req), number of requirements in benchmark (#Req. in Benchmark), the analysis of the results (A: *Matched*, B: *New and Acceptable*, C: *Unmatched but Acceptable* and D: *Unmatched and Unacceptable*) and the number of validated fragments

Ontologies	#Req	#Req in Benchmark	Result Analysis				#Validated Fragments
			A	B	C	D	
Video Game	66	15	12	4	2	7	9
WOT Vicinity	24	8	2	4	3	0	7
BTO	18	4	2	0	0	0	6
BTN100	77	10	3	1	2	0	4
VICINITY Core	127	5	1	1	3	1	3
TOTAL			20	10	10	8	

made by experienced engineers, and highlight how the perception and assessment of similarity vary between the mathematical notion of similarity and human judgement. Human assessment of similarity is directional and asymmetric (unlike mathematical similarity measures): for example, we often say 'the son resembles the father' rather than 'the father resembles the son' [21]. Thus, the emergence of approaches that assess ontologies for reusability with respect to a set of requirements has the potential to facilitate the selection of candidate ontologies for reuse, and reduce decision subjectivity.

5   Conclusions

This paper advocated for an explicit *Reuse Recommendation* phase to be added to ontology development methodologies, to formalise the process of reuse. The proposal is for this phase to be based on assessing the similarity between new and existing ontology requirements, by analogy with established software engineering practices. We formalised the phase into detailed methodological steps and demonstrated its effectiveness through a practical case study, gaining valuable insights. An important caveat is that this phase depends on the actual availability of competency questions, but crucially, despite their utility, CQs are rarely published alongside the ontological artefacts they refer to [10,22]. This does not have to be a hindrance, however, in fact, recent work has attempted to retrofit CQs through Generative AI [5]. Still, we trust that contributions like ours will encourage ontology engineers to share CQs more broadly, aiding application developers and enriching current ontology development practices.

References

1. Abbas, M., Ferrari, A., Shatnawi, A., Enoiu, E., Saadatmand, M., Sundmark, D.: On the relationship between similar requirements and similar software. Require. Eng. **28**, 23–47 (2023)

2. Abdelreheim, M., Soliman, T.H.A., Klan, F.: A personalized ontology recommendation system to effectively support ontology development by reuse. Future Internet **15**(10), 331 (2023)
3. Alharbi, R., Tamma, V., Grasso, F.: Characterising the gap between theory and practice of ontology reuse. In: Proceedings of the 11th K-CAP Conference (2021)
4. Alharbi, R., Tamma, V., Grasso, F.: NLP based framework for recommending candidate ontologies for reuse. In: Proceedings of the AISB Convention (2023)
5. Alharbi, R., Tamma, V., Grasso, F., Payne, T.: An experiment in retrofitting competency questions for existing ontologies. In: Proceedings of the 39th ACM/SIGAPP Symposium on Applied Computing, pp. 1650–1658 (2024)
6. Azzi, S., Assi, A., Gagnon, S.: Scoring ontologies for reuse: An approach for fitting semantic requirements. In: Proceedings of the Reserach Conference on Metadata and Semantic Research, MTSR 2022, pp. 203–208 (2023)
7. Carriero, V.A., et al.: The landscape of ontology reuse approaches. In: Applications and Practices in Ontology Design, Extraction, and Reasoning, vol. 49, pp. 21–38. IOS Press (2020)
8. Felfernig, A., et al.: An overview of recommender systems in requirements engineering. In: Managing Requirements Knowledge, pp. 315–332 (2013)
9. Felfernig, A., Stettinger, M., Falkner, A., Franch, X., Palomares, C.: OpenReq: recommender systems in requirements engineering. In: Proceedings of I-KNOW 2017, pp. 1–4. CEUR-WS.org (2017)
10. Fernández-Izquierdo, A., Poveda-Villalón, M., García-Castro, R.: CORAL: a corpus of ontological requirements annotated with lexico-syntactic patterns. In: Proceedings of the 16th International Conference on The Semantic Web, ESWC 2019, pp. 443–458 (2019)
11. Fernández-López, M., Poveda-Villalón, M., Suárez-Figueroa, M.C., Gómez-Pérez, A.: Why are ontologies not reused across the same domain? J. Web Semant. **57**, 100492 (2019)
12. Irshad, M., Petersen, K., Poulding, S.: A systematic literature review of software requirements reuse approaches. Informa. Softw. Technol. **93**, 223–245 (2018)
13. Jackson, R.C., Balhoff, J.P., Douglass, E., Harris, N.L., Mungall, C.J., Overton, J.A.: ROBOT: a tool for automating ontology workflows. BMC Bioinform. **20**(1) (2019)
14. Kamdar, M.R., Tudorache, T., Musen, M.A.: A systematic analysis of term reuse and term overlap across biomedical ontologies. Semantic web **8**(6), 853–871 (2017)
15. Presutti, V., Daga, E., Gangemi, A., Blomqvist, E.: Extreme design with content ontology design patterns. In: Proceedings of the 2009 International Conference on Ontology Patterns. vol. 516, p. 83–97 (2009)
16. Romero, M.M., Jonquet, C., O'Connor, M.J., Graybeal, J., Pazos, A., Musen, M.A.: NCBO ontology recommender 2.0: An enhanced approach for biomedical ontology recommendation. J. Biomed. Semantics **8**(1), 1–22 (2017)
17. Runeson, P., Höst, M.: Guidelines for conducting and reporting case study research in software engineering. Empirical software engineering, pp. 131–164 (2009). https://doi.org/10.1007/s10664-008-9102-8
18. Ruy, F.B., Guizzardi, G., Falbo, R.A., Reginato, C.C., Santos, V.A.: From reference ontologies to ontology patterns and back. Data Knowl. Eng. **109**, 41–69 (2017)
19. Seidenberg, J., Rector, A.: Web ontology segmentation: analysis, classification and use. In: Proceedings of the 15th International Conference on World Wide Web, pp. 13–22 (2006)

20. Suárez-Figueroa, M.C., Gómez-Pérez, A., Fernández-López, M.: The neon methodology framework: a scenario-based methodology for ontology development. Appl. Ontol. **10**(2), 107–145 (2015)
21. Tversky, A.: Features of similarity. Psychol. Rev. **84**(4), 327–352 (1977)
22. Wiśniewski, D., Potoniec, J., Ławrynowicz, A., Keet, C.M.: Analysis of ontology competency questions and their formalizations in sparql-owl. J. Web Semantics **59**, 100534 (2019)

Toward Ontology-Guided IFRS Standard-Setting

Ivars Blums[1] and Hans Weigand[2]([⊠])

[1] SIA ODO, Riga, Latvia
ivars@odo.lv
[2] University of Tilburg, Tilburg, The Netherlands
h.weigand@uvt.nl

Abstract. This paper addresses the critical gap in the International Financial Reporting Standards (IFRS), widely adopted across 168 jurisdictions, which lack a formal and explicit shared conceptualization, leading to inconsistencies and challenges in financial report comparability. Despite being based on the Conceptual Framework for Financial Reporting (CF), discrepancies such as those between the concepts of transferability and control persist across different frameworks and standards. We propose a novel solution through the grounding of these concepts in the Unified Foundational Ontology (UFO), which has shown to improve framework coherence significantly. Leveraging this approach, we have developed, refined, and herein present the CF Ontology. Using CF Ontology, we conduct an ontological analysis of the IFRS *Revenue from Contracts with Customers* and introduce preliminary ontology model for this standard in OntoUML.

Keywords: UFO · OntoUML · COFRIS · Revenue · Control

1 Introduction

This paper addresses the critical gap in the International Financial Reporting Standards (IFRS) [1], widely adopted across 168 jurisdictions, which lack a formal and explicit shared conceptualization, leading to inconsistencies and challenges in financial report comparability. Despite being based on the Conceptual Framework for Financial Reporting (CF) [2], discrepancies such as those between the concepts of transferability and control persist across different frameworks and standards. We propose a novel solution through the grounding of these concepts in the Unified Foundational Ontology (UFO) [3], which has shown to improve framework coherence significantly [3]. Leveraging this approach, we have developed [4, 5], refined, and herein present the CF Ontology in Sect. 3. The core CF Ontology is an artifact to which Design Science Research (DSR) principles [6] apply. Following the DSR methodology, the subsequent cycle in the evolution of this artifact involves its *practical application (use plan) in the creation and refinement of the IFRS ontologies.* This paper conducts an ontological analysis of the IFRS 15 *Revenue from Contracts with Customers* [1] and introduces a preliminary ontology model for this standard in Sect. 4. This model, crafted within the OntoUML

S. Islam and A. Sturm (Eds.): CAiSE 2024, LNBIP 520, pp. 73–81, 2024.
https://doi.org/10.1007/978-3-031-61000-4_9

language [6], evolves directly from the foundational CF Ontology, illustrating our approach to addressing complex financial reporting standards through ontological analysis and model specialization. The conclusion in Sect. 5 reflects our findings and outlines further validation efforts.

2 Background

Unified Foundational Ontology (UFO). UFO is an axiomatic domain-independent formal Theory. UFO is divided into three layered compliance sets: UFO-A, an ontology of concrete endurants – of substantials and aspects, UFO-B, an ontology of events, and UFO-C, an ontology of intentional and social entities [3]. OntoUML is a graphical language designed for UFO-grounded ontological modeling [3].

Financial Reporting Conceptual Framework, Standards, and Ontologies. Building upon the declarations in [2] the **purpose** of the IASB Conceptual Framework and CF Ontology is to (a) assist the IASB in developing IFRS and IFRS Ontologies that are based on consistent concepts, (b) assist preparers in developing consistent accounting policies and their ontologies, (c) assist all parties in understanding and interpreting the IFRS. Per [2:1], the **objective** of financial reporting is to provide financial information about the reporting entity that is useful to existing and potential investors and creditors in making decisions relating to providing resources to the entity.

3 Ontology of Conceptual Framework for Financial Reporting

The Ontology of the conceptual framework for financial reporting (CF Ontology) is depicted in the white sections of Fig. 1. Its description follows the arrangement of the CF's [2] chapters necessary for processing transactions and events relevant to financial reporting. UFO foundational concepts are denoted in camelCase, e.g., `roleMixin`, `creation`, `bringsAbout`, `phase`, but CF Ontology concepts in Capitalized Words – `Economic Resource`. Some concepts in the diagram are duplicated to ease their specialization.

Reporting Entity and Financial Statements. Per [2:3], "Financial statements provide information about transactions and other events viewed from the perspective of the reporting entity as a whole, not from the perspective of any particular group of the entity's existing or potential investors or creditors. A reporting entity, an `Enterprise`, is a kind of `institutional` agent, and a `Market Participant` in a `Going Concern` phase, who is obliged or committed to preparing Financial Statements [2:3.10].

Statement of Financial Position provides information about the nature and amounts of the entity's `Economic Resources` and `Claims` against the entity at `Measurement Date` [2:3]. Statements of Financial Performance for the `Reporting Period` depict the effects of `Transactions` and `Other Events` with `Enterprise` participation that change an entity's `Economic Resources` and `Claims` against the entity [2:3].

Market Participant – is a roleMixin played in a Market Society by a person, an Enterprise, a collective of persons or Enterprises, or Society itself [2:4.29].

The common practice in financial reporting is calling by the same names both the financial representations in financial statements and the *items* - resources, claims, transactions, or events that they represent. *Elements* of financial statements – assets, liabilities, equity claims, income, and expenses are the classes of items that financial statements comprise [2]. We model items and elements as economic phenomena of the situation of Financial Position underlying Statement of Financial Position, and situation of Financial Performance underlying Statements of Financial Performance.

3.1 Financial Position

Reciprocity Relator mediates an Enterprise with Market Society – a collective of Market Participants (including the Enterprise in another role) and specifies the Commitment to Outflow and the Expectation to Inflow of an Enterprise. The scope of the Reciprocity Relator can be understood to encompass offerings as broad as the entire Enterprise's purpose or as specific as ownership of a particular resource or claim.

Commitment to Outflow mode specifies Types for transfer and termination of complex Resources (and/or receipt and creation of Claims) including Service manifestation and Object termination. The Sacrifice Belief mode specifies Types for the assessed termination of Assets (and/or creation of Liabilities) to produce the Outflow.

Expectation to Inflow mode specifies Types for receipt and creation of the complex Resources (transfer and termination of Claims) including Service manifestation and Object creation. The Benefit Belief mode specifies Types for the assessed creation of Assets (termination of Liabilities) or the Outflow to be produced by the Inflow.

Economic Resource[1] specializes Reciprocity Relator when either:

(a) Non-Agentive Object instantiates the Object Type, and
    Right to Outflow specializes Commitment to Outflow, or
(b) Fulfilled Commitment specializes Commitment to Outflow,
    Right to Inflow against Other Party specializes Expectation to Inflow, and Other Party specializes Market Participant.

For example, the entity has (a) a *property right* to sell inventory (to terminate assets and create resources transferred) and to retain any proceeds (to terminate resources received and create assets), and (b) a *receivable* when the inventory has been transferred.

Asset[2] is a recognized role of the Economic Resource in the Enterprise when:

Control to Outflow specializes Right to Outflow, and

---

[1] *Economic Resource* is a right that has the potential to produce economic benefits [2:4.4].

[2] *Asset* is a present Economic Resource controlled by the entity as a result of past events [2:4.3].

`Control to Inflow` specializes `Expectation to Inflow`.

The meaning of *control* is often taken for granted but requires some attention. Per [2:4.20] "An entity *controls* an economic resource if it has the present *ability* to direct the use of the economic resource (and to prevent others from directing) and obtain the economic benefits that may flow from it (and prevent others from obtaining)." Ontologically, the *ability* is an intrinsic characteristic of an agent [3] tied to the agent's skills, knowledge, competencies, or powers. Abilities are generally not transferable because they are inherently linked to the agent's modes or `qualities`.

Economic Claim against the `Enterprise` specializes the `Reciprocity Relator` as a result that economic benefits have been obtained [2:4.43], and:

`Fulfilled Expectation` specializes `Expectation to Inflow`, `Obligation to Outflow` specializes `Commitment to Outflow`, and `Other Party` specializes `Market Participant`.

Liability[3] is a recognized `role` of the `Economic (Claim)` when:

`Unavoidable Obligation` specializes `Obligation to Outflow`.

Equity[4] **Claim** is a residual `role` of the `Economic Claim` of an `Owner` of the `Enterprise` (aka Holder of Equity Claims), who specializes the `Other Party`.

Contract[5] specializes `Reciprocity Relator` when:

`Obligation to Exchange` specializes `Commitment to Outflow`, `Right to Exchange` specializes `Expectation to Inflow`, and `Other Party` specializes `Market Participant`.

The `Unit of Account`[6] (UOA), a pivotal object of CF Ontology, is a `collective of Reciprocity Relators` that should be recognized, measured, set off, classified, and aggregated according to particular IFRS. UOA can bundle a (consolidated) enterprise, a cash-generating unit, a portfolio of contracts, a contract, economic resources, or claims.

3.2   Financial Performance. Transactions and Other Events

Transactions and Other Events are `Outflow` and `Inflow` events affecting `Economic Resources` and `Claims` of an `Enterprise` either via `interaction` with `Other Parties`, or due to changes in `disposition`, `substance`, or `Value of Resources` and `Claims`. In `Transaction Resources` and `Claims Transferred` and `Received`, play `historicalRoles`. `Market Participants` play `historicalRoleMixins`. `Service` with a `Service Provider` participation is a manifestation of an `Economic Resource` right and a component of a `Transaction`.

Outflow event is a `manifestation` of any non-terminal phase of `Commitment to Outflow`, causing `termination of Resources Transferred`

---

[3] *Liability* is a present obligation of the entity to *transfer* an economic resource. An obligation is a duty or responsibility that an entity has no practical *ability* to avoid [2:4.26].

[4] *Equity* is the residual interest in the assets of the entity after deducting all its liabilities [2:4.63].

[5] An agreement between two or more parties that create enforceable rights and obligations [1].

[6] The *Unit of Account* comprises individual or group of rights, obligations, or both, to which Recognition Criteria and Measurement Concepts are [or will be] applied [2:4.48].

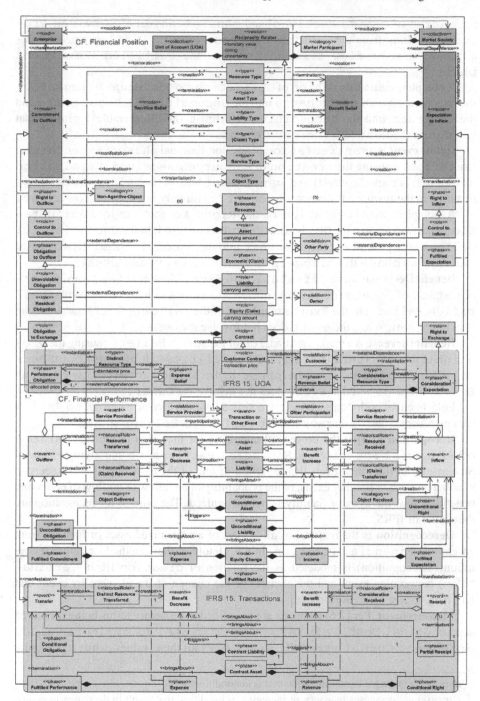

Fig. 1. CF and IFRS 15 Ontology OntoUML diagram. Enterprise perspective. 2 nd order types are depicted in purple, agents in pink, modes in blue, events in yellow, and relators in green. We use (Claim) in parentheses or simply Claim to denote claim *against the enterprise.*

(creation of Claims Received) and manifestation of Services Provided resulting from the Benefit Decrease event. Outflow causes Commitment to Outflow termination into the Fulfilled Commitment phase.

A complete manifestation of Obligation to Exchange bringsAbout the reciprocal Right to Exchange into the Unconditional Right phase and the Contract into the Unconditional Asset (aka Receivable[7]) phase that triggers the Benefit Increase event.

Inflow event is a manifestation of any non-terminal phase of Expectation to Inflow, causing the creation of Resources Received (termination of Claims Transferred) and manifestation of Services Received, resulting in the Benefit Increase event, or directly in the Outflow event.

A complete manifestation of the Right to Exchange manifestation bringsAbout the Obligation to Exchange into the Unconditional Obligation phase and the Contract into the Unconditional Liability (aka Payable) phase that triggers the Benefit Decrease event.

Benefit Decrease is a manifestation of Sacrifice Belief, causing termination of Assets (creation of Liabilities). It bringsAbout Sacrifice Belief into the Expense[8] phase if the Inflow or Outflow causes an Equity Change and the event does not involve the Owner.

Benefit Increase is a manifestation of Benefit Belief, causing the creation of Assets (termination of Liabilities). It bringsAbout Benefit Belief into the Income phase if the Inflow or Outflow causes an Equity Change and that event does not involve the Owner.

Fulfillment of both Commitment to Outflow and Expectation to Inflow bringsAbout the Contract into the Fulfilled Relator phase.

Recognition [2:5] is the process of capturing for inclusion in the situations of Financial Position and Financial Performance underlying Financial Statements, an item that meets the definition of one of the elements. If it is uncertain whether an asset or liability exists, or the probability of an inflow or outflow of economic benefits is low, the asset or liability is not recognized. The criteria for recognition are the matter of IFRS.

Derecognition is the removal of all or part of a recognized asset or liability from an entity's Financial Position. In CF Ontology the specified or actual recognition (derecognition) is modeled as the relation of creation (resp. Termination) between an event and the element or the change of the element by event that bringsAbout element mode.

Measurement. Per [2:6] elements are quantified in monetary terms being measured at Historical Cost, Fair Value, Value in Use, Fulfillment Value, or Current Cost. Conceptually, an item bears all these values, while a particular

---

[7] *Receivable* is a right to consideration that is unconditional [1].

[8] *Expenses* are decreases in assets, or increases in liabilities, that result in decreases in equity, other than those relating to distributions to holders of equity claims [aka owners] [2:4.68]. *Income* is increases in assets, or decreases in liabilities, that result in increases in equity, other than those relating to contributions from holders of equity claims [aka owners] [2:4.68].

one is selected for presentation following the IFRS. **Presentation and Disclosure** [2:7]. Classification of elements based on shared characteristics for presentation and disclosure include the Economic Nature of the item, its Role (Function) in the entity's Activities, and how it is measured.

4 IFRS 15 Ontology: Revenue from Contracts with Customers

IFRS 15 *Revenue from the contracts with customers* [1] Ontology is depicted in the grey sections of Fig. 1 as a specialization of CF Ontology depicted in the white sections.

4.1 Specification of the Main Unit of Account of IFRS 15

IFRS 15 guides how an enterprise should recognize revenue arising from a contract with a customer in four specifications' and one recognition step.

Identify the Customer Contract. The main UOA of IFRS 15 is a Customer Contract which specializes the Contract mediation by the Enterprise and the Customer[9]. The Customer specializes Other Party.

Identify Performance Obligations. Customer Contract Performance Obligations[10] specialize Obligations to Exchange. Performance Obligation mode specifies termination and transfer of the Distinct Resources including Object termination and the manifestation of Services. The Sacrifice Belief mode specifies the assessed termination of Assets to produce the Outflow. Distinct Resources specialize Resources and are complex. Per [1] good or service promised is Distinct if both of the following criteria are met: (a) the customer can benefit from the good or service either on its own or together with other resources that are *readily available* to the customer; and (b) the entity's promise to transfer the good or service to the customer is separately identifiable from other promises in the contract [1].

Issue 1. Case (a) of the definition requires information on the (readily available) resources and abilities of the other parties, which presently is out of the scope of the framework and standards. In contrast, case (b) is in line with COFRIS [5], regarding transfers as productive activities, cf. [1:29] "The nature of the promise, within the contract, is to transfer each of those goods or services individually or, instead, to transfer a combined item or items to which the promised goods or services are inputs."

Determine the Transaction Price. Consideration Expectation specializes Right to Exchange. Consideration specializes Resource whose Fair Value is known. The Transaction Price – the quality of the Customer Contract – is the Consideration Value to which the entity expects to be entitled in exchange for the promised goods or services in the contract [1]. It can be fixed and specified in the contract, but it can also be variable and dependent on different factors which will not be considered further in this paper.

---

[9] A *customer* is a party that has contracted with an entity to obtain goods or services that are an output of the entity's ordinary activities in exchange for consideration [1].

[10] A *performance obligation* is a promise to transfer to the customer either: (a) a good or service that is distinct; or (b) a series of distinct goods or services that are substantially the same [1].

Allocate the Transaction Price to the Performance Obligations in the Contract. The allocation of the Transaction Price to the Performance Obligations is done based on the Standalone Selling Price[11] of the economic resources specified in the performance obligation. The Allocated Transaction Price is a quality of Performance Obligation and Benefit Belief is externally dependent on Performance Obligation.

4.2 Transactions and Other Events Affecting the Unit of Account of IFRS 15

Recognize Revenue. Per [1]: An entity shall recognize Revenue, an Income arising in the course of an entity's ordinary activities when (or as) the entity satisfies a performance obligation by transferring a promised good or service (i.e. an asset) to a customer. In terms of Fig. 1, the Transfer event causes the termination of a Distinct Resource and the manifestation of Services Provided to the Customer, produced by the termination of Assets. This event brings About Contract Asset that triggers Benefit Increase which bringsAbout Revenue in amount reflecting Allocated Transaction Price.

Issue 2. According to [1] "an asset is transferred when (or as) the customer obtains *control* of that asset". In the previous section, we argued that the transfer of control generally is not possible. Information about the abilities of a customer and thus the state of control is out of the scope of the framework and standards. We find that the only reliable criteria for the transfer are obtaining rights or obligations.

Issue 3. Based on the preceding analysis, it is deduced that the transferability attribute does not pertain to an Asset directly, but rather to an Economic Resource.

Complete manifestation of all Obligations and Rights to Exchange result as described in Subsect. 3.2. Their partial manifestation progresses as follows:

Performance Obligation manifestation by the Transfer event causes its termination into the Fulfilled Performance phase and brings About Expectation to Consideration into the Conditional Right (to Consideration) phase and the fulfilled part of the Contract into the Contract Asset[12] phase. Contract Asset triggers the Benefit Increase event that bringsAbout Benefit Belief into the Revenue phase. Revenue recognition could be modeled more directly by the bringsAbout relation (marked green in Fig. 1) connecting the Transfer event with recognized Revenue, also providing the characterization of the transaction. However, the primacy principle of the CF requires to define assets and liabilities first and to define income and expenses as changes in assets and liabilities [2].

---

[11] The price at which an entity would sell a promised good or service separately to a customer.

[12] *Contract Asset* is an entity's right to consideration in exchange for goods or services that the entity has transferred when that right is conditioned on something other than the passage of time (for example, the company's future performance) [1].

Contract Liability is an entity's obligation to transfer goods or services to a customer for which the entity has received consideration (or the amount is due) from the customer [1].

Right to Exchange manifestation by the (partial) `Receipt` event `bringsAbout` part of it into the `Partial Receipt` phase. It `bringsAbout` the `Performance Obligations` (if any) into the `Conditional Obligation` phase and the fulfilled part of the `Contract` into the `Contract Liability` phase. `Contract Liability` increase `triggers` `Benefit Decrease` event that `bringsAbout` `SacrificeBelief` into the `Expense` phase.

5 Conclusion and Future Work

Our investigation into engineering ontologies for IFRS, using specialization of the CF Ontology, reveals significant overlaps. On one hand, standards replicate or even are inconsistent with concepts of the framework. On the other hand, there is a potential for the utilization of shared concepts that might be integrated into the CF Ontology. The entrenched nature of existing practices presents a significant challenge to the development of IFRS Ontologies, transcending mere theoretical complexities. However, this very challenge enhances their practical utility and relevance. Utilizing OntoUML stereotypes enhances the accuracy of our descriptions, though they may diverge from the traditional language of standard setters; for this, a specialized version of stereotypes is required. In [5], a set of specific stereotypes was suggested; however, it was found that their integration into the existing OntoUML plug-in poses considerable challenges. Future efforts should focus on the methodology and developing all IFRS ontologies and validating and elucidating IFRS ontologies through real and hypothetical examples.

References

1. IASB. IFRS 15: Revenue from contracts with customers (2014). https://www.iasb.org/
2. IASB. Conceptual framework for financial reporting, London: IFRS Foundation (2018)
3. Guizzardi, G., et al.: UFO: Unified foundational ontology. Applied Ontology (2022)
4. Blums, I., Weigand, H.: Consolidating economic exchange ontologies for financial reporting standard setting. Data Knowl. Eng.Knowl. Eng. **145**, 102148 (2023)
5. Blums, I., Weigand, H.: Ontological grounding of accounting frameworks. ER (Companion) (2023)
6. Wieringa, R.J.: Design science methodology: for information systems and software engineering (2014)

Towards an Explorable Conceptual Map of Large Language Models

Lorenzo Bertetto[1] , Francesca Bettinelli[2] , Alessio Buda[2] , Marco
Da Mommio[2], Simone Di Bari[1] , Claudio Savelli[1] , Elena Baralis[1] ,
Anna Bernasconi[2(✉)] , Luca Cagliero[1] , Stefano Ceri[2] ,
and Francesco Pierri[2]

[1] Politecnico di Torino, Torino, Italy
[2] Politecnico di Milano, Milano, Italy
anna.bernasconi@polimi.it

Abstract. Large Language Models (LLMs) have revolutionized the current landscape of Natural Language Processing, enabling unprecedented
advances in text generation, translation, summarization, and more. Currently, limited efforts have been devoted to providing a high-level and systematic description of their properties. Today's primary source of information is the Hugging Face (HF) catalog, a rich digital repository for
researchers and developers. Although it hosts several models, datasets,
and applications, its underlying data model supports limited exploration
of linked information.

In this work, we propose a conceptual map for describing the landscape of LLMs, organized by using the classical entity-relationship model.
Our semantically rich data model allows end-users to answer insightful
queries regarding, e.g., which metrics are most appropriate for assessing a specific LLM performance over a given downstream task. We first
model the resources available in HF and then show how this map can
be extended to support additional concepts and more insightful relationships. Our proposal is a first step towards developing a well-organized,
high-level knowledge base supporting user-friendly interfaces for querying and discovering LLM properties.

Keywords: Conceptual Modeling · Knowledge Graph · Large
Language Models · Knowledge Exploration · Knowledge Management

1 Introduction

The recent introduction of Large Language Models (LLMs) has sparked an explo-
sion of interest in generative Artificial Intelligence tools, raising novel opportunities and challenges, but also a pressing need to systematize and comprehend
their intricacies [2]. Currently, Hugging Face (HF) is the most popular and widely
used NLP library [11]. Rooted in the area of Transformer-based applications [21],
HF has been recently extended to support the exploration of LLMs; however, its

S. Islam and A. Sturm (Eds.): CAiSE 2024, LNBIP 520, pp. 82–90, 2024.
https://doi.org/10.1007/978-3-031-61000-4_10

interface fails to provide connected and structured information about the inter-dependencies between models, datasets, and applications, as well as their performance evaluation with suitable metrics. Typical users of the HF platform (e.g., machine learning engineers and developers) know these limitations and carefully consider specific requirements and constraints when utilizing the library. For example, the choice of appropriate metrics to assess model performance over a downstream task requires inspecting dedicated leaderboards.

A promising approach to mitigate these limitations is to leverage conceptual models to represent and connect concepts within the LLM domain, thereby aiding in selecting the most suitable language model and datasets tailored to specific tasks, domains, regulatory requirements, and considerations regarding potential bias or hallucination. Towards this goal, we provide our vision for a new conceptual map[1] that overcomes the limitations of HF; moreover, we present exploratory queries that can be supported by a knowledge base designed on our conceptual map.

In Sect. 2, we present the conceptual map underlying the HF library, which is significantly extended in our proposal (Sect. 3), enabling several queries listed in Sect. 4 on top of our envisioned knowledge base (Sect. 5).

2   HF Conceptual Map and Its Limitations

HF is an online platform that hosts, as of March 2024, over 530,000 open-source models and 110,000 datasets [9]. In Fig. 1 we describe the main concepts and relationships on top of which HF exposes its main services. Notice that the underlying data model is proprietary. Hence, our reverse engineering process is exclusively based on the exposed resources and APIs documentation. Rather than highlighting HF model design issues, our goal is to highlight complementary or additional information about LLM models and applications that is worth considering and build an enriched conceptual data model on top of it.

A LARGELANGUAGEMODEL presents a *Name* (e.g., "gpt2") and the following attributes: *URI* (meaning Unique Resource Identifier) may contain a recognized (bibliographic) reference to the model; *Language* indicates the one or more languages the model was trained on (e.g., "English"); *Library–Framework* indicates which software is adopted by the model (e.g., "JAX", "PyTorch", "TensorFlow"); *ModelCreator* is the company, research institute, university, or individual that has developed/trained the model[2] (e.g. "openai-community"); *LicenseToUse* formally specifies when the model can be used (e.g. "MIT"); *Architecture* is the foundation model underlying the described model (usually a multi-purpose, pre-trained model developed by well-funded institutions, e.g., "T5" by Google [16]); *Fine-tuned* is a Boolean flag indicating foundation models

---

[1] Throughout the text we do not employ the term "model" to avoid overloading the reader when referring to LLMs.

[2] We recall that HF is an open-source community portal, on which everyone can load their model.

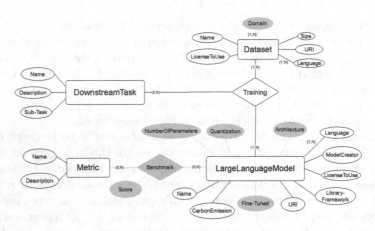

Fig. 1. Conceptual map of HF platform with four entities: LARGELANGUAGEMODEL, DATASET, DOWNSTREAMTASK, METRIC. Attributes and relationships in white are derived from the website/API, whereas those in yellow can only be derived from the HF leaderboard [10] or by inspecting the descriptions of the entities on the HF portal.

(=**False**) or models trained for solving a specific DOWNSTREAMTASK, possibly on a specific *Domain* (=**True**). The *NumberOfParameters* characterizes the model, with larger ones usually performing better but requiring more computational resources for deployment. Scaling laws for the performance-parameters tradeoff are currently an object of study [13]; recent experiments have shown that smaller models can outperform larger ones when trained on bigger text corpora [7]. *Quantization* indicates types of model compression to convert parameters to lower precision (e.g., "LLM.int8()" [6]) so that fewer resources are needed to deploy the model. Finally, *CarbonEmission* tracks the emissions [8] needed to train the model.

A DATASET has a *Name* (e.g., "Wikipedia") and a *Size* expressed in the number of tokens; datasets used for fine-tuning or testing a model are commonly smaller than those used in the pre-training phase. Datasets can be single or multi-language (cf. *Language* attribute); multi-lingual models have been trained on datasets that contain multiple languages. For this reason, models should be evaluated on datasets containing the languages seen by the model in the training phase. It is essential to check the dataset's *LicenseToUse*; publicly available datasets are not necessarily usable for any (commercial) purpose. Datasets can be of interest to one or more *Domains*. When using models on specific DOWNSTREAMTASKS, it could be helpful to fine-tune (or test) specific domains, such as the "legal" or "medical" ones. Recent research has focused on building domain-specific models [3]. Finally, a DATASET contains an external *URI* reference.

The DOWNSTREAMTASK entity has a *Name* (e.g., "Summarization", "Question-Answering (Q-A)", "Translation"), a brief *Description*, and possibly a more specific *Sub-task* (e.g., "Multiple choice Q-A", "Open-domain Q-A", "Extractive Q-A").

Finally, the METRIC entity, with *Name* (e.g., "Perplexity") and a *Description*, measures a model's performance in response to a given task.

Two relationships characterize the HF map. The ternary relationship TRAINING highlights that each LARGELANGUAGEMODEL is trained (and possibly fine-tuned) on one or more DATASETs to solve one or more DOWNSTREAMTASKs. The binary relationship BENCHMARK represents the evaluation of LARGELANGUAGEMODELs through none, one, or more METRICs with a resulting *Score*.

HF's map presents several limitations. While some attributes are categorized on the main webpage for both the LARGELANGUAGEMODELs and the DATASETs and can be easily used as filters, some are included in a generic category denoted as 'Others'. That is the case of *Quantization* for LARGELANGUAGEMODELs and *Domain* for DATASETs. Other attributes, such as *Architecture* for LARGELANGUAGEMODELS – which is used as a tag for models fine-tuned on a common base (e.g., "T5") – can be retrieved via the API but do not appear on the main webpage. Conversely, other information is available on the website but not accessible via the API (for instance, the *NumberOfParameters* in MODELs, which is associated with an optional tag). The METRIC entity is particularly critical; all the related information is unstructured (available as a textual description). The issues in the map described so far limit the queries readily available to the user. Even though information on the TRAINING relationship can be retrieved from the web interface, several attributes of the involved entities are not immediately accessible. Instead, the BENCHMARK relationship can be reconstructed exclusively through the available leaderboards, which are user-defined and based on arbitrary METRICs.

3   Extended Conceptual Map

We propose an extended conceptual map for better representing the landscape of LLMs, shown in Fig. 2. It comprises the same four entities described in Sect. 2; however, it provides additional information to support relevant queries involving attributes, entities, and relationships that were not available in the HF map. We highlight in green all the entities/attributes/relationships that are currently not present in the conceptual map of Fig. 1, as not exposed in HF.

The LARGELANGUAGEMODEL is uniquely identified by the pair ⟨*Name*, *Version*⟩; this distinction is not formalized and sometimes missing/not exposed in HF (e.g., "Llama-2" in HF is split into "Llama", "2" in our map). To enrich the HF information, we add the *NumberOfParameters* of the model, the *ModelCreator*, i.e., the original author of a model (e.g., "Meta") and the *Developer*, i.e., whoever has fine-tuned the model to serve a specific need – starting from a foundation model. All the remaining HF attributes are preserved. In addition, we introduce the *ContextLength*, which characterizes the number of tokens that the model can handle (e.g., "4k"), and a *Tokenizer* that determines how the input prompt (and the output answer) are divided into tokens (e.g., "SentencePiece Byte-Pair Encoding"). The Boolean attribute *OpenSource* identifies whether or not a model is utterly transparent in terms of its architecture, training data, and

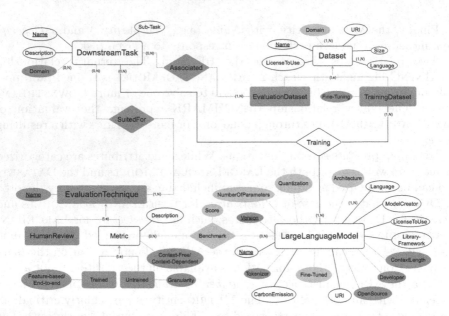

Fig. 2. Extended conceptual map. Green entities/attributes/relationships are new, as they are not present in the conceptual map of Fig. 1.

methodologies; all models hosted on the HF portal are open-source (then, it is possible to have access to their weights), but this is not valid in general.

The DATASET entity is identified by its *Name*. We further define a total, exclusive, specialization of this entity in TRANINGDATASET and EVALUATION-DATASET, assigned depending on the role assigned by the creator of the dataset. A TRAININGDATASET can be used to train or fine-tune the model on a specific downstream task (in the latter case, the *Fine-tuned* attribute is **True**). EVALU-ATIONDATASETs often provide a target associated with a sequence of tokens to allow comparison.

The DOWNSTREAMTASK entity presents the same attributes as in the HF map, except for introducing the possibility of assigning one or more *Domain*s to which the task refers.

The EVALUATIONTECHNIQUE entity represents different forms of evaluation of the performance of a model and is identified by its *Name*. It relies on a computed METRIC or a HUMANREVIEW of the model. A metric is characterized by a *Description* and a *Context-Free/Context-Dependent* flag. Context-free metrics only need the model's output and a ground truth text to use as a reference. Context-dependent metrics, instead, need the model's input, such as a table, a document, etc. For this reason, most context-free metrics are task-agnostic and can be adapted to many scenarios, while most context-dependent metrics are task-specific.

Metrics are TRAINED or UNTRAINED. TRAINED metrics have trainable parameters and need human annotations to be trained on. An example of trained metrics can be the recognition of hallucinations of LLMs as occurs in [1], where some prompts and responses of LLMs are manually annotated by humans as hallucinated or not to train NLP models for their automatic recognition. They can use other metrics/heuristics as input features or can be taught in an end-to-end manner, requiring the input given to the model, the output of the model, and the ground truth; we encode this information in the *Feature-based/End-to-end* attribute. UNTRAINED metrics can operate at the Word-Character level or use Embeddings to evaluate the output of the models. Embeddings-based metrics are usually able to capture the semantics of the phrase. We represent this information in the *Granularity* attribute. Note that both trained and untrained metrics can be context-free or context-dependent, but context-dependent metrics are usually trained. The described taxonomy represents an important addition to the HF map, allowing queries to be performed on previously unstructured information.

The extended map includes the TRAINING and the BENCHMARK relationships shown in Fig. 1 and adds two new relationships. The SUITED_FOR relationship can connect none, one or more DOWNSTREAMTASKs with one or more EVALUATIONTECHNIQUEs. An EVALUATIONTECHNIQUE must be suited for at least one DOWNSTREAMTASK (e.g., ROUGE for the summarization task [14]). Similarly, the ASSOCIATED relationship connects EVALUATIONDATASET to DOWNSTREAMTASK (e.g., the SQuAD dataset for Question-Answering [17]).

4 Exploratory Queries

In the following, we propose a few queries that can be performed on our map while are not supported on HF.

Query 1. *"Find all the LLaMA-based large language models fine-tuned for the chat task."* This query exploits the TRAINING relationship between LARGE-LANGUAGEMODEL and DOWNSTREAMTASK and filters the "LLaMA" *Architecture* and a "True" *Fine-tuned* attribute of LARGELANGUAGEMODEL, as well as the "Chat" *Name* of the DOWNSTREAMTASK. **Example output.** Vicuna [4], an open-source ChatBot that achieves promising performances on the chat task [23]. **User advantage.** Currently, filtering models on specific tasks and architectures is not supported in HF.

Query 2. *"Find the models with less than 8 billion parameters, fine-tuned on question answering (Q-A) in the medical domain."* The query considers the TRAINING relationship between the LARGELANGUAGEMODEL and DOWNSTREAMTASK entities. We filter on the attributes *NumberOfParameters* ($\leq 8B$) and *Fine-tuned* (True) for LARGELANGUAGEMODEL, and the *Name* and *Domain* of the DOWNSTREAMTASK ("Question Answering" and "medical"). **Example output.** MEDITRON-7B [3]. **User advantage.** Hardware limitations must be considered when looking for models that solve a specific task. Here, we can determine which model is both suitable for the Q-A task in the medical domain and not too big so that it can be easily deployed. Currently, this possibility is absent on HF, which does not include the *NumberOfParameters* attribute; moreover, it is not possible to look for *Fine-tuned* models on a specific *Domain*.

Query 3. *"Find all the models fine-tuned on the legal domain for text summarization, with a context length greater than 32k tokens."* The query considers the TRAINING relationship between the LARGELANGUAGEMODEL and DOWNSTREAMTASK entities, filtering on the *ContextLength* attribute ($\geq 32k$) and the *Name/Domain* of the DOWNSTREAMTASK ("text summarization" and "legal"). **Example output.** SaulLM7B [5], based on Mistral 7B [12]. **User advantage.** Summarizing long documents is an essential task, which requires models to have a reasonable context length (in our case, $32k$). This filter is not supported in HF, which lacks the *ContextLength* attribute in LARGELANGUAGEMODEL and *Domain* in DOWNSTREAMTASK.

Query 4. *"Find a suitable untrained metric with character-based granularity suitable for machine translation."* This query considers the SUITED_FOR relationship between the EVALUATIONTECHNIQUE and DOWNSTREAMTASK entities. Considered attributes are the *Granularity* of UNTRAINED metric ("character"), and the *Name* of DOWNSTREAMTASK ("Machine Translation"). **Example output.** The chrF metric [15]. **User advantage.** Enabling filtering on evaluation techniques based on specific downstream tasks, a link currently lacking in HF.

Query 5. *"Find open-source Large Language Models that are specialized in Code Generation and were trained for the Python language on at least 50 billion tokens."* The query takes into account the TRAINING relationship between the LARGELANGUAGEMODEL, DATASET, and DOWNSTREAMTASK entities. The attributes considered are *OpenSource* ("True") for LARGELANGUAGEMODEL; *Size* and *Language* of the DATASET (requiring that the sum of datasets' sizes for the "Python" language is $\geq 50B$); and the *Name* and *Sub-task* of the DOWNSTREAMTASK ("Text Generation"/"Code Generation"). **Example output.** Code Llama Python [18], a model trained on publicly available code, discussions about code and code snippets. **User advantage.** The search for LLMs specialized in a particular programming language, forcing the minimum training data, is important. This complex query is not possible in HF.

5   Conclusions and Vision

We identified specific high-quality information sources and will exploit them to instantiate a knowledge base of LLMs enriching the information exposed by the Hugging Face library. Primarily, we will employ HF APIs to retrieve immediately-available information (e.g., Tasks/sub-tasks, Models, Datasets, and Licenses). This will be compared and integrated with other up-to-date sources, such as scientific publications (tasks and related training datasets from Sanh et al. [20], Large Language Models from Zhao et al. [22], evaluation techniques from Sai et al. [19]).

Next, to scale up the instantiation of the knowledge base, we also aim to experiment with NLP techniques, supporting automatic scraping of information about LLMs from online resources. In the future, we aim to have the content fed using crowdsourcing approaches.

Overall, this vision paper proposes a conceptual map of LLM-related information. We will provide API services to query the content of each entity (i.e., retrieving a list of objects with their attributes) and run queries connecting instances. Once fully functioning, this knowledge map can be extended to an interactive web app that supports all researchers in exploring and explaining this new arising domain, guiding the design and engineering of LLM usage, comparisons, and evaluations.

Acknowledgement. The authors are thankful to other members of the ChatIMPACT project of Alta Scuola Politecnica: Andrea Clerici, Flavio Giobergia, Pietro Pinoli, and Piercesare Secchi.

References

1. Borra, F., et al.: MALTO at SemEval-2024 Task 6: Leveraging Synthetic Data for LLM Hallucination Detection. arXiv:2403.00964 (2024)
2. Chang, Y., et al.: A survey on evaluation of large language models. ACM Trans. Intelligent Syst. Technol. (2024)
3. Chen, Z., et al.: MEDITRON-70B: Scaling Medical Pretraining for Large Language Models. arXiv:2311.16079 (2023)
4. Chiang, W.L., et al.: Vicuna: An Open-Source Chatbot Impressing GPT-4 with 90%* ChatGPT Quality. https://lmsys.org/blog/2023-03-30-vicuna/
5. Colombo, P., et al.: SaulLM-7B: A pioneering Large Language Model for Law. arXiv:2403.03883 (2024)
6. Dettmers, T., et al.: LLM.int8(): 8-bit Matrix Multiplication for Transformers at Scale. arXiv:2208.07339 (2022)
7. Hoffmann, J., et al.: An empirical analysis of compute-optimal large language model training. In: Advances in Neural Information Processing Systems (2022)
8. Hugging Face: Displaying carbon emissions for your model. https://huggingface. co/docs/hub/model-cards-co2
9. Hugging Face: Hub documentation. https://huggingface.co/docs/hub/index
10. Hugging Face: Open LLM Leaderboard. https://huggingface.co/spaces/ HuggingFaceH4/open_llm_leaderboard
11. Hugging Face: The Hugging Face portal. https://huggingface.co/
12. Jiang, A.Q., et al.: Mistral 7B. arXiv:2310.06825 (2023)
13. Kaplan, J., et al.: Scaling laws for neural language models. arXiv:2001.08361 (2020)
14. Lin, C.Y.: ROUGE: a package for automatic evaluation of summaries. In: Text Summarization Branches Out, pp. 74–81. ACL, Barcelona, Spain (2004)
15. Popović, M.: chrF: character n-gram F-score for automatic MT evaluation. In: Proceedings of the 10th Workshop on Statistical Machine Translation, pp. 392–395 (2015)
16. Raffel, C., et al.: Exploring the limits of transfer learning with a unified text-to-text transformer. J. Mach. Learn. Res. **21**(1), 5485–5551 (2020)

17. Rajpurkar, P., et al.: SQuAD: 100,000+ questions for machine comprehension of text. In: Su, J., et al. (eds.) Proceedings of the 2016 Conference on Empirical Methods in Natural Language Processing, pp. 2383–2392. ACL (2016)
18. Roziere, B., et al.: Code Llama: Open Foundation Models for Code. arXiv:2308.12950 (2023)
19. Sai, A.B., et al.: A survey of evaluation metrics used for NLG systems. ACM Comput. Surv. (CSUR) **55**(2), 1–39 (2022)
20. Sanh, V., et al.: Multitask prompted training enables zero-shot task generalization. In: International Conference on Learning Representations (2022)
21. Vaswani, A., et al.: Attention is all you need. In: Guyon, I., et al. (eds.) Advances in Neural Information Processing Systems, vol. 30 (2017)
22. Zhao, W.X., et al.: A survey of large language models. arXiv:2303.18223 (2023)
23. Zheng, L., et al.: Judging LLM-as-a-judge with MT-Bench and Chatbot Arena. In: 37th Conference on Neural Information Processing Systems Datasets and Benchmarks Track (2023)

Demo Papers

ProReco: A Process Discovery Recommender System

Tsung-Hao Huang[1]([✉])(ID), Tarek Junied[2]([✉])(ID), Marco Pegoraro[1](ID),
and Wil M. P. van der Aalst[1](ID)

[1] Process and Data Science (PADS), RWTH Aachen University, Aachen, Germany
{tsunghao.huang,pegoraro,wvdaalst}@pads.rwth-aachen.de
[2] RWTH Aachen University, Aachen, Germany
tarekjunied@icloud.com
http://www.pads.rwth-aachen.de/

Abstract. Process discovery aims to automatically derive process models from historical execution data (event logs). While various process discovery algorithms have been proposed in the last 25 years, there is no consensus on a dominating discovery algorithm. Selecting the most suitable discovery algorithm remains a challenge due to competing quality measures and diverse user requirements. Manually selecting the most suitable process discovery algorithm from a range of options for a given event log is a time-consuming and error-prone task. This paper introduces **ProReco**, a **Pro**cess discovery **Reco**mmender system designed to recommend the most appropriate algorithm based on user preferences and event log characteristics. ProReco incorporates state-of-the-art discovery algorithms, extends the feature pools from previous work, and utilizes eXplainable AI (XAI) techniques to provide explanations for its recommendations.

Keywords: Process Mining · Process Discovery · Recommender System · Explainable Recommendations · Explainable AI

1 Introduction

Process discovery [1] is a discipline that aims to automatically obtain formal representation through models of the operating mechanisms in a process. The input of such methods is a collection of data related to the historical execution of a process, often in the form of discrete *events*. Discovery algorithms read events and their *attributes* from a dataset (often called an *event log*), and output a process model, to provide a representation as close as possible to the real process operations.

Since the inception of the discipline in the early 2000s, many discovery algorithms have been proposed [2], as well as numerous metrics to assess their desirability and quality. Nevertheless, the systematic review and benchmark [3] show no algorithm dominating all other methods in terms of model quality measures. Moreover, producing a satisfactory process model is still an open challenge, although there exists extensive literature dedicated to measuring the quality of

S. Islam and A. Sturm (Eds.): CAiSE 2024, LNBIP 520, pp. 93–101, 2024.
https://doi.org/10.1007/978-3-031-61000-4_11

models obtained through discovery. This is because (i) some of the most widely adopted quality measures are competing (i.e., there exist trade-offs between them), and (ii) depending on the final use of the discovered model, different (and sometimes opposite) characteristics are desirable. Under such a circumstance, users are left with the task of manually selecting the most prominent process discovery algorithm for the event log at hand. The procedure is time-consuming and error-prone even for process mining experts, let alone inexperienced users.

To address the aforementioned problems and to assist process mining users, previous works [6,7] proposed using recommender systems for process discovery. The approaches [6,7] abstract from the actual values of model quality by calculating the final score based on the rankings. Also, the approach in [7] does not incorporate user preferences for the recommendation, assuming every user wants to maximize all measures simultaneously. Lastly, the recommendations offered by both works lack accompanying explanations. Intransparent recommendations could hamper the acceptance of a recommender system [9].

This paper proposes ProReco, a **Pro**cess discovery **Reco**mmender system. Given an event log and user preferences regarding model quality measures, ProReco recommends the most appropriate process discovery algorithm tailored to the users' needs. Internally, ProReco utilizes machine learning models to predict the values for each quality measure before computing the weighted (user preferences) sum of the final score. The scores are then used to rank and recommend the discovery algorithm. ProReco not only expands the features pool from previous work but also includes state-of-the-art process discovery algorithms. Last but not least, for every recommendation made by ProReco, explanations are available to the user thanks to the incorporation of the eXplainable AI (XAI) technique [5] in ProReco.

The remainder of the paper is structured as follows. Section 2 illustrates some preliminary notions. Section 3 describes the components and mechanics of ProReco. Lastly, Sect. 4 concludes the paper and indicates directions for future research.

2   Preliminary Concepts

In this section, we introduce the necessary concepts before presenting ProReco in Sect. 3.

Event Log. The starting point of process mining is the event log where each event refers to a case (an instance of the process), an activity, and a point in time. The existence of these three attributes is the minimal requirement for an event log, whereas more attributes can be recorded and/or extracted. Event data can be extracted from various sources such as a database, a transaction log, a business suite/ERP system, etc. An event log can be seen as a collection of cases, whereas a case is a trace/sequence of events. Figure 1a shows a synthetic event log for the purchasing process of an online retail site. Each row corresponds to an event.

Case ID	Activity	Timestamp
4268	place order	2/13/2023 14:29
1968	place order	2/13/2023 16:17
7426	place order	2/13/2023 17:53
7426	send invoice	2/19/2023 9:20
1968	send invoice	2/19/2023 16:08
4268	send invoice	2/21/2023 9:38
4268	pay	3/2/2023 12:39
7426	pay	3/5/2023 15:46
1968	cancel order	3/6/2023 10:17
4268	prepare delivery	3/7/2023 13:50
4268	make delivery	3/7/2023 16:41
4268	confirm payment	3/7/2023 16:53
7426	prepare delivery	3/7/2023 17:05
7426	confirm payment	3/7/2023 17:59
7426	make delivery	3/8/2023 9:54

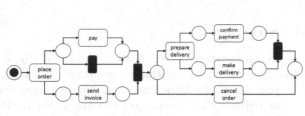

(a) An example event log   (b) A process model represented using Petri net

Fig. 1. An example of an event log and the corresponding process model.

Process Model. A process model is a structured representation of the activities and their relationships within a business process. It plays a crucial role in understanding, analyzing, and improving organizational workflows. Various process modeling notations exist such as Petri nets, BPMNs, BPEL models, or UML Activity Diagrams [1]. In ProReco, we focus on Petri net since it is one of the simplest formalisms that explicitly model concurrency. Moreover, it is trivial to convert process models in other notations into Petri nets.

Figure 1b shows the corresponding process model (in the form of a Petri net) for the event log in Fig. 1a. The process starts with the activity *"place order"* followed by the concurrent executions of activity *"pay"* and *"send invoice"*, where activity *"pay"* is optional. Then, the process might be either *"cancel"* or followed by a delivery procedure.

Process Discovery. Process discovery aims at constructing process models to describe the observed behaviors of information systems from event logs. In general, the problem of process discovery can be defined as follows: A process discovery algorithm is a function that maps an event log L onto a process model N such that the model N is representative of the behaviors seen in the log L. Despite the development of process discovery algorithms, manually finding the most appropriate algorithm is a challenging and error-prone task. To assist users with identifying the most prominent discovery algorithm, we present ProReco in the next section.

3   ProReco: A Process Discovery Recommender System

The backend of ProReco is developed in Python, to leverage the capabilities of the PM4py[1] package. The package provides a comprehensive suite of algorithms and tools for process mining. The source code for ProReco can be found on a GitHub repository[2], which provides detailed instruction for installation. In

---

[1] https://pm4py.fit.fraunhofer.de/.
[2] https://github.com/TarekJunied/ProReco.

the following, we introduce the structure and the main functions of `ProReco`. Additionally, a demo video of `ProReco` is available[3].

3.1   Structure

The overall structure of `ProReco` is shown in Fig. 2. To recommend the most prominent discovery algorithm for event log L, `ProReco` takes a vector of weights W representing the importance of different measures in addition to L. The weights (within the interval [0,100]) are given by the users and will be used to calculate the final score of the algorithm.

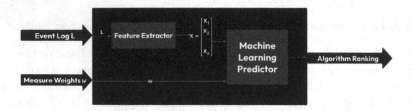

Fig. 2. General structure of `ProReco`

The output of `ProReco` is a ranking for each discovery algorithm in our portfolio, as well as the corresponding score calculated based on the weighted sum of the quality measures. The higher the score, the better the algorithm adapts to the users' preferences. In the following, we briefly describe the target quality dimensions used in `ProReco`.

As we aim to quantify the most common quality measures of a process model, the four primary quality measures [1] (*fitness*, *simplicity*, *precision*, and *generalization*) are used. A model with good fitness represents (and can replay) behavior seen in the log. The simplicity dimension refers to the complexity of the model. In the context of process mining, this means that a simpler model is advantageous, as long as it can explain the behaviors seen in the log. A precise process model does not allow too much unseen behavior, as it is trivial to create a model that allows any behavior (the flower model [1]). Lastly, a model with good generalization can represent behavior unseen in the event log. Since the four quality dimensions compete with each other, a single ideal model often does not exist [1]. The ideal model highly depends on the use case of the users. This motivates the use of weights to incorporate the user preferences w.r.t. the importance of the four quality measures.

Next, we introduce each component (the feature extractor and the machine learning predictor) in more detail.

Feature Extractor. Based on previous work [6–8], we extract an initial pool of various features. Moreover, the initial pool is filtered considering two criteria.

---

[3] https://bit.ly/prorecodemo.

First, we remove the computationally expensive features. As efficiency is one of the motivations for developing such a recommender system, using features that are expensive to compute does counteract the benefit. Second, we remove redundant features. Features are considered redundant if there is already another feature representing the same concept. For instance, the feature representing the number of trace variants is implemented as n_unique_traces in [7] and as "Number of distinct traces" in [6]. These redundancies lead to higher execution time and adversely affect the performance of some machine learning models. Thus, we remove such redundancies using the Pearson correlation coefficient. Lastly, we add ten Directly-Follows Graph (DFG)- and footprint matrix-based features. In the end, 162 features were extracted. The introduction to all features is out of scope. The corresponding function (called *Featurer*) providing insight for all features is available in ProReco and introduced in Sect. 3.2 in more detail.

Machine Learning Predictor. As shown in Fig. 3a, the machine learning predictor consists of a score predictor for each algorithm in the algorithm portfolio, which consists of Alpha Miner, Alpha-Plus Miner, Heuristics Miner, Inductive Miner (classic, infrequent, direct), ILP Miner, and Split Miner.

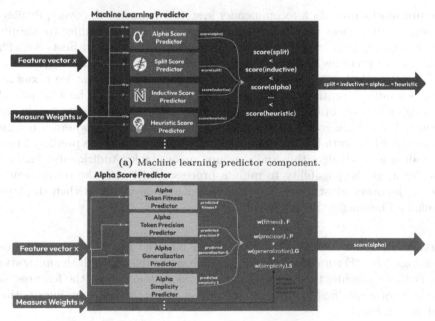

(a) Machine learning predictor component.

(b) Score predictor for a single algorithm (Alpha Miner as an example)

Fig. 3. Machine learning predictor and its sub-components: score predictors.

The structure for an algorithm score predictor is shown in Fig. 3b using Alpha Miner as an instance. The Score Predictor consists of individual predictors for each of the four measures (fitness, precision, generalization, and simplicity). Each measure predictor accepts a feature vector derived from the event log as input and forecasts the value of the corresponding measure for the process model that would have been generated based on the provided event log. The measure weights W provided by the user are then used for the final computation of the overall score for a discovery algorithm. During this computation, each predicted measure value is multiplied by its corresponding measure weight and subsequently aggregated.

The choice of the predictor to predict the measure values for each algorithm is of little importance here, as it is flexible to switch among different predictors whenever suitable. In `ProReco`, we adopt the `xgboost` [4] regressor as an instantiation for the predictor. To train the predictors, we included 12 real-life event logs from the 4TU repository[4] and 785 synthetic event logs generated by the PLG tool[5]. The data is available for download[6]. We used 5-fold cross-validation for each experiment with an 80/20 training/test split.

3.2   ProReco's Functions

In this section, we introduce the main functions of `ProReco`.

Recommendation. As a recommender system for process discovery, `ProReco` recommends the most prominent algorithm for the user according to the predicted weighted sum of the four quality measures discussed in Sect. 3.1. The inputs are an event log L and the user preferences w.r.t. measure weights W.

To initiate the recommendation, users have to upload an event log (`.xes` format) as input. Then, they are redirected to a page where they have to provide the weights for each of the four quality measures. Once the measure weights are submitted, users are redirected to the recommendation page, where a ranking of the algorithm portfolio, the score for each algorithm, and the predicted measure values for each algorithm and measure are available. Additionally, `ProReco` provides users the possibility to mine a process model with the recommended process discovery algorithms. The discovered process model is then displayed through an interactive Petri net viewer.

Feature Insights. `ProReco` offers insights into the features extracted from event logs. The *"Featurer"* (shown in Fig. 4) is accessible through the navigation bar. *Featurer* provides the user with detailed information about the features. By searching for a specific feature name, users can access the following information, as shown in Fig. 4:

- Description: a brief description of the feature.
- From: the source of the feature.
- Used in: the number of regressors that use this feature.

---

[4] https://data.4tu.nl/.
[5] https://plg.processmining.it/.
[6] http://bit.ly/allEventLogsProReco.

- Most important for: the regressor that gains the most advantage from the feature.
- Ranking: the importance of the feature among all features.
- Feature Score: a metric used to determine the feature's ranking.

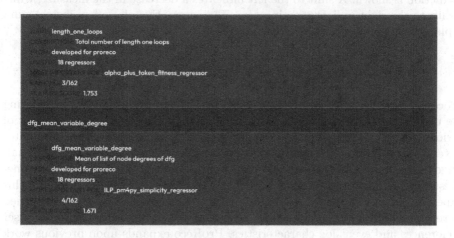

Fig. 4. The user interface for the feature insights.

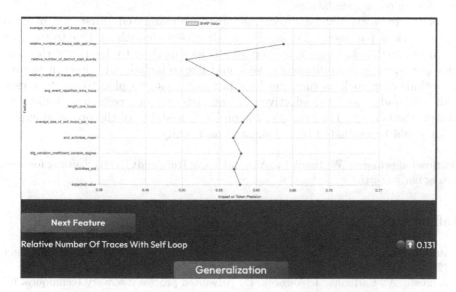

Fig. 5. The user interface for explaining an individual recommendation.

Explainable Recommendation. As recommendations without explanations can hinder the transparency, trustworthiness, and satisfaction of a recommender system [9], `ProReco` incorporates techniques from explainable AI (XAI) to provide explanations for individual predictions made by the regressors. Users can access the explanations by clicking on "Explain the Predictions" on the resulting recommendation page. Then, users will be redirected to an interactive plot based on SHAP values [5]. The plot begins at the bottom, displaying the expected measure for the selected algorithm. As each feature is added, its effect on the prediction is shown. A shift to the left indicates a decrease in the measure, while a shift to the right indicates an increase. The interactive plot offers insights and explanations for the recommendations (Fig. 5).

4   Conclusion and Future Work

Process discovery aims to automatically generate process models representing the underlying information system from event logs. Despite the development of various discovery algorithms and quality metrics, no single algorithm dominates in terms of model quality measures [3]. Consequently, users often face the challenge of manually selecting suitable discovery algorithms, a process that is time-consuming and error-prone, even for experts in process mining. In response, this paper introduces ProReco, a process discovery recommender system designed to recommend the most appropriate process discovery algorithm based on user preferences and event log characteristics. ProReco expands upon previous work by incorporating state-of-the-art algorithms and providing transparent explanations for its recommendations.

As future work, several directions can be investigated. First, we plan to explore various parameter settings for the discovery algorithms. Due to the vast search space, the challenge is finding an efficient method to determine the best value per technique. Additionally, we would like to include additional measures for optimization such as runtime. Last but not least, we plan to conduct user studies to understand the effectiveness and usability of ProReco as well as to validate the benefits. For example, the understandability of the provided explanation could be evaluated by a dedicated user study.

Acknowledgement. We thank the Alexander von Humboldt (AvH) Stiftung for supporting our research.

References

1. van der Aalst, W.M.P.: Process Mining - Data Science in Action, 2nd edn. Springer (2016). https://doi.org/10.1007/978-3-662-49851-4
2. Augusto, A., Carmona, J., Verbeek, E.: Advanced process discovery techniques. In: van der Aalst, W.M.P., Carmona, J. (eds.) Process Mining Handbook, Lecture Notes in Business Information Processing, vol. 448, pp. 76–107. Springer (2022). https://doi.org/10.1007/978-3-031-08848-3_3
3. Augusto, A., et al.: Automated discovery of process models from event logs: review and benchmark. IEEE Trans. Knowl. Data Eng. **31**(4), 686–705 (2019)
4. Chen, T., Guestrin, C.: Xgboost: A scalable tree boosting system. In: KDD, pp. 785–794. ACM (2016)

5. Lundberg, S.M., Lee, S.: A unified approach to interpreting model predictions. In: NIPS, pp. 4765–4774 (2017)

6. Ribeiro, Joel, Carmona, Josep, Mısır, Mustafa, Sebag, Michele: A recommender system for process discovery. In: Sadiq, Shazia, Soffer, Pnina, Völzer, Hagen (eds.) BPM 2014. LNCS, vol. 8659, pp. 67–83. Springer, Cham (2014). https://doi.org/10.1007/978-3-319-10172-9_5

7. Tavares, G.M., Junior, S.B., Damiani, E.: Automating process discovery through meta-learning. In: CoopIS. LNCS, vol. 13591, pp. 205–222. Springer (2022). https://doi.org/10.1007/978-3-031-17834-4_12

8. Zandkarimi, F., Decker, P., Rehse, J.R.: Fig4pm: A library for calculating event log measures (extended abstract) (2021)

9. Zhang, Y., Chen, X.: Explainable recommendation: a survey and new perspectives. Found. Trends Inf. Retr. 14(1), 1–101 (2020)

RecPro: A User-Centric Recommendation Tool for Business Process Execution

Sebastian Petter[✉] and Stefan Jablonski

University of Bayreuth, Bayreuth, Germany
{sebastian.petter,stefan.jablonski}@uni-bayreuth.de

Abstract. This paper introduces RecPro, a novel tool in the field of Business Process Management (BPM), fostering the integration of human-centric computing by integrating methods from recommender systems. Unlike existing approaches that enrich BPM by recommendation techniques, RecPro is not restricted to a specific recommendation method. This adaptability allows for the utilization of various algorithms to create personalized recommendations. By offering users task recommendations based on their individual likes and dislikes, RecPro fosters a more user-centric approach, addressing the often overlooked aspect of personal preferences in BPM. This integration signifies a move towards a more inclusive, efficient, and personalized BPM.

Keywords: Business Process Management · Recommender systems · User-centered process improvement

1 Introduction

Today, Business Process Management (BPM) is a widely adopted practice across various industries, essential for companies pursuing specific business objectives and maintaining competitive advantage [5,15]. However, integrating human-centric approaches into BPM remains an ongoing challenge. These approaches aim to consider users' unique needs, preferences, and abilities during process execution and optimization - elements often overshadowed by a strong focus on enhancing process efficiency [7,10,16]. This tendency limits the potential for improved efficiency and overlook the valuable perspectives contributed by individuals, leading to a noticeable divide between traditional process-centric and human-centric BPM methodologies. This deficiency begs the question: How can we make BPM more responsive to individual human needs and expectations while maintaining and enhancing process efficiency?

In response to this challenge, we develop RecPro (RECommender systems for Business PROcess Management), a tool addressing these concerns[1] by linking recommender systems with BPM. RecPro offers users recommendations about activities to be performed next based on their preferences, marking a paradigm

---

[1] RecPro has been developed within the project PRIME (Process-based integration of human expectations in digitized work environments). https://prime-interaktionsarbeit.de - https://gitlab.com/2024-caise-forum.

S. Islam and A. Sturm (Eds.): CAiSE 2024, LNBIP 520, pp. 102–110, 2024.
https://doi.org/10.1007/978-3-031-61000-4_12

shift from traditional process-centric BPM tools to a more user-centric approach. Unlike existing solutions, which typically adhere to static recommendation methods or algorithms [3,9,13], RecPro is designed to emphasize a more flexible and adaptive framework. This design choice aims at integrating a variety of recommendation algorithms to meet the diverse needs and preferences of individual users.

This paper aims at demonstrating the functionality, utility, and unique features of RecPro within the BPM context, addressing the question of enhancing BPM with personalized user engagement. We will illustrate how RecPro meets the aforementioned challenges by capturing and analyzing employee preferences, thus facilitating a more personalized and human-centric approach to BPM. The integration of user preferences into the BPM lifecycle suggests a step towards more inclusive business process practice, considering the unique environments and requirements of different organizations and their staff.

The remainder of this paper is organized to provide thorough overview of RecPro's capabilities. After this introduction, we will review the background and literature relevant to RecPro's development and application. Subsequent sections will elaborate on the analysis of requirements, the specific features, and the design of the architecture of RecPro, followed by an example of its practical application in a real-world setting. The conclusion will summarize our findings and discuss potential directions for future work.

2   Related Work

BPM serves to enhance organizational workflows, improving efficiency and effectiveness while adapting to an ever-changing environment [5,6,15]. Central to BPM are components such as a worklist, which assigns tasks to users within a Process-Aware Information System (PAIS); the event log, recording all actions within the PAIS; and the PAIS itself, facilitating business process execution and alignment with organizational goals [11,12].

Emerging from sectors like e-commerce and content streaming, personalized recommendation systems can enhance BPM's focus on human resources. These systems use algorithms to analyze user data and provide tailored suggestions, significantly improving user experience and satisfaction [1]. However, integrating these systems into the BPM landscape requires understanding the intricate details of user needs, business processes, and their operational execution [8].

While there are approaches linking recommender systems with BPM, they often face limitations. Many proposals remain conceptual without practical implementation or rely solely on single algorithms, constraining their adaptability and breadth [2,3,14]. Additionally, these systems seldom utilize comprehensive user feedback to generate suggestions, a critical component for personalizing recommendations within the BPM context [9]. Additionally, in cases where explicit user feedback is considered, only one type of user feedback is typically examined, neglecting the diversity of user perspectives and insights.

3   RecPro

3.1   Requirements Analysis

The development of RecPro necessitates a meticulous approach in identifying and defining a set of critical requirements. These requirements emerge from the gaps and limitations highlighted in Sect. 2, focusing on enhancing the human-centric aspect of BPM. In this context, we outline the primary requirements essential for the successful implementation and operation of RecPro:

RQ1 **Integration of various recommendation methods:** RecPro must support various recommendation methods (like collaborative filtering and content-based filtering) within a PAIS to support personalized user experiences.

RQ2 **Integration of existing process engines:** RecPro must facilitate the integration of existing process engines.

RQ3 **User feedback mechanisms:** The system should include efficient ways to collect and analyze user feedback, both explicit (e.g., ratings) and implicit (e.g., usage patterns), to continuously refine and improve recommendations.

RQ4 **Extensibility:** RecPro should have a modular design, allowing easy integration of new recommendation methods and feedback systems to adapt to evolving needs and technologies.

RQ5 **User-centric design and accessibility:** The interface should be intuitive and accessible to all users, promoting engagement and inclusivity without sacrificing functionality or security.

3.2   Features

RecPro distinguishes itself with functional and non-functional features. The functional features are categorized into two main areas: modeling and execution. The modeling features comprise *Filter*, *Feedback*, *Attribute*, and *Process Modeling*. Altogether, they enable the customization of the system to align with specific business processes and user preferences. The first three features facilitate to model recommendation specific issues and cover requirements RQ1 and RQ4 (Sect. 3.1). The execution related features, including *Filter*, *Feedback*, *Attribute*, and *Process Execution*, put the modeling related features into action. They enact personalized recommendations and feedback during process execution enhancing BPM with personalized recommendations and responsive feedback mechanisms. They meet the requirements RQ1, RQ3, and RQ4 by supporting a range of recommendation methods. Besides, seamless integrating with existing process engines is enabled by its modular architecture (Sect. 3.3) what covers requirement RQ2 from above. Furthermore, RecPro is designed with a user-friendly interface (Sect. 4), ensuring accessibility for users of different expertise and responsibility (requirement RQ5).

3.3 Architecture

RecPro shows a scalable and modular architecture to meet the diverse needs of recommendation systems, especially the integration of various recommendation methods and the connection to various PAIS. It comprises four key modules: *Frontend Application*, *Backend Application*, *Workflow Engine Connector*, and *Recommendation Engine* (Fig. 1).

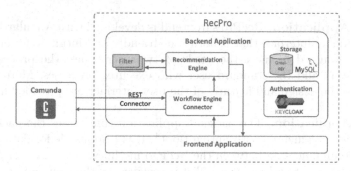

Fig. 1. RecPro architecture.

Workflow Engine Connector. The core component of a PAIS is the workflow engine that controls the execution of business processes. RecPro depends on *external* PAIS like Camunda[2]. A workflow engine is connected to RecPro through the Workflow Engine Connector via a REST connector. The main task of the external PAIS is to determine next process steps eligible to be executed. However, the external PAIS does not communicate this to users directly. Instead, RecPro takes this data, revises and augments it and delivers it to the worklists of designated users, i.e. worklists are provided by RecPro instead of an external PAIS. In our prototype, Camunda serves as an illustrative example of integrating an external PAIS into RecPro.

Recommendation Engine. RecPro supplies a comprehensive recommendation engine by itself. This engine is responsible for analyzing user data and generating personalized recommendations. It employs various recommendation techniques, such as collaborative filtering, content-based filtering, and knowledge-based filtering to offer accurate recommendations based on factors such as user preferences, historical behavior, and process execution context. The system is flexibly adaptable to new algorithms. This allows process owners to experiment with different recommendation methods. In our current RecPro implementation, three filters are implemented: content-based filtering using Bayes Classifier algorithm [1], collaborative filtering using Pearson correlation coefficient in a user-based approach [1], and knowledge-based filtering implemented through comparison-based algorithm. In addition to providing personalized recommendations, it is crucial to highlight that the recommendation algorithms

---

[2] https://camunda.com/.

employed by RecPro do not alter the priority of individual tasks. This means that if optimization algorithms have already been applied to the worklist for purposes such as reducing turnaround times, those outcomes remain untouched. The new recommendation capabilities are designed to work in accordance with existing optimizations, ensuring that personalized recommendations do not override or disrupt any pre-established task prioritization based on process efficiency objectives.

Frontend Application. RecPro's frontend is developed with Angular 16[3], aiming to provide an interface that is both user-friendly and intuitive for end-users. Its GUI is designed to meet the needs of two user types: the process owner (administrator) and the standard user who executes processes. More detailed insights into the design and features of the user interface are provided in Sect. 4.

Backend Application. The backend application constitutes the backbone of RecPro. It is implemented with Spring Boot[4]. It is responsible for data management and communication between the RecPro modules.

When a request to a RecPro worklist is received by the frontend application, it is forwarded to the workflow engine connector by the backend application; from there it is send to the external PAIS, in our case Camunda. Camunda then processes this request and provides the updated content for a worklist refresh. Subsequently, these worklist data, along with other available data about users, contexts, etc., are worked on by the recommendation engine to generate personalized recommendations. The latter are processed together with Camunda's worklist data for reorganizing the worklist in a personalized way. The new and individualized worklist is then returned and displayed to a user through the frontend application. This ensures that each user is presented with a unique and personalized worklist, enhancing the user-centric nature of RecPro.

The backend application holds all the necessary input data for creating these recommendations. It stores execution data, including event logs and user ratings, in a MySQL database. Data related to process models, e.g. augmented business processes, is stored in an ontology developed specifically for this purpose. Furthermore, Keycloak 23.0.5[5] - a user management system - has been incorporated into the backend application to handle user authentication, authorization, and profile management.

4   Demonstration

Initial testing of a first RecPro prototype reveals that is has the potential to allow users to incorporate their individual preferences in real time when executing tasks, resulting in a more personalized execution of business processes. According to [4], this enhances user experience and consequently has a positive impact on

---

[3] https://angular.io/.

[4] https://spring.io/projects/spring-boot/.

[5] https://keycloak.org/.

process execution. Figure 2 depicts the user interface of RecPro; it illustrates how recommendation mechanisms are combined with BPM within one integrated application.

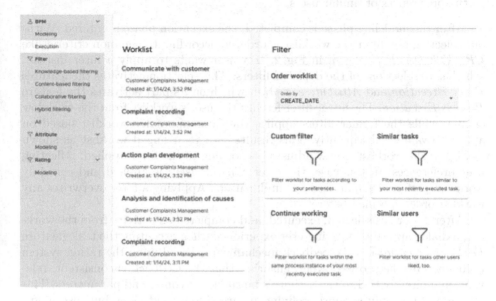

Fig. 2. RecPro user interface.

Before executing processes, they must first be modeled and integrated into RecPro. This step lies in the domain of a process owner and unfolds in the *Modeling* phase of an application. It is arranged on the left side of the application (Fig. 2). One key aspect is to enrich processes and activities with descriptive attributes, a fundamental step necessary to enable content-based filtering (feature *Attribute modeling*). For collecting user feedback, required by content-based and collaborative filtering methods, a process owner defines custom ratings, varying from straightforward binary (thumbs up/down) to more nuanced ordinal and continuous scales, like a five-star rating system (feature *Feedback modeling*). One of the main task of a process owner is to define filters (feature *Filter modeling*). This involves selecting the filter type (e.g. knowledge-based) and meticulously specifying the data (for instance, which types of processes) and algorithm to be used, starting from a basic Pearson correlation coefficient to potentially more sophisticated algorithms. The filters are offered to the process participants during process execution on the right side of the user interface (Fig. 2). In our sample application depicted in this figure we have configured four distinct filters:

- **Custom filter:** This is a knowledge-based filter that selects tasks according to manually defined user preferences.
- **Similar tasks:** This content-based filter recommends tasks similar to the task most recently executed by the user.

- **Continue process:** This knowledge-based filter selects the open tasks of the process instance the user is currently working on.
- **Similar users:** This is a collaborative filter that recommends tasks based on the preferences of similar users.

After the modeling phase is completed, the execution phase is entered. Without selecting any filter the worklist is ordered according to common criteria like *CREATE_DATE* as shown in Fig. 2. If a user wants to apply a filter instead, s/he has to select one of the depicted filters. This selection activates the features *Filter Execution* and *Attribute execution* which on its part activates the feature *Process Execution*. The latter filter fetches the user's worklist from the workflow engine, while the former filters applies the filter upon this worklist based on attribute values subsequently. This results in a re-arranged worklist as shown in Fig. 3. The worklist is now adjusted according to the filter applied, reflecting user preferences. In this case, the filter *Similar users* is applied and certainly works on preferences inherited by similar users. Applying a filter overwrites any worklist order specified before.

After a user has selected, executed, and completed an activity from the worklist, a dialog appears, inquiring user experience when executing the task (feature *Feedback execution*). This feedback mechanism is based upon the rating system predefined by the process owner, ensuring that the feedback is consistent, relevant, and directly tied to the activity's intended outcomes and parameters. This interaction not only supports refining future recommendations but also aligns user feedback directly with the activity instance.

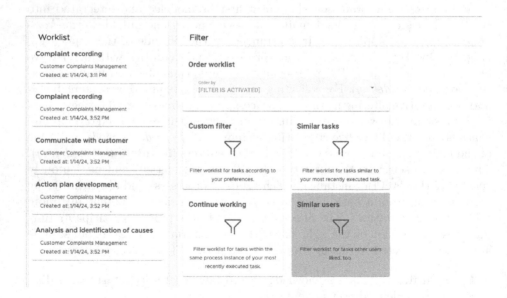

Fig. 3. Similar tasks filter applied.

5   Conclusion

In conclusion, this paper introduces RecPro, a novel tool designed to improve BPM by integrating user-centric recommendation approaches. Being developed within the PRIME project, RecPro has already undergone preliminary testing by project members, demonstrating its potential to facilitate personalized user engagement and streamline process management. Despite promising feedback, there is room for further development and validation across different organizational contexts: refining the user interface to enhance user experience, customizing algorithms to specific process needs, and conducting a project-based user study to assess its impact on user satisfaction. These future endeavors aim at optimizing the performance of the tool and user engagement.

References

1. Aggarwal, C.C.: Recommender Systems - The Textbook. Springer, Heidelberg (2016). https://doi.org/10.1007/978-3-319-29659-3
2. Barba, I., Weber, B., Del Valle, C.: Supporting the Optimized Execution of Business Processes Through Recommendations. In: Daniel, F., Barkaoui, K., Dustdar, S. (eds.) BPM 2011. LNCS, vol. 99, pp. 135–140. Springer, Heidelberg (2012). https://doi.org/10.1007/978-3-642-28108-2_12
3. Bidar, R., ter Hofstede, A.H.M., Sindhgatta, R., Ouyang, C.: Preference-based resource and task allocation in business process automation. In: Panetto, H., Debruyne, C., Hepp, M., Lewis, D., Ardagna, C., Meersman, R. (eds.) OTM 2019. LNCS, vol. 11877, pp. 404–421. Springer, Heidelberg (2019). https://doi.org/10.1007/978-3-030-33246-4_26
4. Bryson, A., Forth, J., Stokes, L.: Does worker wellbeing affect workplace performance? Technical Report 9096, Bonn (2015). http://hdl.handle.net/10419/111548
5. Dumas, M., Rosa, M.L., Mendling, J., Reijers, H.A.: Fundamentals of Business Process Management. Springer, Heidelberg (2013). https://doi.org/10.1007/978-3-662-56509-4
6. Jablonski, S., Bussler, C.: Workflow management - modeling concepts, architecture and implementation. International Thomson (1996)
7. Kubrak, K., Milani, F., Nolte, A., Dumas, M.: Prescriptive process monitoring: Quo vadis? PeerJ Comput. Sci. **8**, e1097 (2022). https://doi.org/10.7717/peerj-cs.1097
8. Lu, J., Wu, D., Mao, M., Wang, W., Zhang, G.: Recommender system application developments: a survey. Decis. Supp. Syst. **74**, 12–32 (2015)
9. Petter, S., Fichtner, M., Schönig, S., Jablonski, S.: Content-based filtering for worklist reordering to improve user satisfaction: a position paper. In: Proceedings of the 24th International Conference on Enterprise Information Systems, ICEIS, vol. 2, pp. 589–596. SciTePress (2022). https://doi.org/10.5220/0011092900003179. ISBN 978-989-758-569-2. ISSN 2184-4992
10. Petter, S., Jablonski, S.: Recommender systems in business process management: a systematic literature review. In: Proceedings of the 25th International Conference on Enterprise Information Systems, ICEIS, vol. 2, pp. 431–442. SciTePress (2023). https://doi.org/10.5220/0012039500003467. ISBN 978-989-758-648-4. ISSN 2184-4992

11. Reichert, M., Weber, B.: Enabling Flexibility in Process-Aware Information Systems - Challenges, Methods, Technologies. Springer, Heidelberg (2012). https://doi.org/10.1007/978-3-642-30409-5
12. Rosemann, M., vom Brocke, J.: The six core elements of business process management. In: vom Brocke, J., Rosemann, M. (eds.) Handbook on Business Process Management 1. International Handbooks on Information Systems. Springer, Heidelberg (2015). https://doi.org/10.1007/978-3-642-45100-3_5
13. Schonenberg, H., Weber, B., van Dongen, B.F., van der Aalst, W.M.P.: Supporting flexible processes through recommendations based on history. In: Dumas, M., Reichert, M., Shan, M.C. (eds.) BPM 2008. LNCS, pp. 51–66. Springer, Heidelberg (2008). https://doi.org/10.1007/978-3-540-85758-7_7
14. Valentin, C.D., Emrich, A., Werth, D., Loos, P.: Context-sensitive and individualized support of employees. IEEE (2014)
15. Weske, M.: Business Process Management: Concepts, Languages, Architectures. Springer (2007). https://doi.org/10.1007/978-3-540-73522-9
16. Eili, M.Y., Rezaeenour, J.: A survey on recommendation in process mining. Concurrency Comput. Pract. Exp. **34** (2022). https://doi.org/10.1002/cpe.7304

Predictive Maintenance in a Fleet Management System: The Navarchos Case

Apostolos Giannoulidis[1]([✉]), Anna-Valentini Michailidou[2],
Theodoros Toliopoulos[1,2], Ioannis Constantinou[2], and Anastasios Gounaris[1]

[1] Aristotle University of Thessaloniki, Thessaloniki, Greece
{agiannous,tatoliop,gounaria}@csd.auth.gr
[2] Istognosis Ltd., Nicosia, Cyprus
valentina@navarchos.com, ioannis@istognosis.com

Abstract. This work presents a state-of-the-art predictive maintenance (PdM) framework, which is tailored to demanding cases, where information is dynamic and partial, and non-supervised solutions should be applied. Moreover, it discusses and aims to demonstrate the application of this framework to the Navarchos Fleet Management System (FMS).

1 Introduction

Fleet Management Systems (FMS) play a pivotal role in maintaining the operational safety and efficiency of vehicle fleets, especially in the face of escalating fleet sizes. A critical responsibility within this domain is the meticulous scheduling of vehicle maintenance, aimed at averting potential failures that not only endanger driver safety but also disrupt vehicle uptime. As we navigate the landscape of Industry 4.0, the integration of Predictive Maintenance (PdM) emerges as a crucial paradigm shift for enhancing FMS capabilities.

Traditionally, many FMS rely on Diagnostic Trouble Codes (DTCs) sourced from original equipment manufacturers (OEMs) as a primary means of identifying and addressing vehicle issues. These codes, emanating from the engine control unit (ECU), serve to pinpoint faulty behavior based on predefined rules applied to sensor data. However, a main limitations of this approach is that serious vehicle failures evade detection through DTCs, highlighting a need for a more proactive and comprehensive solution. Furthermore, while DTCs excel at detecting malfunctions, their primary focus contrasts with the broader scope of PdM, which not only identifies existing issues but anticipates potential failures.

In a FMS, PdM constitutes a holistic end-to-end application encompassing data collection, pre-processing, storage, and the generation of predictive alarms within a dynamic streaming environment. Implementing such a solution comprises many challenges, including the dynamic nature of vehicle operations,

The research is funded under the programme of social cohesion "THALIA 2021–2027" co-funded by the European Union, through Research and Innovation Foundation.

insufficient information about past services and repairs, and the absence of readily available expert guidance. The intricacies of these challenges underscore the complexity involved in establishing a robust PdM framework for FMSs. In this work, we delve into the application of PdM in the FMS of Navarchos proposed in [2], presenting detailed information and insights gained from real-world implementation. While frameworks like COSMO, as presented in [5], exist for PdM in vehicles, we distinguish ourselves in several ways. Firstly, our fleet is heterogeneous, comprising various vehicle types operating in diverse areas, both urban and non-urban. Additionally, we address the challenge of partial information concerning the state of vehicles, derived solely from our limited access to a subset of the vehicles' service logs. Overall, we aim to contribute valuable perspectives to the evolving landscape of working PdM systems in fleet management.

Structure . The next section provides the architecture of Navarchos FMS. Section 3 deals with the PdM framework design principles, while Sect. 4 discusses its implementation. We conclude with the demo description.

2   Navarchos Architecture Overview

The NAVARCHOS AI Fleet Management System (FMS) has been developed as a cloud-native solution, deployed on a Kubernetes infrastructure directly on bare metal. This system adopts a microservices architecture, where each Internet of Things (IoT) subsystem is a distinct, independently deployable service. This architecture enables autonomous scaling of each subsystem, significantly enhancing the system's overall scalability, simplifying updates to individual components, and allowing for the selection of the most appropriate technology for each subsystem based on its unique requirements.

Each subsystem, as well as the FMS as a whole, is continuously monitored to quickly identify and rectify failures, ensuring swift service recovery. The majority of subsystems communicate over REST/HTTPS with JSON payloads; JSON is chosen due to its human-readable format. Nevertheless, for critical performance subsystems like the GPS tracking gateway, which utilize inherently binary protocols, a binary communication protocol has been implemented to assure high performance.

Subsystems are deployed in isolated environments, such as containers, taking full advantage of Kubernetes' dynamic workload management and advanced scalability features. This configuration permits the system to dynamically adjust resources (either scaling up or down) in near real-time in response to evolving business needs. Additionally, the system embraces Continuous Integration (CI) and Continuous Delivery (CD) practices, enabling frequent updates and maintaining the system's currency with minimal downtime. The NAVARCHOS FMS architecture has been meticulously developed, showcasing a comprehensive, multi-layered approach to fleet management. This system seamlessly integrates a broad array of functionalities, specifically designed to meet the advanced needs of modern vehicle tracking, data processing, and analysis. Below is a detailed overview of the developed subsystems, also presented in Fig. 1:

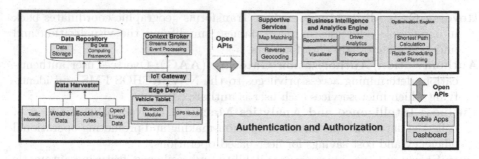

Fig. 1. NAVARCHOS FMS architecture

Edge Devices: Installed across the fleet, these devices capture GPS locations and vehicle diagnostics, ensuring secure data exchange with the cloud.

Vehicle Data Gateway/Hub: Acts as a secure conduit for GPS locations and vehicle diagnostics data, compatible with a diverse range of vehicle tracking protocols.

Data Harvester: This subsystem interfaces with various external data sources (e.g., via APIs) to aggregate, process, and store both real-time and historical data, such as weather and traffic conditions, within the NAVARCHOS FMS infrastructure. This capability is vital for generating timely notifications, alerts, and underpinning business intelligence and analytics.

Context Broker: Serves as the intermediary for sharing context information between input subsystems (such as the data gateway and data aggregator, known as context producers) and other subsystems or users (context consumers) who require this information. It accommodates dynamic roles, allowing entities to act as either producers, consumers, or both, and manages updates as subscribable events.

Stream Processor: Incorporated within the context broker or as an independent subsystem, it processes data streams and integrates them with business processes, enabling real-time responses to recognized events with notifications and alerts.

Routing Optimizer Microservice: Processes a sequence of GPS locations to determine the most efficient route, providing detailed turn-by-turn navigation instructions to optimize travel paths.

Scheduling Optimizer Microservice: Solves the Vehicle Routing Problem (VRP) by calculating the optimal delivery routes for a fleet of vehicles, considering various constraints and objectives, and then providing detailed navigation guidelines.

Map-Matching Microservice: Matches recorded geographic coordinates to a logical representation of the real world, minimizing storage needs for trip data, facilitating quicker trip visualization, and standardizing geodata for subsequent analysis.

Reverse Geocoding Microservice: Transforms geographic coordinates back into readable addresses or place names, simplifying the visualization and understanding of trip data for users.

Authentication/Authorization Gateway (AAG): Oversees user authentication, determining access privileges to the NAVARCHOS FMS and identifying which microservices each user is authorized to use.

Business Intelligence and Analytics Machine: Delivers a holistic view of collected data, enabling informed decision-making and promoting operational efficiency and cost savings for fleet-based operations.

Data Storage: Guarantees data availability and resilience, featuring automatic failover and maintenance operations without causing system downtime.

Visualizer: Provides visualization tools for data, analytics, and insights, especially regarding driver behavior, and supports the management of vehicles, devices, and user interfaces.

REST API: Makes system data accessible and supports the integration of NAVARCHOS FMS with other applications, thereby enhancing both interoperability and extensibility.

3   Our PdM Solution

Navarchos's fleet comprises a variety of vehicles operating in different conditions in terms of driving behavior, route types, weather conditions and so on. The objective of PdM is this context is to detect which vehicles should perform maintenance tasks (i.e., unscheduled, non-periodic service) to avoid serious damage, based on their operational state derived solely from sensor data and (partial) past maintenance event recordings. The absence of appropriate and/or adequate labels and historical data led us to a non-supervised solution upon Parameter IDs (PIDs) signals[1]; DTCs (Diagnostic Trouble Codes)[2] are also monitored, but, after investigation, they cannot serve our purpose. The main rationale is to detect deviations from the normal operating condition in vehicles; such deviations are interpreted as early signs of a forthcoming damage. In conclusion, the primary challenge lies in the requirement to offer precise indications for maintenance requirements while safeguarding the trust of drivers and mechanics. This underscores the need for enhanced precision in our anomaly score-based alarms. Such alerts serve to notify both drivers and maintenance managers of abnormal vehicle operation, prompting the necessary inspections.

To address all the aforementioned challenges, we build a PdM framework, which does not rely on domain expert active involvement, handles the dynamicity of the operating conditions, and maintains high precision in predicting failures. This framework consists of three main modules forming a 3-stage pipeline: 1) transformation of data in a form that highlights behavioral changes, 2) the construction of a normal reference state of a vehicle, and 3) use of a non-supervised

---

[1] https://en.wikipedia.org/wiki/OBD-IIPIDs.

[2] https://github.com/mytrile/obd-trouble-codes/blob/master/obd-trouble-codes.csv.

model to produce an anomaly score. Full details and evaluation results are in [2], and here we present only a summary.

The first module's objective is to transform the data into a form where changes related to the failure state of a vehicle are highlighted. The final choice of these steps depends on the variety and volume of the data that our system collects. Key alternatives include delta transformation, correlation between signals, frequency-domain transformation, histograms, and so on.

The second module deals with constructing a reference state of vehicle's normal operating condition and is closely related to the support of non-supervised solutions. The idea behind this stage is that, based on the normal operation state of a vehicle despite the existence of noise, we can calculate a deviation of that vehicle in real-time by comparing its current state to the reference one. The extraction of such knowledge (i.e., the normal reference profile), depends on the actual case and characteristics of the problem. In most PdM cases, we expect that, in general, a failure state is rarer than healthy/normal operation. Different approaches exist in the literature regarding this step, for example, in [3], the authors selected the data of an asset in its starting state as healthy, while in [1], the authors based the selection of healthy data on the concept of the wisdom of the crowd, i.e., in any given time point, the majority of a bus fleet performing the same routes is in a good condition.

Finally, the third module concerns the actual detection of abnormal operational behavior and thus the need for maintenance. Here, a non-supervised model that leverages the transformed data and the knowledge regarding the reference data produces a deviation level (a.k.a, an anomaly score) and alarms for each vehicle in the fleet in a streaming fashion. The choice for such a model can vary, where any non-supervised model is applicable without excluding supervised ones if enough trustworthy data have been gathered. Navarchos currently operates in a non-supervised manner and three well-known representative types of techniques employed are similarity-based, reconstruction (deep-learning) models, and regression (or forecasting) ones. We note that the performance of a model depends on many factors, such as the size of the reference data, the underlying hypothesis used by the model to predict anomalies (e.g., proximity-based techniques use distance, statistic-based techniques use some kind of distribution, where many different approaches exist in literature).

Framework Instantiation in our FMS. We provide more details about how the framework above is instantiated within Navarchos FMS to become operational and effective. As previously, more details are in [2]. Regarding the first stage, the correlation between the raw features is selected, which lets us observe behavioral changes between two different periods of vehicle operation. Correlation transformation refers to the calculation of the cross-correlation between the different data features. Using a sliding window over raw data, we calculate the correlation between the collected signal data. In more detail, if we consider that the number of the initial data features are f_n, after cross-correlation, we result in a symmetric $f_n \times f_n$ matrix, which can be considered as a vector with

$\frac{f_n*(f_n-1)}{2}$ features. The idea behind this transformation is that different usages of vehicles may produce similar correlations. For example, we expect that speed and rpm are positively correlated regardless of whether the vehicle performs urban or regional rides under different weather conditions, while a difference in the correlation of two signals may refer to a failure state.

For the second stage, to define a reference state, we use a period of vehicle operation after maintenance (or standard service), assuming that the vehicle operates normally after such events without seeking more guarantees. Note that building the reference state based on such events yields a dynamic solution, where the reference vehicle profile is updated upon known completion of maintenance tasks. Moreover, towards being more flexible, the framework allows the recollection of the reference data upon request, where data from the current period can be used for reference.

To instantiate the final stage of our framework, we use the *Closest Pair Detection* technique, inspired by solutions such as those in [3,4]. The technique calculates the deviation of upcoming data by leveraging a healthy reference. However, instead of producing a single score for each vehicle, the technique calculates the distance of upcoming data from the reference data, in each feature separately. So, if the dimensionality of our data, or the number of features is f_n, then the technique produces f_n anomaly scores, by computing the minimum difference between the value of its feature from the values of the same feature in the reference data. Alarms are produced from violation of the threshold in any of f_n anomaly scores and are accompanied by a description with the feature that triggered it.

The above methodology relies on appropriate tuning. For setting the threshold for each score, we decided to use the self-tuning thresholding from [3], which is useful in dynamic environments and, using the same parameters, a different threshold is calculated for each vehicle.

4   Navarchos PdM Service Implementation

In this section, we present the pipeline and data flow through the system. The process begins with data collection from GPS tracking devices installed on vehicles. These data undergo parsing and transformation to become suitable input for the PdM module. This module then processes the input to generate predictions and trigger alarms when necessary. Figure 2 provides an overview of the pipeline, presenting the technologies employed at each stage and the type of data being transmitted. In the following sections, we will detail each step of this process, starting with data parsing, followed by data processing, and concluding with an overview of the PdM module.

Data Parsing. Vehicles are equipped with edge devices (GPS tracking devices) that monitor and report the status of various vehicle sub-systems in real-time. Each tracking device utilizes a specific communication protocol to periodically

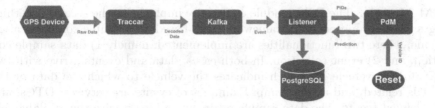

Fig. 2. Data flow of NAVARCHOS PdM

exchange data with a server in the form of data packets. These packets contain information such as device ID, timestamp, location, speed, temperature, and so on. The tracking device and communication protocol used in this work is manufactured by Sinocastel[3]. The transmitted packets are represented in a hexadecimal format and need to be decoded to extract the information. This decoding is performed by Traccar[4], an open-source GPS tracking server that supports multiple models of GPS tracking devices and protocols, by providing real-time tracking in fleet management scenarios. Upon receiving a data packet from a tracking device, Traccar identifies the protocol used, decodes the incoming data packet, and extracts information such as device ID, timestamp, location, and several PID signals. These data are then transformed into a human-readable format, specifically to JSON, and are then sent to an Apache Kafka topic for further analysis.

Data Processing. To continuously consume vehicle data from the Kafka topic to which Traccar sends data, a Spring application was developed. More specifically, a Kafka listener that consumes sensor data related to pressure, speed, and temperature of the vehicle engine from this topic was implemented. When a new message arrives, the listener receives it and stores the important information in a database table; the database we utilized is PostgreSQL with provisions for the cases where data volumes grow very large. If the message contains all six of the required PID features without any outliers, based on specified thresholds, it is also stored in a buffer table. This buffer is used to implement the first stage of the PdM framework (Sect. 3), which is the data correlation transformation. More specifically, the Pearson correlation coefficient between the PID features is calculated using the last m (m=300) stored signals. This calculation of the correlation between features takes place every 100 new samples, and the results are submitted along with the timestamp and vehicle ID to the PdM Module through an API. In return, the PdM Module for each submitted message returns a response with the anomaly scores for all features and corresponding thresholds, an indication for alarms, and a description.

---

[3] https://www.sinocastel.com/.
[4] https://www.traccar.org/.

PdM Module. The PdM module essentially implements the second and third stages of the proposed PdM framework. It is based on a simple communication scheme, where two functionalities are implemented, namely 1) data sample collection, and 2) event collection. In both cases, data and events arrive with two tag values, a vehicle ID, which indicates the vehicle to which the data or the event is related, and a timestamp. Examples of events are services, DTCs, and user-defined events. The data sample represents a record with the available features. When a new event or data sample from a vehicle (or source) arrives, the system checks if corresponding models exist for that vehicle; if not, it creates one. After that, in the case of data samples, the corresponding model before calculating anomaly scores, checks if reference data exist for that source. When no reference data are available, the PdM module takes care of creating the reference set from the upcoming data; this will stop when criteria regarding the size of the reference set are met. When a reference set exists, the method produces the anomaly scores for all features and returns the decision (along with scores and thresholds). Finally, the events are used to trigger the reset of the models i(i.e., the recalculation of reference data with the new upcoming data) on the fly. To this end, the models are saved on a separate database, so that, in case of system failure, to start from their last state.

5   Demo Description and Conclusions

The demo will showcase a successful scenario of detecting failures in operating a vehicle using NAVARCHOS FMS bringing all the aforementioned functionalities together. The scenario involves a stream of raw data produced by a specific vehicle, emphasizing crucial stages of the data flow, encompassing the computation of the anomaly score in a streaming fashion, illustrating how this aids in mitigating upcoming failures. The demo commences with the presentation of upcoming vehicular raw data while the vehicle is in operation. Subsequently, the next stage of the data flow reveals the transformation of raw data into a readable format (JSON), which also encapsulates the signals used for failure prediction. Moving forward, the results of data collection in batches and the extraction of correlation features are displayed. Lastly, in the concluding part of the scenario, the anomaly score is computed and presented for each feature as described in Sect. 3. The analytical results, encompassing raw anomaly scores and a user-friendly indicator for the vehicle, will be visible as part of NAVARCHOS FMS.

Overall, we present a state-of-the-art PdM framework and an exemplary instantiation of it to serve the needs of a real-world FMS.

References

1. Fan, Y., Nowaczyk, S., Rögnvaldsson, T.: Evaluation of self-organized approach for predicting compressor faults in a city bus fleet. In: INNS Conference on Big Data, pp. 447–456 (2015). https://doi.org/10.1016/j.procs.2015.07.322
2. Giannoulidis, A., Gounaris, A., Constantinou, I.: Exploring unsupervised anomaly detection for vehicle predictive maintenance with partial information. In: EDBT, pp. 753–761 (2024)
3. Giannoulidis, A., Gounaris, A., Nikolaidis, N., Naskos, A., Caljouw, D.: Investigating thresholding techniques in a real predictive maintenance scenario. SIGKDD Explor. Newsl. **24**(2), 86-95 (2022). https://doi.org/10.1145/3575637.3575651
4. Linardi, M., Zhu, Y., Palpanas, T., Keogh, E.J.: Matrix profile goes MAD: variable-length motif and discord discovery in data series. Data Min. Knowl. Disc. **34**(4), 1022–1071 (2020)
5. Rögnvaldsson, T., Nowaczyk, S., Byttner, S., Prytz, R., Svensson, M.: Self-monitoring for maintenance of vehicle fleets. Data Min. Knowl. Disc. **32**(2), 344–384 (2018). https://doi.org/10.1007/s10618-017-0538-6

CDMiA: Revealing Impacts of Data Migrations on Schemas in Multi-model Systems

Annabelle Gillet[✉] and Éric Leclercq

Laboratoire d'Informatique de Bourgogne - EA 7534, University of Burgundy, Dijon, France
{annabelle.gillet,eric.leclercq}@u-bourgogne.fr

Abstract. To produce quality results from artificial intelligence (AI) pipelines, data consistency and structure must be finely controlled. This control must take into consideration the heterogeneity of data, and more specifically the heterogeneity of their models. Indeed, multi-model data are at the core of current systems, such as data lakes or polystores, that supply data for AI pipelines. To benefit the most of multi-model systems, data migrations are used to ingest data with a more suitable model than the original model, to apply operators available only for a specific model or to optimize queries, by sending data into a system capable of processing data faster than the original system, even when the migration time is included. However, data migrations are complex in a multi-model environment, in particular because the models do not support the same types of constraints. Thus, such constraints can be preserved, weakened, created or dropped during the migration process. Furthermore, the impact of a migration on a schema is contextual. Indeed, if a schema does not apply a constraint of its source model, it is not important that it is not supported in the destination model. Thus, it is essential to control data migrations, and to assess the impact of a migration on a schema. To do so, we propose the Categorical Data Migration Assessor tool (CDMiA), that relies on category theory to automatically detect the required creations and losses of constraints when migrating a schema from a model to another.

Keywords: Multi-model data · Data migration · Category theory

1 Introduction

Data are at the core of AI pipelines. The quality of the result greatly depends on input data, that may undergo multiple transformations in these pipelines. Furthermore, data are heterogeneous by their very nature, regarding their source, their content, their quality and their model [1]. Thus, it is essential to have a fine control over data, and more specifically over their consistency and structure, to build robust AI pipelines. To do so, this control must occur as early as possible, namely over storage systems.

To cope with the diversity of data models, storage systems have evolved towards multi-model systems. Some database management systems (DBMSs)

S. Islam and A. Sturm (Eds.): CAiSE 2024, LNBIP 520, pp. 120–128, 2024.
https://doi.org/10.1007/978-3-031-61000-4_14

propose several models at the same time [19], but they often rely on a main model, and thus are less specialized in the minor models. Other systems such as polystores [24], data lakes [12] or data spaces [13] aim at benefiting from each model and their specific operators individually (e.g., path finding queries in the graph model) by using jointly different DBMSs, but at the cost of an increased complexity.

In these systems, data migrations are essential for multiple use cases. When ingesting data, the source model might not be the most suitable model for manipulating data, and it might require to migrate data into a system supporting another data model. For example, social network data are generally supplied under the JSON format, that can be transformed into a graph model to study the interaction among users, into a relational model to store the main characteristics of messages such as the hashtags or the publication time, and into a textual model to study the content of publications [7,11]. Once data are stored, they can be used for querying or for further data processing. For example, it can consist in the application of an operator not available in the current system, or in the execution of an algorithm on data originating from multiple sources that must be integrated into a common model suitable for the algorithm [14,18]. Query optimization in multi-model systems may also lead to data migration. As some models are best tailored to execute some types of query, the performances can be enhanced by migrating data from its source DBMS to a DBMS that can better handle the query, even when the migration time is included [3,22]. Optimizations can also be applied with operators processing data of multiple systems, as for example with the bind join between a large and a small datasets [16], that sends the small dataset into the system of the large dataset to filter it and to avoid retrieving unnecessary data.

However, in multi-model environments data migration is a daunting process [20]. Indeed, modifying the model of data may require to add constraints (e.g., adding a foreign key constraint on the attribute of the referencing table stating that it must be equal to a primary key attribute of the referenced table when migrating from the graph model to the relational model) or to lose expressivity (e.g., loosing a primary key constraint when migrating from the relational model to the JSON model). The acceptability of these alterations depends on the context of the migration. One may want to use an equivalent model if the goal is to change the system used for storing data, but could accept some losses regarding the constraints of the data if the goal is only to execute an analysis algorithm. Furthermore, there are multiple ways to transform a model into an other, and a transformation also depends on the schema of the data (e.g., if there is no primary key constraint applied on data stored with the relational model, it is not important that the JSON model does not support such constraint). Thus, as data migrations can be costly to process and can lead to errors or data inconsistencies, it is essential to identify beforehand the constraints that must be dropped or created in a schema.

To this end, we propose CDMiA[1], a tool based on category theory able to assess the impacts of a migration on a given schema, i.e., which constraints and specificities of the destination model must be created and which ones are preserved from the source model to the destination model. This tool assists data engineers when migrating data, to evaluate if the losses and creations are acceptable for their use case. The article is organized as follows: Sect. 2 presents related works on multi-model data migrations, Sect. 3 gives a glimpse of the category theoretical background, Sect. 4 details how CDMiA assesses the impact of a migration on a schema, and Sect. 5 opens up perspectives of future work.

2 Related Work

Data migrations in a multi-model context have particular needs that must be taken into account. First, multiple levels of abstraction are needed to link a schema to its model, or models among them. Second, enabling the expression of constraints in a schema or in a model is essential to consider individual characteristics of models and differentiate them. In the remainder of this section, we study how related works have taken into consideration these aspects.

In [15], authors proposed a tool to support model transformation and data migration from relational database to MongoDB. They used tags and action tags to guide model transformations, and proposed a transformation algorithm to perform automatic data migrations. However, this method is not generalizable for other data models, and shows the need for a formal framework.

In [4], authors focused on model transformations and argued that model transformations can be abstracted as being transformation models. They proposed an UML/MOF framework including OCL constraints. Nonetheless, focusing only on transformation models hinders transformations for specific use cases that do not necessarily fit predefined transformations.

Cluet et al. [6] studied data conversions for mediator/wrapper architectures. They proposed YAT (Yet Another Tree-based system) which includes a graph data model to capture data from heterogeneous sources and a rule based language based on pattern matching facilities and Skolem functions as well as a type checking system. The proposed language is used to specify data conversions.

Ehrig et al. [8] focused on bi-directional model transformations defined with triple graph grammars. They demonstrated their proposal on a transformation between a relational model and a class model. They showed under which conditions a transformation has an inverse. However, they did not consider the case for which the transformations induce an information loss.

Alagic and Bernstein in [2] proposed a theoretical framework for generic schema management to express schemas and data transformations independently of a particular model. Based on category theory principles, they proposed to define transformations as schema morphisms and the same at the data level. They applied their formal paradigm only on XML schema.

---

[1] Available at: https://github.com/AnnabelleGillet/CDMiA.

Some other proposals, such as CQL [5] and MMQL [17], have already used category theory to represent multi-model systems. However, they focused on providing a unified schema regardless of the model of data. Therefore, they lose the individual advantages and drawbacks of each model, and cannot rely on their specificities to fully benefit from multi-model systems.

Many of the articles in this field contain elements borrowed from category theory, such as monads for generalizing list, set and bag structures [10] or algebraic structures induced by morphisms (pullback, pushout) for controlling data transformations, without fully embracing this theory. However, on top of providing all these elements, category theory proposes advanced mechanisms useful for handling data migrations: 1) specific constructs such as particular morphisms, path equalities [23] and limits/colimits can be used to express specificities and constraints in a category; and 2) functors naturally allow to navigate among abstraction levels and guarantee by definition the preservation of the structure of the source category, by defining the mapping for each objects and morphisms of the source category towards the destination category. Our work propose to rely on these mechanisms to assess the impact of data migrations on schema in multi-model systems.

3   Theoretical Background

Category theory focuses on relationships between objects with morphisms, allowing to define the global structure of data models and schemas. Some special organisations of objects and morphisms known as limits "(e.g., products and pullback)" and "(e.g., coproducts and pushout)" enforce different properties over a category, that can be used to represent constraints of models. Functors map two categories and ensure that the destination category preserves the structure of the source category, therefore they are optimal to define migrations and to guarantee that a schema matches its model.

Due to space restriction, the definitions of the concepts of category theory are not given here, but can be found in the literature [9,21]. We only present which concepts of category theory are used for our multi-model data representation at the abstraction levels of model and schema, and for the migrations' specifications.

In our representation, a model is defined by a category. The objects of the category define structures such as tables, documents or data types, and morphisms are connections between structures, such as attributes or relationships.

Constraints of models are supported directly with categorical concepts. An identifier is supported by an isomorphism and referential constraints are represented by morphism equalities (including equalities of compositions). An association of several structures (e.g., an edge in a graph) is a product, and an association with constraint (e.g., a foreign key for which the attribute of the referencing table must be equal to the attribute of the referenced table) is a pullback.

To illustrate the capabilities of this representation, the categories of the property graph and the relational models are given in Fig. 1. For the property graph

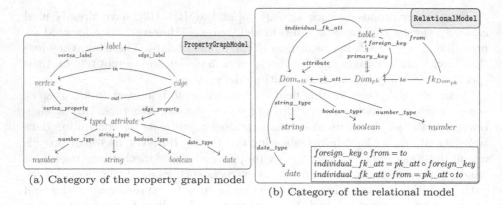

(a) Category of the property graph model

(b) Category of the relational model

Fig. 1. Two categories of data models

model, the edge and vertex properties are morphisms towards *typed_attribute*, itself mapped to its type (only major types have been represented in this article), and the labels are objects mapped by vertices and edges. An *edge* is a product constructed with the morphisms *in* and *out* towards the object *vertex*. The relational model, on top of simple attributes connected to their domain, can have primary keys, that are isomorphisms between a table and the domain of the primary key, and foreign keys, that are pullbacks for which the morphism equality $to = foreign\_key \circ from$ holds. The composite primary and foreign keys are represented respectively by a morphism pk_att and $individual\_fk\_att$ for each attribute.

A schema is a category along with a functor mapping the schema category to its model category. Thus, to respect the definition of a functor and the functorial law, the schema must follow the rules imposed by the model.

A model transformation is defined with a functor between the category of the schema to migrate and the destination model. As a functor preserves the structure of the source category into the destination category, it is an efficient mechanism to represent a migration and to assess its impacts. We distinguish two types of migration: 1) a migration following a template, in which case it is automatically computed by composing the functor from the schema to its source model and the functor of the template transformation from the source model to the destination model; or 2) a custom migration that is directly defined by a functor between the category of the schema and the destination model. A template migration forces all elements of a schema of a same type to be mapped to the same element of the destination model, whereas a custom migration allows to map individually each element (e.g., an attribute of a JSON schema can be mapped to a standard attribute in the relational model, and another attribute to a primary key).

4   Assessing Impacts of Data Migrations

The tool we propose aims at simulating a data migration to evaluate its impact on a schema. A user can select a schema along with its associated model, a destination model (in this version of the tool, the relational, JSON and property graph models are available), and define a migration (or choose a template one). From the specified theoretical background, CDMiA includes a core module implementing the concepts of category theory, on which it relies to assess the impacts of the migration on the schema. It is done by verifying which specific morphisms or patterns are preserved by the functor of the migration.

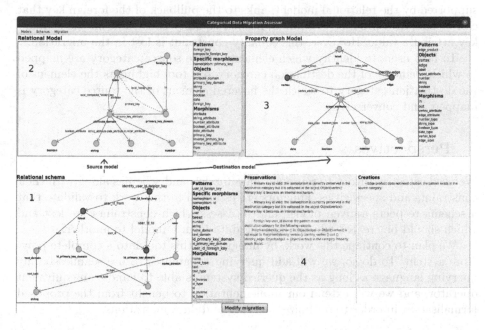

Fig. 2. An example of the output of a migration using CDMiA (highlighted elements concern the already fulfilled creation of the product of the edge)

Two verifications are performed: 1) the need to drop constraints when specific morphisms or patterns that exist in the source category are not preserved by the functor; and 2) the need to create constraints when specific morphisms or patterns of the destination category are partially mapped by some elements of the source category without fully respecting them.

Figure 2 is a screenshot of CDMiA which illustrates this mechanism for a relational schema (panel 1) to migrate towards the property graph model. This schema has two different tables, *user* and *tweet*. A *user* has a primary key *id* of type *number* and a *name* attribute of type *string*. A *tweet* also has a primary key *id* and an attribute *text* of type *string*, as well as a foreign key towards the table *user*, through the local attribute *user_id*. This schema follows the relational model (panel 2), thus it has a functor towards it. We apply a migration for which the tables are transformed into vertices, and the foreign key into an edge.

The performed migration is represented by a functor from the schema towards the property graph model category (panel 3). The panel 4 displays the constraints of the source model that are preserved in green and those that are not in red, and the creations of constraints in the destination model that are already supported in the source model in green and those that must be applied on the schema in red. In our relational schema example, the product of the edge is already supported by the relational model thanks to the pullback of the foreign key that can be seen as a product with an additional equality constraint on the primary key attribute value. However, this equality constraint is lost in the migration.

To help users to identify which elements of the source category are mapped to which elements of the destination category, our tool highlights the element of the destination category to which the hovered element of the source category is mapped, and conversely.

5   Perspectives

We used category theory to represent data models and schemas along with their constraints and specificities. Functors are essential in this work to validate that a schema respects a given model, and to assess which constraints are lost and which should be created when migrating data form a model to another.

We plan to continue this work, by integrating this tool into a complete polystore system. To do so, we will add querying capabilites to use seamlessly any querying language as long as the queried system is able to handle an equivalent operator, and we will extend our implementation to benefit from the proposed formalisation in order to optimize querying and data migrations.

References

1. Abiteboul, S., et al.: Research directions for principles of data management. Dagstuhl Manifestos **7**(1), 1–29 (2018)
2. Alagić, S., Bernstein, P.A.: A model theory for generic schema management. In: Ghelli, G., Grahne, G. (eds.) DBPL 2001. LNCS, vol. 2397, pp. 228–246. Springer, Heidelberg (2002). https://doi.org/10.1007/3-540-46093-4_14
3. Alotaibi, R., Bursztyn, D., Deutsch, A., Manolescu, I., Zampetakis, S.: Towards scalable hybrid stores: constraint-based rewriting to the rescue. In: Proceedings of the 2019 International Conference on Management of Data, pp. 1660–1677 (2019)

4. Bézivin, J., Büttner, F., Gogolla, M., Jouault, F., Kurtev, I., Lindow, A.: Model transformations? Transformation models! In: Nierstrasz, O., Whittle, J., Harel, D., Reggio, G. (eds.) MODELS 2006. LNCS, vol. 4199, pp. 440–453. Springer, Heidelberg (2006). https://doi.org/10.1007/11880240_31
5. Brown, K.S., Spivak, D.I., Wisnesky, R.: Categorical data integration for computational science. Comput. Mater. Sci. **164**, 127–132 (2019)
6. Cluet, S., Delobel, C., Siméon, J., Smaga, K.: Your mediators need data conversion! In: Proceedings of the 1998 ACM SIGMOD International Conference on Management of Data, pp. 177–188 (1998)
7. Dasgupta, S., Coakley, K., Gupta, A.: Analytics-driven data ingestion and derivation in the awesome polystore. In: 2016 IEEE International Conference on Big Data (Big Data), pp. 2555–2564. IEEE (2016)
8. Ehrig, H., Ehrig, K., Ermel, C., Hermann, F., Taentzer, G.: Information preserving bidirectional model transformations. In: Dwyer, M.B., Lopes, A. (eds.) FASE 2007. LNCS, vol. 4422, pp. 72–86. Springer, Heidelberg (2007). https://doi.org/10.1007/978-3-540-71289-3_7
9. Eilenberg, S., MacLane, S.: General theory of natural equivalences. Trans. Am. Math. Soc. **58**(2), 231–294 (1945)
10. Fernandez, M., Simeon, J., Wadler, P.: A semi-monad for semi-structured data (ICDT version). In: Van den Bussche, J., Vianu, V. (eds.) ICDT 2001. LNCS, vol. 1973, pp. 263–300. Springer, Heidelberg (2001). https://doi.org/10.1007/3-540-44503-X_18
11. Gillet, A., Leclercq, É., Cullot, N.: Lambda+, the renewal of the lambda architecture: category theory to the rescue. In: La Rosa, M., Sadiq, S., Teniente, E. (eds.) CAiSE 2021. LNCS, vol. 12751, pp. 381–396. Springer, Cham (2021). https://doi.org/10.1007/978-3-030-79382-1_23
12. Hai, R., Koutras, C., Quix, C., Jarke, M.: Data lakes: a survey of functions and systems. IEEE Trans. Knowl. Data Eng. **35**, 12571–12590 (2023)
13. Halevy, A., Franklin, M., Maier, D.: Principles of dataspace systems. In: Proceedings of the Twenty-Fifth ACM SIGMOD-SIGACT-SIGART Symposium on Principles of Database Systems, pp. 1–9 (2006)
14. Jarke, M., Quix, C.: Federated data integration in data spaces. In: Otto, B., ten Hompel, M., Wrobel, S. (eds.) Designing Data Spaces, pp. 181–194. Springer, Cham (2022). https://doi.org/10.1007/978-3-030-93975-5_11
15. Jia, T., Zhao, X., Wang, Z., Gong, D., Ding, G.: Model transformation and data migration from relational database to MongoDB. In: 2016 IEEE International Congress on Big Data (BigData Congress), pp. 60–67. IEEE (2016)
16. Kolev, B., et al.: Parallel polyglot query processing on heterogeneous cloud data stores with LeanXcale. In: 2018 IEEE International Conference on Big Data (Big Data), pp. 1757–1766. IEEE (2018)
17. Koupil, P., Holubová, I.: A unified representation and transformation of multi-model data using category theory. J. Big Data **9**(1), 61 (2022)
18. Lenzerini, M.: Direct and reverse rewriting in data interoperability. In: Giorgini, P., Weber, B. (eds.) CAiSE 2019. LNCS, vol. 11483, pp. 3–13. Springer, Cham (2019). https://doi.org/10.1007/978-3-030-21290-2_1
19. Lu, J., Holubová, I.: Multi-model databases: a new journey to handle the variety of data. ACM Comput. Surv. (CSUR) **52**(3), 1–38 (2019)
20. Manolescu, I.: Understanding and querying data regardless of the data model. In: VLDB Summer School 2023 (2023)
21. Milewski, B.: Category Theory for Programmers. Blurb (2018)

22. She, Z., Ravishankar, S., Duggan, J.: BigDAWG polystore query optimization through semantic equivalences. In: 2016 IEEE High Performance Extreme Computing Conference (HPEC), pp. 1–6. IEEE (2016)
23. Spivak, D.I., Kent, R.E.: Ologs: a categorical framework for knowledge representation. PLoS ONE **7**(1), e24274 (2012)
24. Tan, R., Chirkova, R., Gadepally, V., Mattson, T.G.: Enabling query processing across heterogeneous data models: a survey. In: 2017 IEEE International Conference on Big Data (Big Data), pp. 3211–3220. IEEE (2017)

MApp-KG: Mobile App Knowledge Graph for Document-Based Feature Knowledge Generation

Quim Motger[✉], Xavier Franch, and Jordi Marco

Universitat Politècnica de Catalunya, Barcelona, Spain
{joaquim.motger,xavier.franch,jordi.marco}@upc.edu

Abstract. Mobile app repositories serve as large-scale crowdsourced information systems used for various document-based software engineering tasks, leveraging product descriptions, user reviews, and other natural language documents. Particularly, feature extraction (i.e., identifying functionalities or capabilities of a mobile app mentioned in these documents) is key for product recommendation, topic modelling, and feedback analysis. However, researchers often face domain-specific challenges in mining these repositories, including the integration of heterogeneous data sources, large-scale data collection, normalization and ground-truth generation for feature-oriented tasks. In this paper, we introduce MApp-KG, a combination of software resources and data artefacts in the field of mobile app repositories aimed at supporting feature-oriented knowledge generation tasks. Our contribution provides a framework for automatically constructing a knowledge graph that models a domain-specific catalog of natural language documents related to mobile applications. We distribute MApp-KG through a public triplestore, enabling its immediate use for future research and replication of our findings.

Keywords: Mobile Apps · Knowledge Graph · User Reviews · Natural Language Document · Feature Extraction · RDF

1 Introduction

Mobile apps have become an essential commodity for users worldwide and a fundamental environment for researchers in multiple data management and knowledge generation tasks [17]. This has led to a surge in research on effectively utilizing text-based documents associated with these apps, such as changelogs and reviews, across various domains. A particularly challenging NLP task in the mobile app domain is feature extraction [7], which refers to automatically identifying text references to functionalities or capabilities of a given mobile app (e.g., *send messages, video calling, GPS navigation, file sharing, track running*). Feature extraction is key for multiple software and requirements engineering tasks, including user validation of new features, elicitation of requirements based on feature requests, and prioritization of requirements based on user feedback [7].

© The Author(s), under exclusive license to Springer Nature Switzerland AG 2024
S. Islam and A. Sturm (Eds.): CAiSE 2024, LNBIP 520, pp. 129–137, 2024.
https://doi.org/10.1007/978-3-031-61000-4_15

Knowledge graphs have proved useful for leveraging text-based documents through NLP techniques [4,5,9]. However, building a knowledge graph from scratch involves several time-consuming challenges, including data collection, integration, normalization, and analysis. Researchers often replicate processes or use existing data sets, leading to limitations like outdated data and lack of control. Furthermore, to the best of our knowledge, there is no free open-access software- or data-based resource in the field of mobile apps integrating and regularly updating natural language documents (e.g., descriptions, reviews) and app features extracted from these documents.

This paper introduces MApp-KG, a software-based approach for constructing a comprehensive knowledge graph of mobile apps and their associated documents, augmented with explicit feature mentions. Our contributions include: (i) an end-to-end mechanism for the construction of a domain-specific knowledge graph of mobile apps and related documents; (ii) a schema-based extension to support deductive knowledge for explicit modelling of app features; (iii) a continuously updated instance of MApp-KG publicly available for further research in the field, augmented with app feature mentions; and (iv) a data snapshot of MApp-KG to facilitate reuse in further studies. We provide a replication package[1] and the source code for the software resources (see Sect. 2).

2   System Overview

Figure 1 presents a high-level overview of MApp-KG. **Software resources** facilitate replicating the knowledge graph construction, embedding automatic mechanisms to support data collection, schema and data integration, and storage. Deductive knowledge generation is detailed in Sect. 3.3.

- **AppDataScannerService** is a Python-based data collection service integrating access to multiple decentralized, heterogeneous mobile app repositories[2]. The service covers two main data collection mechanisms: web scraping and API consumption. Its interface-based design offers adaptive mechanisms to extend its scope with new repositories.
- **KnowledgeGraphRepository** is a Java-based service acting as a repository component between the data collection service and the database management system[3]. It encompasses all CRUD operations for the entities of the data model, as well as some advanced queries based on inductive knowledge generation on the knowledge graph instance. The database is developed using GraphDB, an RDF Graph Database compliant with W3C standards.

Additionally, as **data artefacts**, we distribute **MApp-KG** as a continuously evolving catalogue of millions of text-based documents (i.e., summaries, descriptions, changelogs, reviews) related to 832 mobile apps. The README

---

[1] Available at https://doi.org/10.6084/m9.figshare.24760032.
[2] Available at https://github.com/gessi-chatbots/app_data_scanner_service/.
[3] Available at https://github.com/gessi-chatbots/app_data_repository/.

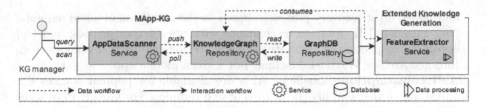

Fig. 1. MApp-KG overview.

file of the replication package contains examples of SPARQL queries to navigate through the public instance of MApp-KG. In addition, a static **MApp-KG data snapshot** in Terse RDF Triple Language (Turtle) format is also available.

3 Knowledge Graph Construction

3.1 Data Collection

We conducted a narrative literature review to identify relevant Android mobile app repository types using search terms such as *mobile apps* and *repositories* alongside their synonyms. We identified three types of mobile app repositories:

- **App stores:** application store programs which allow users to discover, download, install, update, review and remove mobile apps through a specific software tool [1]. As a representative, we selected Google Play Store[4], as the major source of Android mobile apps worldwide [1].
- **Sideloading repositories:** these repositories store the *Android Package Kit* (APK) which can be downloaded and installed into any Android device, allowing a flexible alternative to the constraints of official app stores [1], which might become a barrier for some developers (e.g., the open source community). We selected F-Droid[5] due to its focus on Open-Source Software.
- **App search engines:** indexation websites giving centralized access to popular mobile applications published in third-party repositories. We selected AlternativeTo[6], especially for the potential of crowd-sourced user annotated data, including suggestions to related/similar apps, list of app features and tag-based app categorization.

Based on these repositories, we designed two data collection mechanisms:

- **Web scraping:** applied to both dynamic and static web-based data source types (i.e., F-Droid and AlternativeTo). Web-based data extraction conveyed into network access limitations and specialized network security access protection from these web-based repositories, for which we combined multiple solutions, including: (*i*) sequential and delayed source consumption patterns; (*ii*)

---

[4] https://play.google.com/store/apps.
[5] https://f-droid.org/es/.
[6] https://alternativeto.net/.

automated error-recovery protocols, based on the repetition of failed requests; (*iii*) automated IP rotation mechanisms with open-access proxies; and (*iv*) automatic inspection of alternative sources storing web-cached versions (e.g., Internet Archive Wayback Machine[7]) of a given mobile app.

- **API consumption:** nonofficial APIs are available for popular sources like app stores, which simplify the process of web scraping. For Google Play, some examples include free, open-source components like the Google-Play-Scraper Python module[8], and real-time commercial API services like SerpApi[9].

For each of these data collection techniques, we define the following operations to support the construction of the data set used for this research:

- **Query:** given a set of keywords, we use the search function available in every data source to enumerate related apps to those keywords. The result of this operation is a list of app packages and names.
- **Scan:** given a set of packages and names, we use all data sources to collect available data items for each app. The result of this process is the integration of metadata fields and natural language documents. MApp-KG utilizes a cron job to regularly scan new user reviews, allowing users to customize update frequency (by default set to weekly updates).

3.2   Schema and Data Integration

We designed the data model as a directed edge-labelled graph using the Resource Description Framework (RDF) model from W3C [6], focusing on the standardization and interoperability of the knowledge graph towards its integration on third-party software systems [11]. We formalized the definition of a semantic data schema modelling the high-level elements (i.e., nodes) and relationships (i.e., edges) stored in the knowledge graph using the RDF Schema (RDFS) [3], focusing mainly on subclass and property relations between nodes. Figure 2 depicts the semantic data schema using the Data Catalog Vocabulary (DCAT) specification aligned with existing schema entities from Schema.org[10].

We formalize the schema integration process using RDF Mapping Language (RML) as a declarative mapping language to transform heterogeneous schemas from mobile app repositories into the unified schema defined in Fig. 2. The generated RML files and the DCAT vocabulary are available in the replication package, including a sample snapshot to manually verify the schema integration process. Concerning data integration, we focused on two NLP-based techniques:

- **App key normalization.** Different mobile repositories use different keys to identify a single mobile app (i.e., entity recognition), from the application package (i.e., Google Play, F-Droid) to the published app name (i.e.,

---

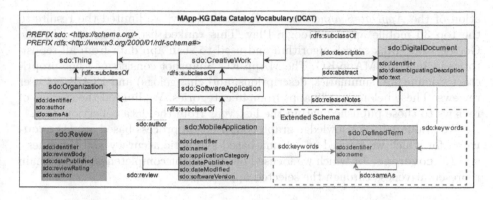

Fig. 2. MApp-KG Data Catalog Vocabulary (DCAT) schema

AlternativeTo), for which in some scenarios a customized text-based variant of the name is used for app reference. Consequently, to increase app coverage, we extended the data integration process with a syntactic-based custom pipeline for the automatic generation of alternative app keys, using all potential ordered combinations between the tokens composing the app name with the application of minor lexical transformations (e.g., text cleaning, stemming).

- **Document merging.** We extended the integration of natural language documents with a simplified TF-IDF duplicate detection process to identify redundant content and merge documents by removing duplicated content.

3.3 Deductive Knowledge Generation

MApp-KG encompasses a catalogue of text-based documents for app-related natural language deductive and inductive knowledge generation tasks. Public version of MApp-KG is augmented with explicit feature mentions extracted using the feature extraction method described in our previous work [10], which was evaluated for the use case of system (i.e., mobile app) recommendation [14]. Extracted features are explicit extensions of the data model, which include the automated generation of new nodes (i.e., *DefinedTerm* in Fig. 2) and new edge relations (i.e., *keywords* property of a given *DigitalDocument*). The feature extraction process also includes explicit link generation between semantically similar features (i.e., *sameAs* property of a given *DefinedTerm*) to support topology-based analysis of related mobile apps based on their features [14]. Public version of MApp-KG is augmented with features and similarity links (see the replication package for instructions on how to query such knowledge extension).

4 Evaluation Report

MApp-KG is built and populated with the most popular apps from Google Play. We used the full set of Google Play app categories as input for the query operation of the *AppDataScannerService*. For each query, we limited the results to the top 30 mobile apps in Google Play. This ranked list is generated by the Google Play Rank search algorithm and used to scan app data from all repositories included in MApp-KG. The MApp-KG Snapshot consists of 1,666 proprietary documents (summaries, descriptions, and changelogs) and 13,478,744 user reviews. These belong to 832 apps from 46 categories. We limited the storage of reviews to those published within the last year from the data collection date.

We evaluated the knowledge graph construction process based on: (1) **accuracy**, for which we focused on schema-based syntactic accuracy and timeliness; and (2) **coverage**, for which we focused on document completeness and domain representativeness through the selected apps [11].

- **Syntactic accuracy**: measured for each property of the RDF Schema entities in our data set. The schema and data integration processes depicted in Sect. 3.2 prove to majorly comply with the semantic RDF Schema depicted in Fig. 2, for which only some formatted properties like *datePublished* and *softwareVersion* report a syntactic accuracy below 100%.
- **Timeliness**: rebuilding the MApp-KG snapshot from scratch takes around 17 h. The weekly review polling apps takes 5 h on average. Given that the lowest median value of days between updates reported in Google Play is 14 [16], we argue that timeliness is achieved through MApp-KG polling feature to automatically collect new reviews weekly.
- **Coverage**: we measured completeness based on the population of proprietary and user documents, aiming at the concept of the *ideal knowledge graph* [8]. We refer to this ideal knowledge graph as an instance with at least one sample of each proprietary document and a balanced amount of user documents. Concerning proprietary documents, the MApp-KG Snapshot reports 100% completeness for summaries and descriptions and 85.4% for changelogs or release notes. Concerning reviews, the review polling mechanism forces a balanced distribution of available user-generated documents.
- **Representativeness**: we qualitatively elicited high-level biases on the inclusion and exclusion of entities and properties, as suggested by Baeza-Yates et al. [2]. We identify four potential biases: (1) limitation of data sources, for which we only selected one major representative for each mobile repository type (see Sect. 3.1); (2) excluded mobile applications, conditioned by the Google Play Rank search algorithm, whose output triggers the data scan process; (3) excluded proprietary document types, given that we limited the scope to three of the most commonly available documents, leaving out additional natural language corpora (e.g., websites, code repositories); and (4) excluded user reviews (i.e., published more than 1 year ago).

Concerning threats to validity, the selection of mobile app repositories is limited to a restricted set of app repositories, and the selection of mobile apps and documents is limited in terms of size. To mitigate these threats, we conducted a narrative literature review on app repositories and focused on popularity for repository selection. For repository coverage, at least one representative of each repository type was selected. For data completeness and relevance, we relied on Google Play due to its pervasiveness among users worldwide [12]. Beyond these, decisions on the design and technical specification of the solution entail several constraints in terms of reusability, interoperability, and generalization. However, we argue that our approach (e.g., RDF schema, RML-based schema integration, SPARQL-based public access) is aligned with Semantic Web standards.

5 Related Work

There is some existing work in the field of mobile app knowledge graph construction. The most restricting limitation is the lack of public access to the data set for reusability [13,15,18], or even information about the data model and schema used to build the data set [18]. All surveyed contributions are limited to app stores from vendors, using web scraping (often referred to as crawling) as the main data collection technique. Consequently, they exclude relevant sources like sideloading repositories (e.g., F-Droid) or search engines (e.g., AlternativeTo), which have proven to provide a large data set of complementary apps as well as additional data like user reviews and crowdsourced annotations [1]. Finally, none of the surveyed alternatives offers an up-to-date, continuously updated data set. Furthermore, they do not report on specific mechanisms or computational effort (including execution time) for updating their data sets to a timely representation. This timeliness dimensionality is key, especially in the context of mobile app repositories as constantly evolving environments.

Among the surveyed studies, MAKG [19], a mobile app knowledge graph to support cybersecurity research, is revealed as the most similar contribution to MApp-KG. Its major limitation lies in its static dataset, limited to 2021. Additionally, software resources are limited to the schema integration, data integration and storage processes. Notably, MAKG lacks automatism in data collection and formalization/exemplification of extended knowledge generation. Finally, they neglect quality assessment of the resulting knowledge graph and a discussion on dataset generalization or replicability beyond cybersecurity contributions. Finally, none of the previous contributions offer feature-oriented persistent knowledge augmentation, which is one of the main contributions of MApp-KG.

6 Conclusions

In this paper, we presented MApp-KG, a set of software resources and data artefacts designed for researchers and developers in the field of mobile software ecosystems. MApp-KG provides a solid foundation for document-based and feature-oriented research on mobile software ecosystems, providing a rich data set that can be leveraged to address a wide range of research questions. Researchers interested in the outcomes of this resource can use the software components as independent tools for customizing their own data collection and knowledge graph construction processes. In addition, they can also integrate the public instance of MApp-KG for the consumption of a timely catalogue of text-based documents related to mobile apps. In the future, we plan on exploring more sophisticated NLP techniques and incorporating additional repositories and data artefacts, such as extended metadata fields and developer documentation. We also plan to apply Shapes Constraint Language (SHACL) to evaluate the integrity and quality of our knowledge graph. Additionally, focusing on generalization, we plan on adapting MApp-KG to curate a knowledge graph instance tailored for AI-based tools and products. We envisage that MApp-KG can potentially contribute to the field of document-based mobile app analysis, and can be used to open up new possibilities for research and development of practical solutions.

Acknowledgments. With the support from the Secretariat for Universities and Research of the Ministry of Business and Knowledge of the Government of Catalonia and the European Social Fund. This paper has been funded by the Spanish Ministerio de Ciencia e Innovación under project / funding scheme PID2020-117191RB-I00 / AEI/10.13039/501100011033.

References

1. ACM: Market study into mobile app stores (Report ACM/18/032693)
2. Baeza-Yates, R.: Bias on the Web. Commun. ACM **61**(6), 54–61 (2018)
3. Brickley, D., Guha, R.V.: RDF Schema 1.1 (2014). https://www.w3.org/TR/2014/REC-rdf-schema-20140225/
4. Chang, S., et al.: AppGrouper: knowledge-graph-based interactive clustering tool for mobile app search results. In: Intelligent User Interfaces, IUI (2016)
5. Chen, J., et al.: Knowledge graph enhanced third-party library recommendation for mobile application development. IEEE Access **8**, 42436–42446 (2020)
6. Cyganiak, R., et al.: RDF 1.1 Concepts and Abstract Syntax (2014). https://www.w3.org/TR/2014/REC-rdf11-concepts-20140225/
7. Dabrowski, J., et al.: Analysing app reviews for software engineering: a systematic literature review. Empir. Softw. Eng. **27**(2), 43 (2022)
8. Darari, F., et al.: Completeness management for RDF data sources. ACM Trans. Web **12**(3), 1–53 (2018)
9. Dong, X., et al.: An ontology enhanced user profiling algorithm based on application feedback. In: Computer Software and Applications, COMPSAC (2019)
10. Gallego, A., et al.: TransFeatEx: a NLP pipeline for feature extraction. In: REFSQ-2023 Posters & Tools Track (2023)
11. Hogan, A., et al.: Knowledge graphs. ACM Comput. Surv. **54**, 1–37 (2021)
12. Kamei, F., et al.: Grey literature in software engineering: a critical review. Inf. Softw. Technol. **138**, 106609 (2021)
13. Li, W., et al.: Combining knowledge graph embedding and network embedding for detecting similar mobile applications. In: Natural Language Processing and Chinese Computing, NLPCC (2020)
14. Motger, Q., Franch, X., Marco, J.: Mobile feature-oriented knowledge base generation using knowledge graphs. In: Abelló, A., et al. (eds.) New Trends in Database and Information Systems, ADBIS 2023. CCIS, vol. 1850, pp. 269–279. Springer, Cham (2023). https://doi.org/10.1007/978-3-031-42941-5_24
15. Rizun, M., Strzelecki, A.: Knowledge graph development for app store data modeling. In: Information Systems Development, ISD (2019)

16. Semrush: Number of days since the highest-ranking mobile apps in the Google Play Store were last updated worldwide as of February 2022, by category, February 2022. https://www.statista.com/statistics/1296548/. Accessed 27 Apr 2023

17. Steglich, C., et al.: Revisiting the mobile software ecosystems literature. In: International Workshop on Software Engineering for Systems-of-Systems, SESoS (2019)

18. Zhang, M., Zhao, J., Dong, H., Deng, K., Liu, Y.: A knowledge graph based approach for mobile application recommendation. In: Kafeza, E., Benatallah, B., Martinelli, F., Hacid, H., Bouguettaya, A., Motahari, H. (eds.) ICSOC 2020. LNCS, vol. 12571, pp. 355–369. Springer, Cham (2020). https://doi.org/10.1007/978-3-030-65310-1_25

19. Zhou, H., Li, W., Zhang, B., Ji, Q., Tan, Y., Na, C.: MAKG: a mobile application knowledge graph for the research of cybersecurity. In: Qin, B., Jin, Z., Wang, H., Pan, J., Liu, Y., An, B. (eds.) CCKS 2021. CCIS, vol. 1466, pp. 321–328. Springer, Singapore (2021). https://doi.org/10.1007/978-981-16-6471-7_28

CAKE: Sharing Slices of Confidential Data on Blockchain

Edoardo Marangone[1]([✉]) [ID], Michele Spina[1] [ID], Claudio Di Ciccio[2] [ID],
and Ingo Weber[3,4] [ID]

[1] Sapienza University of Rome, Rome, Italy
marangone@di.uniroma1.it, spina.1711821@studenti.uniroma1.it
[2] Utrecht University, Utrecht, The Netherlands
c.diciccio@uu.nl
[3] School of CIT, Technical University of Munich, Munich, Germany
ingo.weber@tum.de
[4] Fraunhofer Gesellschaft, Munich, Germany

Abstract. Cooperative information systems typically involve various entities in a collaborative process within a distributed environment. Blockchain technology offers a mechanism for automating such processes, even when only partial trust exists among participants. The data stored on the blockchain is replicated across all nodes in the network, ensuring accessibility to all participants. While this aspect facilitates traceability, integrity, and persistence, it poses challenges for adopting public blockchains in enterprise settings due to confidentiality issues. In this paper, we present a software tool named Control Access via Key Encryption (CAKE), designed to ensure data confidentiality in scenarios involving public blockchains. After outlining its core components and functionalities, we showcase the application of CAKE in the context of a real-world cyber-security project within the logistics domain.

Keywords: Cyphertext Policy · Attribute-Based Encryption · Cryptography · Blockchain technology · Smart Contract

1 Introduction

Blockchain technology is increasingly being applied in information systems of diverse enterprise domains due to its capacity to facilitate the establishment and execution of cooperative processes involving multiple parties with limited mutual trust [26,28]. The decentralized structure of public permissionless blockchains ensures that each participant in the network possesses a replicated ledger, thereby allowing for unrestricted accessibility of all data. This transparency, in conjunction with the immutability of data and the non-repudiable nature of transactions, makes blockchains a robust foundation for verifiable and trustworthy interactions.

In scenarios where there is a lack of mutual trust among parties, hiding some data from the majority of users can be advantageous. Indeed, when blockchain technology is discussed, the security and privacy topics are the critical issues

S. Islam and A. Sturm (Eds.): CAiSE 2024, LNBIP 520, pp. 138–147, 2024.
https://doi.org/10.1007/978-3-031-61000-4_16

and their importance is underlined and well recognized [6,9,32]. A solution to guarantee data secrecy and confidentiality among parties was presented in [20] under the name of Control Access via Key Encryption (CAKE). The parties can securely exchange information using the CAKE architecture, hiding data or parts thereof from others. This paper demonstrates the CAKE tool, illustrating its implementation and the newly introduced features. We used CAKE as a core component of a larger platform designed and realized in the context of a national cyber-security research and innovation project for international logistics: Blockchain Register for Import-Export (BRIE).[1] We employ the case study to showcase the maturity and integration of the tool within a real-world setting. At large, our research provides security-minded practitioners with a tool to securely transact confidential data: A whole public blockchain network permanently stores the transactions attesting to the validity and integrity of the data, but only authorized parties can read the actual information in-clear.

In the following, Sect. 2 outlines the CAKE architecture and the core concepts it builds upon. In Sect. 3, we demonstrate our proof-of-concept implementation with the BRIE real-world use case. Section 4 provides implementation details about our tool. Section 5 presents the related work in the literature. Finally, Sect. 6 concludes the paper and draws some avenues for future work.

2   Core Concepts and Tool Architecture

In the following, we outline the key methodologies and techniques underpinning our solution. Equipped with these notions, we describe the core components of CAKE thereafter.

Core Concepts. Distributed Ledger Technologies (DLTs) are protocols that facilitate transactional storage, processing, and validation within a decentralized network without the need for central authorities or intermediaries. These transactions come along with cryptographic signatures. The resulting shared transaction log collectively constitutes a ledger accessible to all participants in the network. In a **blockchain**, a specific type of DLT, transactions are organized in blocks, which are linked to form an append-only singly linked list, namely a chain. DLTs, including blockchains, are tamper-resistant thanks to cryptographic techniques such as hashing and decentralized validation of transactions. Public blockchain platforms such as Ethereum [30] and Algorand [5] require the payment of fees for submitting and processing transactions on the platform. These platforms enable the utilization of **smart contracts**, which are programs deployed, stored, and executed directly on-chain [7,33]. Ethereum and Algorand support smart contracts through the Ethereum Virtual Machine (EVM) and the Algorand Virtual Machine (AVM), respectively. These contracts are deployed and invoked via transactions. Their code is stored on the blockchain and executed by the nodes within the distributed system. The results of contract invocations are subject to blockchain consensus, thereby being verified by the network and completely traceable. To reduce the costs associated with invoking

---

[1] https://brie.moveax.it/en, accessed 2024-03-11.

smart contracts, external Peer-to-Peer (P2P) systems are employed for storing significant volumes of data [31]. Among the facilitating technologies is the **InterPlanetary File System (IPFS)**. IPFS is a distributed system utilizing a Distributed Hash Table (DHT) to distribute stored files across multiple nodes. It employs hashing to generate a uniquely identifying resource locator for every file. In a conventional blockchain integration, the locator is subsequently transmitted to a smart contract for permanent storage on the blockchain [16]. Notice that such an address is content-based: changing even a single bit in the data entails the modification of the hash, thus the original locator does not match the modified data. **Attribute-Based Encryption (ABE)** is a type of public-key encryption scheme where the ciphertext (i.e., an encrypted plaintext) and its corresponding decryption key are linked via attributes [4,25]. In Ciphertext-Policy Attribute-Based Encryption (CP-ABE) [3,15], a set of such attributes is assigned to potential users. Policies are linked to ciphertexts and articulated as propositional formulae over the attributes. The formulae are evaluated to determine whether a user holds the necessary properties to grant access to the unencrypted data.

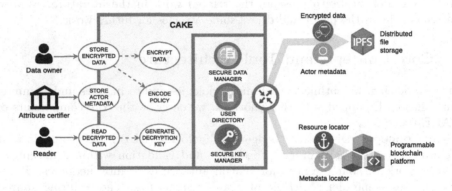

Fig. 1. An overview of the CAKE architecture

Tool Architecture. Figure 1 depicts the core traits of CAKE's architecture. It offers three core functionalities, drawn as use cases in the figure: *(i)* storing encrypted data, which in turn requires the encryption of the transmitted artifacts via ABE and the encoding of ciphertext policies to control access; *(ii)* storing actor metadata, mapping ABE attributes to specific users to later determine their suitability to read the stored information; *(iii)* reading decrypted data, which entails the generation of decryption keys depending on the attributes that the requesting user bears. Those three functionalities are realized by the interplay of three basic components: *(i)* the Secure Data Manager (SDM), which is responsible for the encryption of data based on the policies and the subsequent storage thereof; *(ii)* the User Directory (UD), recording the association of users with the attributes they bear in the context of the collaborative process enactment; *(iii)* the Secure Key Manager (SKM), which generates decryption keys for users who wish to read data in clear based on their attributes. CAKE is interfaced with an IPFS distributed file storage to save the files with encrypted data and with the actor metadata. It resorts to a programmable blockchain platform to record the locators of those files via smart contracts. The *attribute certifier* writes the actor metadata via UD in a file uploaded onto IFPS, the locator of which is later stored on-chain. A *data owner*, namely a process actor that wants to share data with selected users, sends the data in clear and the policies to encrypt it to the SDM. The latter performs the encryption based on the encoded policy, stores the secured data on IPFS, and notarizes the locator thereof on chain. To access the data, a *reader* asks for a decryption key to the SKM, which in turn retrieves the users' attributes from the UD and uses them to generate the key. If those attributes satisfy the policy originally used to encrypt the data, the reader can access the contents in clear. Note that the transactions stored on-chain do not disclose core information. The hash-based resource locator is stored on chain, but the sender of the transaction is the SDM itself, and the recipient is a smart contract. Thus, even if any network node can fetch the public ledger, it cannot extract any information on the exchanged data, its owner, or the intended readers therefrom.

The detailed explanation of the above passages goes beyond the scope of this demo paper. More information can be found in the paper describing the CAKE approach [20]. Next, we provide further details about the implementation of CAKE.

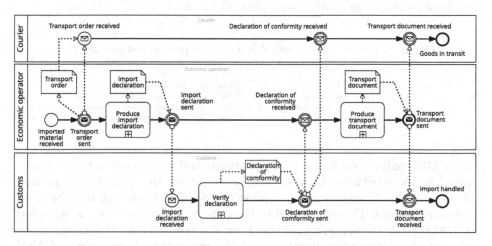

Fig. 2. An excerpt of a process workflow in the BRIE project

3   Demonstration Through a Real-World Case Study

BRIE (Blockchain Register for Import-Export) (see Footnote 1) is a project aimed at the design and realization of a blockchain-based solution for the monitoring and optimization of international logistics processes. The primary goal is to support stakeholders by facilitating the tracking of shipments, the effective management of pertinent documentation, and the establishment of novel synergies to enhance the management, storage, and transit of goods within Europe.

Figure 2 shows a Business Process Model and Notation (BPMN) collaboration diagram [8] illustrating a model fragment of a process handled in the BRIE project. The process actors involved are the *Courier*, the *Economic Operator*, and *Customs*. A new process instance begins when the Economic Operator sends a *transport order* to a Courier. Then, the Economic Operator compiles an *import declaration* for Customs. This document describes the goods, the country of destination, the buyer, and the selected courier for the import. The import declaration is subsequently verified and confirmed by Customs emitting a *declaration of conformity* which can be accessed both by the Economic Operator and the Courier. After this confirmation, the Economic Operator produces a *transport document* with the mode of transport, the Courier, the data and address for goods collection, the expected delivery date, and the delivery address.

Since we utilize ABE, we associate the process actors with users, each having attributes that characterize their role. We assume here that the importing country's Chamber of Commerce and the competent ministerial body acted as attribute certifiers to register the actors involved as licensed operators. In our example, the involved Courier, Economic Operator and Customs are associated with attributes `courier`, `economic_operator`, and `customs`, respectively. We represent the participation in the process identified by number 29837 with an attribute recalling the number itself (`29837`) for short.

Table 1. Documents exchanged in Fig. 2 for process instance 29837

Document	Sender	Recipients	Policy
Transport order	Economic Operator	Courier	`(29837 and ((economic_operator) or (courier)))`
Import declaration	Economic Operator	Customs	`(29837 and ((economic_operator) or (customs)))`
Declaration of conformity	Customs	Economic Operator; Courier	`(29837 and ((customs) or (economic_operator) or (courier)))`
Transport document	Economic Operator	Courier; Customs	`(29837 and ((economic_operator) or (customs) or (courier)))`

In ABE, policies are linked with ciphertexts and articulated as propositional formulae over attributes. They serve to ascertain whether a user is authorized for access. Table 1 contains the encryption policies associated with the aforementioned documents. The one related to the import declaration, e.g., is expressed as `(29837 and ((economic_operator) or (customs)))` as it is meant to be accessed by the Economic Operator and Customs involved in case 29837. CAKE encrypts every document with the corresponding policy to let only the intended actors read it. Notice that if the writer of a document wants to be able to decrypt the shared document later on, they need to include themselves in the set of authorized readers. Once the document is encrypted, it is uploaded on IPFS, and the resulting resource locator (e.g., `QmTnDqWf[...]i9wZUgYp`), is stored on the blockchain alongside a unique message ID.

To access the import declaration later, Customs must ask for a decryption key and obtain the document in clear. In this example, the attributes of Customs satisfy the policy used to encrypt the import declaration, so they can obtain the document and read its decrypted content. On the contrary, the Courier has attributes that do not satisfy the policy, so they cannot access that document's content. After the Customs agency verifies the conformity of the declaration, the process can progress. As for the transport document, all the three players considered in this example can read the document. Their attributes satisfy the ciphertext policy, so their key is apt for decryption.

The above scenario was used during the final review meeting of the BRIE project and involved a larger integrated platform for logistics data collection and exchange. Next, we provide an overview of the implementation of CAKE and its integration with the BRIE platform.

4   Implementation

We implemented CAKE and its communication channels in Python. The CAKE components expose their interfaces as APIs to a bundled service provider to ease communication and integration with other systems. The communication infrastructure is thus external to the blockchain and IPFS and relies on the Secure Sockets Layer (SSL) protocol. We used this protocol to mitigate the risk of packet sniffing by potential malicious third parties aiming to intercept the transmitted data. Moreover, the communication from the data owner to the Secure Data Manager and from the reader to the Secure Key Manager is preceded by an initial authentication phase via a preliminary handshake. Without this security measure, any malicious peer could submit requests on behalf of the authentic reader, having obtained their address and conjecturing a file to which access might be granted. CAKE allows for the encryption of different types of documents. It is possible to handle a single text file, with the option of applying different policies to different parts thereof. Alternatively, multiple text or binary documents can be uploaded, each being associated with a separate policy.

The source code of CAKE is openly available at https://github.com/apwbs/CAKE. In the code repository, we provide two implementations of CAKE, distributed within Docker containers: one for the EVM and one for the AVM. The smart contracts we employ are encoded in Solidity for the EVM and in PyTeal for the AVM. They are deployed on the Sepolia testnet[2] and the Algorand testnet,[3] respectively. The AVM-based version of CAKE was used for the BRIE project described in Sect. 3. To integrate our tool with the BRIE platform, we developed a plug-in named Secrecy and Privacy Enhancer for Ciphered Knowledge (SPECK, available at github.com/MichaelPlug/SPECK), including a collection of scripts to automatically retrieve information from a shared data repository and interact with the APIs of CAKE.

Next, we provide a comparative summary of research endeavors that relate to CAKE.

---

[2] https://sepolia.etherscan.io/, accessed 2024-03-11.
[3] https://app.dappflow.org/dashboard/home, accessed 2024-03-11.

5 Related Work

Numerous research endeavors have focused on automating collaborative processes utilizing blockchain technology. Weber et al. [28] introduce a method leveraging this technology to facilitate the conduction of business among parties in the absence of mutual trust. Their work demonstrates how actors can mutually agree on executed behaviors without relying on a central enforcement authority. López Pintado et al. [17] introduce Caterpillar, a process execution engine based on Ethereum. Caterpillar enables users to generate process instances and monitor their progress. Madsen et al. [18] investigate the execution of distributed declarative workflows, particularly in situations involving collaboration among adversarial entities. Corradini et al. [6] introduce ChorChain, a tool that executes and monitors process choreographies on the Ethereum blockchain platform. These studies enhance the fusion of blockchain and process management, unlocking security and traceability opportunities. However, they lack mechanisms to ensure fine-grained access control over data stored on a public platform. In contrast, our work addresses this aspect in a collaborative business process scenario.

Another research area within our domain concerns the privacy and integrity of data stored on-chain. Hawk [14] is a decentralized system that leverages user-defined private smart contracts to execute cryptographic techniques autonomously. In contrast, our approach eliminates the need for custom smart contract encoding, as it relies on on-chain policies for message encryption. Rahulamathavan et al. [24] introduce a novel privacy-preserving blockchain architecture tailored for Internet of Things (IoT) applications, utilizing Attribute-Based Encryption (ABE) techniques. While we also utilize ABE, we aim to augment existing software architectures. In contrast, their model alters the blockchain protocol itself. Benhamouda et al. [2] propose a solution enabling a public blockchain to function as a repository for confidential data. In their system, a secret is initially stored on the blockchain, followed by the specification of conditions for its release, with the secret disclosed only if these conditions are satisfied. In contrast, our approach involves the utilization of shared secrets among components. However, it does not entail utilizing the blockchain as a storage system for secret data or disclosing the secret. Differently from these methodologies, our approach addresses the challenge of regulated data access within a multi-party process scenario. This scenario involves the exchange of multiple information artifacts, where various actors can read specific segments of messages based on access policies.

Wang et al. [27] propose an electronic health record framework integrating Attribute-Based Encryption (ABE), Identity-Based Encryption (IBE), and Identity-Based Signature (IBS) mechanisms with blockchain technology. Unlike the CAKE model, this system design empowers hospitals with patient data ownership while patients delineate access policies. In our architecture, no central authority is intended to manage the data except the data owners, who, in healthcare processes, would be the patients. Pournaghi et al. [23] propose a framework named MedSBA that leverages blockchain technology and Attribute-

Based Encryption. The distinction in their architecture lies in using two private blockchains. Instead, we consider only a public blockchain scenario.

6 Conclusion and Future Developments

In this paper we presented CAKE, a tool integrating public blockchain platforms, Attribute-Based Encryption (ABE) and the InterPlanetary File System (IPFS) for controlled data access within multi-party processes. IPFS serves as a tamper-proof repository for storing information artifacts, access policies, and actor metadata. Smart contracts manage user attributes, determine access permissions for process participants, and establish connections to IPFS files for notarization. Thereby, CAKE offers the ability to define precise specifications of access privileges, while ensuring data integrity, immutability, non-repudiation, and ultimately facilitating auditability. The maturity and integration of the tool is testified by its adoption in the context of a real-world cybersecurity project (BRIE) (see Footnote 1) in the area of international logistics. Testing the adoption of our tool in further industry settings, thereby gathering feedback, extracting practical implications and devising theory from on-field experience [10,29] represents a future, highly interesting endeavor. Nevertheless, our solution exhibits limitations that we aim to address in future work, too. To begin with, whenever a data owner wishes to withdraw access to data from a specific reader, the only possibility is modifying the policy and re-encrypting the messages. However, the data previously uploaded on IPFS remains accessible. We are considering InterPlanetary Name System (IPNS) to overcome this limitation. Recently, we introduced an alternative approach to blockchain-based secure data sharing in cooperative settings, which divides the tasks of the attribute certification and key forging among multiple computing nodes in a distributed fashion [19]. The full distribution of computing (and the additional overhead it entails) was deemed as unnecessary in the BRIE setting among the stakeholders, due to the involvement of authoritative bodies for the attribution of user metadata and keys in the project. It is in our plans to implement the latter solution on multiple blockchain platforms and reach a level of maturity that is akin to CAKE in order to conduct comparative analyses on the applicability and trade-offs of the two approaches. Also, we plan to incorporate oracles in our solution to enable smart contracts' validation of off-chain data [1,22]. This integration empowers system designers to set the balance between complete transparency in the decision-making process and access control. Achieving this equilibrium entails strategically managing the storage of data both on-chain and off-chain, as discussed in [11]. Finally, combining our solution with techniques for process analytics based on blockchain data [12,13,21] paves the path for future research avenues.

Acknowledgements. The work of E. Marangone was partly funded by projects PIN-POINT (B87G22000450001), under the PRIN MUR program, and BRIE (Cyber 4.0).

References

1. Basile, D., Goretti, V., Di Ciccio, C., Kirrane, S.: Enhancing blockchain-based processes with decentralized oracles. In: BPM Blockchain and RPA Forum, pp. 102–118 (2021)
2. Benhamouda, F., et al.: Can a public blockchain keep a secret? In: TCC (2020)
3. Bethencourt, J., Sahai, A., Waters, B.: Ciphertext-policy attribute-based encryption. In: SP, pp. 321–334 (2007)
4. Chase, M.: Multi-authority attribute based encryption. In: Vadhan, S.P. (ed.) TCC 2007. LNCS, vol. 4392, pp. 515–534. Springer, Heidelberg (2007). https://doi.org/10.1007/978-3-540-70936-7_28
5. Chen, J., Micali, S.: Algorand: a secure and efficient distributed ledger. Theor. Comput. Sci. **777**, 155–183 (2019)
6. Corradini, F., Marcelletti, A., Morichetta, A., et al.: Engineering trustable and auditable choreography-based systems using blockchain. ACM Trans. Manage. Inf. Syst. **13**(3), 1–53 (2022)
7. Dannen, C.: Introducing Ethereum and Solidity. Apress, Berkeley, CA (2017). https://doi.org/10.1007/978-1-4842-2535-6
8. Dumas, M., La Rosa, M., Mendling, J., Reijers, H.A.: Fundamentals of Business Process Management, 2nd edn. Springer, Heidelberg (2018)
9. Feng, Q., He, D., Zeadally, S., Khan, M.K., Kumar, N.: A survey on privacy protection in blockchain system. J. Netw. Comput. Appl. **126**, 45–58 (2019)
10. Ghaisas, S., Rose, P., Daneva, M., Sikkel, K., Wieringa, R.J.: Generalizing by similarity: lessons learnt from industrial case studies. In: CESI, pp. 37–42 (2013)
11. Haarmann, S., Batoulis, K., Nikaj, A., Weske, M.: Executing collaborative decisions confidentially on blockchains. In: BPM (Blockchain and CEE Forum), pp. 119–135 (2019)
12. Hobeck, R., Weber, I.: Towards object-centric process mining for blockchain applications. In: BPM (Blockchain and RPA Forum), pp. 51–65 (2023)
13. Klinkmüller, C., Ponomarev, A., Tran, A.B., Weber, I., van der Aalst, W.M.P.: Mining blockchain processes: extracting process mining data from blockchain applications. In: BPM Blockchain and CEE Forum, pp. 71–86 (2019)
14. Kosba, A., Miller, A., Shi, E., Wen, Z., Papamanthou, C.: Hawk: the blockchain model of cryptography and privacy-preserving smart contracts. In: SP, pp. 839–858 (2016)
15. Liu, Z., Jiang, Z.L., Wang, X., et al.: Multi-authority ciphertext policy attribute-based encryption scheme on ideal lattices. In: ISPA/IUCC/BDCloud/SocialCom/SustainCom, pp. 1003–1008 (2018)
16. López-Pintado, O., Dumas, M., García-Bañuelos, L., Weber, I.: Controlled flexibility in blockchain-based collaborative business processes. Inf. Syst. **104**, 101622 (2022)
17. López-Pintado, O., García-Bañuelos, L., Dumas, M., et al.: Caterpillar: a business process execution engine on the Ethereum blockchain. Softw. Pract. Exper. **49**(7), 1162–1193 (2019)
18. Madsen, M.F., Gaub, M., Høgnason, T., et al.: Collaboration among adversaries: distributed workflow execution on a blockchain. In: FAB, pp. 8–15 (2018)
19. Marangone, E., Di Ciccio, C., Friolo, D., Nemmi, E.N., Venturi, D., Weber, I.: MARTSIA: enabling data confidentiality for blockchain-based process execution. In: Proper, H.A., Pufahl, L., Karastoyanova, D., van Sinderen, M., Moreira, J. (eds.) Enterprise Design, Operations, and Computing, EDOC 2023. LNCS,

vol. 14367, pp. 58–76. Springer, Cham (2024). https://doi.org/10.1007/978-3-031-46587-1_4

20. Marangone, E., Di Ciccio, C., Weber, I.: Fine-grained data access control for collaborative process execution on blockchain. In: BPM Blockchain and RPA Forum, pp. 51–67 (2022)

21. Mühlberger, R., Bachhofner, S., Di Ciccio, C., et al.: Extracting event logs for process mining from data stored on the blockchain. In: BPM Workshops, pp. 690–703 (2019)

22. Mühlberger, R., Bachhofner, S., Ferrer, E.C., et al.: Foundational oracle patterns: connecting blockchain to the off-chain world. In: BPM 2020 Blockchain and RPA Forum, pp. 35–51 (2020)

23. Pournaghi, S., Bayat, M., Farjami, Y.: MedSBA: a novel and secure scheme to share medical data based on blockchain technology and attribute-based encryption. JAIHC 11, 4613–4641 (2020). https://doi.org/10.1007/s12652-020-01710-y

24. Rahulamathavan, Y., Phan, R.C.W., Rajarajan, M., Misra, S., Kondoz, A.: Privacy-preserving blockchain based IoT ecosystem using attribute-based encryption. In: ANTS, pp. 1–6 (2017)

25. Sahai, A., Waters, B.: Fuzzy identity-based encryption. In: Cramer, R. (ed.) EUROCRYPT 2005. LNCS, vol. 3494, pp. 457–473. Springer, Heidelberg (2005). https://doi.org/10.1007/11426639_27

26. Stiehle, F., Weber, I.: Blockchain for business process enactment: a taxonomy and systematic literature review. In: Marrella, A., et al. (eds.) Business Process Management: Blockchain, Robotic Process Automation, and Central and Eastern Europe Forum, BPM 2022. LNBIP, vol. 459, pp. 5–20. Springer, Cham (2022). https://doi.org/10.1007/978-3-031-16168-1_1

27. Wang, H., Song, Y.: Secure cloud-based EHR system using attribute-based cryptosystem and blockchain. J. Med. Syst. 42(8), 152 (2018). https://doi.org/10.1007/s10916-018-0994-6

28. Weber, I., Xu, X., Riveret, R., Governatori, G., Ponomarev, A., Mendling, J.: Untrusted business process monitoring and execution using blockchain. In: La Rosa, M., Loos, P., Pastor, O. (eds.) BPM 2016. LNCS, vol. 9850, pp. 329–347. Springer, Cham (2016). https://doi.org/10.1007/978-3-319-45348-4_19

29. Wieringa, R., Daneva, M.: Six strategies for generalizing software engineering theories. Sci. Comput. Program. 101, 136–152 (2015)

30. Wood, G.: Ethereum: a secure decentralised generalised transaction ledger (2014)

31. Xu, X., Weber, I., Staples, M.: Architecture for Blockchain Applications. Springer, Switzerland (2019). https://doi.org/10.1007/978-3-030-03035-3

32. Zhang, R., Xue, R., Liu, L.: Security and privacy on blockchain. ACM Comput. Surv. 52(3), 1–34 (2019)

33. Zheng, Z., et al.: An overview on smart contracts: challenges, advances and platforms. Fut. Gener. Comput. Syst. 105, 475–491 (2020)

PADI-web for Plant Health Surveillance

Mathieu Roche[1,3](✉) iD, Julien Rabatel[1] iD, Carlène Trevennec[2,5,6] iD,
and Isabelle Pieretti[1,4,7] iD

[1] CIRAD, 34398 Montpellier, France
{mathieu.roche,julien.rabatel,isabelle.pieretti}@cirad.fr
[2] INRAE, 34398 Montpellier, France
[3] TETIS, Univ Montpellier, AgroParisTech, CIRAD, CNRS, INRAE,
Montpellier, France
[4] PHIM, Univ Montpellier, CIRAD, INRAE, Institut Agro, IRD, Montpellier, France
[5] ASTRE, Univ Montpellier, CIRAD, INRAE, Montpellier, France
carlene.trevennec@cirad.fr
[6] Plateforme Nationale d'Épidémiosurveillance en Santé Animale,
Montpellier, France
[7] Plateforme Nationale d'Épidémiosurveillance en Santé Végétale,
Montpellier, France

Abstract. Due to the increasing number of new and reemerging pests resulting from intensification, globalisation and climate change, monitoring of plant health is crucial. In this context, outbreak detection in digital media could be useful for improving plant disease surveillance. But manually extracting relevant information from unofficial sources is time-consuming. The Platform for Automated extraction of Disease Information from the web (PADI-web) has been developed initially for animal health surveillance, and recently for plant disease surveillance. In order to identify relevant news and information with this new PADI-web instance dedicated to plant health, machine learning approaches and language models (RoBERTa) have been integrated for monitoring plant diseases. This paper presents the PADI-web algorithms and visualisations implemented for specific case studies (i.e. Xylella fastidiosa and Fusarium Oxysporum Tropical) using text-mining approaches tuned on the plant disease domain.

Keywords: Epidemic intelligence · Event-based surveillance · Web monitoring · Text mining · Plant health

We thank Rémy Decoupes (INRAE, TETIS) for the recommendations regarding language models fine-tuned with labeled data manually built by the authors and/or provided by the French General Directorate for Food (DGAL) and the French Plant Health Surveillance Platform (ESV Platform). This study was partially funded by EU grant 874850 MOOD. This work has also been funded by DGAL and the French National Research Agency under the Investments for the Future Program: ANR-16-CONV-0004 (#DigitAg) and 20-PCPA-0002 (BEYOND project).

1   Introduction

Global disease outbreak detection and monitoring rely on official sources, such as intergovernmental organizations, as well as digital media and other unofficial outlets. Manually extracting relevant information from unofficial sources is time-consuming. The Platform for Automated extraction of Disease Information from the web (PADI-web) is an automated biosurveillance system devoted to online news source monitoring for the detection of emerging/new animal infectious diseases by the French Epidemic Intelligence System.

In the field of plant health, surveillance involves gathering information from diverse sources (e.g. field observations, official reports, records from the literature and public databases, online media). A recent study retrospectively examined three online data aggregators, including data from social networks, to identify key information for two plant pest species [4]. The study concludes that web-based information, although unstructured in format, is abundant, promising and complementary to official information for the detection of weak signals, i.e. early warning information of low intensity but likely to become important. For collecting and identifying epidemiological information into unofficial and unstructured data (i.e. news, social media, etc.) in the context of animal and/or plant health, Event-Based Surveillance (EBS) systems (e.g. MedISys, GPHIN, HealthMap, etc.) have been proposed [3,5]. In this context, PADI-web[1] [5] automatically collects news via customized multilingual queries, classifies them and extracts epidemiological information. This tool was mainly developed for animal disease surveillance, but a new version of PADI-web is dedicated to plant health to address the One Health context. This new instance of this tool that contains 8900 news collected is available at the following address: https://plant.padi-web.cirad.fr (see Fig. 1 that highlights data collected with PADI-web).

The rest of the paper is organized as follows. Section 2 presents the PADI-web pipeline and the new implementations integrated into this platform. Section 3 describes the experimental setup and the obtained results. Finally, Sect. 4 concludes and highlights future perspectives.

2   New Methods Implemented into PADI-web

2.1   The PADI-web Pipeline

PADI-web collects news articles based on Google News due to its international coverage and flexible RSS feeds. Moreover, specific sources (e.g., https://medisys.newsbrief.eu/, https://emm.newsbrief.eu/) have been integrated to improve the coverage of the news collection for plant disease surveillance. To detect news dealing with dedicated diseases (i.e., diseases caused by *Xylella fastidiosa* and *Fusarium oxysporum* f. sp. *cubense* Tropical Race 4), the RSS feeds use specific keywords (e.g., disease names, association of terms on hosts and symptoms). For plant diseases the keywords used are "Xylella" for *Xylella fastidiosa* and "FOC

---
[1]   https://www.padi-web-one-health.org.

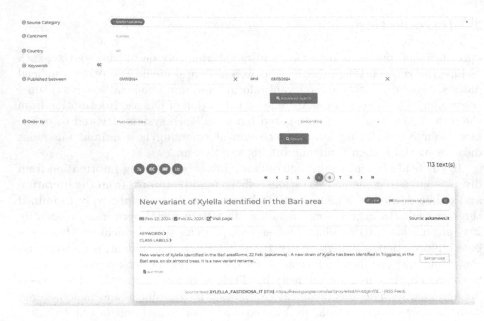

Fig. 1. Examples of text collected with PADI-web dealing with Xylella fastidiosa disease - 01/01/2024-03/03/2024

TR4", "FOC RT4", "Fusarium Oxysporum", "Fusarium Oxysporum Tropical" and "Fusarium Oxysporum Cubense" for *Fusarium Oxysporum Tropical*.

The collected news items are automatically classified as "relevant" or "irrelevant" using machine learning techniques. The relevant news corresponds to recent or current infectious plant health events. Moreover, a more fine-grained classification of documents using machine learning approaches and/or language models has been implemented to highlight more accurate topics. To identify key pieces of epidemiological information in the news (i.e., location, date of outbreaks, affected hosts, etc.), PADI-web integrates information extraction (IE) methods. Finally, our system proposes automatic notifications to end-users. To sum-up, the PADI-web pipeline involves 5 steps ranging from online news collection to the extraction of epidemiological features: (1) data collection, (2) data processing, (3) data classification, (4) information extraction, (5) visualization and user notification.

The next section details new methods recently integrated into the PADI-web tool regarding data classification (step 3) and visualization/notification (step 5). The other steps are detailed in [5].

2.2   The PADI-web Classification for Plant Disease Surveillance

The objective of classification is to identify collected texts dealing with plant disease outbreaks and associated information. The first step for applying classification to new articles is to train a classification model by exploiting previously user-labeled articles. Note that all texts that are not in English are automatically translated into English using the *Microsoft Azure* tool.

For simple classification tasks (e.g. classifying an article as relevant or not) PADI-web includes a fully automated pipeline to use articles labeled by users within PADI-web and train new models. For most complex tasks (e.g. topic classification) it is also possible to import externally trained classification models.

For the fully automated classification training integrated to PADI-web, the following process is implemented:

– **Training datasets construction.** For each kind of classification (e.g., relevance classification), a distinct model is trained. A set of articles (the amount is defined in the application configuration) is selected in random order. The obtained subset of articles defines the training dataset.
– **Training dataset pre-processing.** To exploit the training datasets for the classification models, the data must be pre-processed and converted into a format that is well-adapted to the classification training step. The data format includes the following article database fields: text, title, source domain and RSS feed. For textual data (text and title fields), the TfidfVectorizer scikit-learn[2] class is used to convert them into a vector of features with TF-IDF (Term Frequency - Inverse Document Frequency) criterion to give a discriminative weight to the linguistic features. For each categorical variable (source domain and RSS feed), some dummy variables are built instead (i.e., each distinct value on the field is replaced by a distinct boolean feature). A feature selection process reduces the total number of features to 200 by applying the SelectKBest class of scikit-learn.
– **Training for supervised machine learning.** A selection of more than 10 supervised machine learning models are trained on the datasets. These models include Random Forests (with various parameters), Linear Support Vector Classification, Neural networks, Gaussian-based models, K-nearest neighbors, etc. For each model, a cross-validation scheme is applied and the accuracy score for each fold is computed (the fold number is defined in the application settings, default is 5). The best model is considered to be the one with the highest mean accuracy score along the folds. Once the best model is selected, it is trained on the whole dataset (until now, it was only trained on separate folds). This model will later be used to classify new articles.
– **Classifying texts.** Each new article created through the scraping process is classified for each classification task based on the selected models. The results of the conducted experiments are summarized in Sect. 3.

For topic classification (i.e. classifying articles into a set of predefined topics), another model has been trained outside of the automatic training pipeline described above and imported into PADI-web. A language model called RoBERTa (Robustly Optimized BERT Pretraining Approach) [2] is used. It is based on the BERT (Bidirectional Encoder Representations from Transformers) [1] model, which is designed to pre-train deep bidirectional representations from

---

[2] https://scikit-learn.org/.

unlabeled text by jointly conditioning on both left and right context in all layers. The pre-trained model can be fine-tuned with additional output layers for specific tasks, such as topic classification issues implemented into PADI-web.

As this model is trained outside of PADI-web, the training process is not described here. The model is imported into PADI-web and used to classify new articles. Its use and results are summarized in Sect. 3.

2.3 New Spatial Visualization Integrated into PADI-web

Mapping disease events is commonly used in epidemiology to monitor the incidence and prevalence of pathogens in specific territories, to detect incursion in new areas or to get a better understanding of disease spatial patterns. Interactive maps and automatic clustering allow for various levels of precision and adjustment according to the objective of the epidemiologist. When dealing with official outbreak data, maps are very useful tools to monitor disease events and assist decision makers to assess, prevent and mitigate the risk.

The spatial extraction process integrated into PADI-web is based on a named entity recognition tool, i.e. spaCy[3], and the geocoding step to provide spatial coordinates is supported by the Geonames API[4]. PADI-web provides a feature to generate maps in order to visualize the geographical data contained in the articles. A map can be generated with the "Generate Map" button. It displays markers on the world map for the articles that are returned by the current search criteria. The map generation can be customized with the following options:

- **Only show article countries.** If checked, only one marker per article is shown, and this marker corresponds to the country that has been automatically associated with each article (See Fig. 2). To address this issue, in each article, the most frequently mentioned country when considering all locations (i.e., cities, regions, countries) is selected.
  If unchecked (See Fig. 3), all spatial information extracted from each article in the search is displayed on the map. There are therefore many more markers, potentially noisy (i.e. false positives), but the information is sometimes much more precise (i.e. cities, areas, regions, etc.).
  If the users check the button "Clusters", nearby markers on the map are grouped together as clusters. The user can click on a cluster to zoom in and explore it.
- **Exclude countries and continents.** When the "Only show article countries" box is unchecked, all types of places found are displayed, from the most specific to the most general (cities, areas, rivers, regions, countries, continents, etc.). Checking this box prevents markers for countries and continents from being displayed, as they are sometimes considered too general to be of interest on the map.

---

[3] https://spacy.io/.
[4] https://www.geonames.org/.

Individual markers on the map display several pieces of information: For instance the color stands for the number of articles that are contained in the corresponding location (the darker a map marker, the most articles it contains).

Clicking on a map marker displays a pop-up window with the list of associated articles (See Fig. 4). Each article is a link to the article's Web page. The source language of the article is shown at the right of the article link between parentheses. The header of the pop-up window for a map marker contains (from left to right) the name of the map marker location, the number of articles associated with this location, and a search icon. This icon only exists when the "Only show article countries" is checked. If clicked, the current search is filtered to only show articles associated with this country.

Fig. 2. Examples of texts collected with PADI-web dealing with Xylella fastidiosa - 01/01/2024-03/03/2024 - Option 'Only show article countries' selected

Fig. 3. Examples of texts collected with PADI-web dealing with Xylella fastidiosa - 01/01/2024-03/03/2024 - Option 'Only show article countries' not selected

3   Experiments

Each article collected by PADI-web is classified on two levels: The first one determines whether the article is relevant or not, and the second one detects the topics of interest addressed within the article content.

Fig. 4. Examples of text collected with PADI-web dealing with Xylella fastidiosa - 01/01/2024-03/03/2024 - articles associated with Italy

3.1   Relevance Classification

Relevance classification is a binary classification task that determines whether an article is of interest to the platform. It is performed using a Random Forest Classifier (RFC) trained on a dataset of 257 annotated articles. The RFC has been experimentally selected as the best for this task among the classifier types described in Sect. 2.2. Its accuracy score is 0.79 in a 5-fold cross-validation process. Relevance classification uses a Random Forest Classifier, which is fast to train and use while providing good performance. This choice is made because the relevance classification model can be retrained very frequently to take into account the new articles that users of the platform can annotate daily. Therefore, the model has to be fast to train without using a lot of server resources.

3.2   Topic Classification

Each relevant article collected by PADI-web is then classified into one of the eight categories (listed in Table 1) defined by the experts to detect the topics addressed within the article content. Topic classification is a harder task than relevance classification, so a more complex model has been used to perform it.

Experts have annotated a curated dataset of 6173 texts to train a binary classification model for each category, with two classes *yes* and *no* indicating whether the article belongs to the category. The dataset is split into two parts: a training dataset (80% of the whole dataset) and an evaluation dataset (20% of the whole dataset). The classification uses a RoBERTa model [2] that has been fine-tuned on the annotated dataset to build a new classifier. RoBERTa is based on the BERT model [1] and has been optimized for training on large corpora. The performance metrics computed on the evaluation dataset are reported in Table 1 for each category. Note that the precision and recall metrics are calculated as a weighted average over the two classes of each classification task.

Table 1. Results of topic classification with RoBERTa

Class	Accuracy	Precision	Recall
Communication/popularization	0.85	0.84	0.85
Genetic and molecular scale	0.90	0.89	0.90
Health statuses and interceptions	0.87	0.86	0.87
Fighting measures	0.85	0.84	0.85
Methods of analysis and detection	0.97	0.96	0.97
Regulation	0.94	0.88	0.94
Epidemiological, socio-economic and environmental risk	0.96	0.95	0.96
Monitoring	0.89	0.80	0.89

4   Conclusion

Epidemic intelligence integrates two components: indicator-based (e.g. official disease reports), and event-based surveillance (EBS) which looks at reports, stories, rumours, and other information about health events. Because they are based on published reports which take time to produce and lack geographical precision, EBS tools may monitor digital media and other unofficial outlets. In this context, a new instance of an automated biosurveillance system called PADI-web has been proposed for plant health surveillance. This paper presents new contributions based on the use of language models (RoBERTa) for topic classification and spatial visualisations to enhance the result analysis. These new approaches are generic, they are also integrated into the PADI-web platform dedicated to animal disease surveillance.

In future work, we plan to evaluate how these visualisations and language model methods can improve the identification of (i) weak signals and (ii) duplication of events. Moreover, syndromic surveillance tasks implemented for animal health monitoring could be integrated (with specific RSS feeds and keywords associated with) in order to identify unknown plant diseases (i.e. disease X).

References

1. Devlin, J., Chang, M.W., Lee, K., Toutanova, K.: BERT: Pre-training of deep bidirectional transformers for language understanding (2018). arXiv:1810.04805
2. Liu, Y., et al.: RoBERTa: a robustly optimized BERT pretraining approach. arXiv, 1907.11692 (2019)
3. Roberts, S.L.: Signals, signs and syndromes: tracing [digital] transformations in European health security. Eur. J. Risk Regul. **10**(4), 722–737 (2019)
4. Tateosian, L.G., Saffer, A., Walden-Schreiner, C., Shukunobe, M.: Plant pest invasions, as seen through news and social media. Comput. Environ. Urban Syst. **100**, 101922 (2023). https://doi.org/10.1016/j.compenvurbsys.2022.101922
5. Valentin, S., et al.: PADI-web 3.0: a new framework for extracting and disseminating fine-grained information from the news for animal disease surveillance. One Health **13**, 100357 (2021). https://doi.org/10.1016/j.onehlt.2021.100357

PROMISE: A Framework for Model-Driven Stateful Prompt Orchestration

Wenyuan Wu[1]([✉]), Jasmin Heierli[2], Max Meisterhans[2], Adrian Moser[2],
Andri Färber[2], Mateusz Dolata[1]([✉]), Elena Gavagnin[2]([✉]), Alexandre
de Spindler[2]([✉]), and Gerhard Schwabe[1]([✉])

[1] University of Zurich, Zürich, Switzerland
{wenyuan,dolata,schwabe}@ifi.uzh.ch
[2] Zurich University of Applied Sciences, Winterthur, Switzerland
{heej,meix,mosa,faer,gava,desa}@zhaw.ch

Abstract. The advent of increasingly powerful language models has raised expectations for conversational interactions. However, controlling these models is a challenge, emphasizing the need to be able to investigate the feasibility and value of their application. We present PROMISE (Available at: https://github.com/zhaw-iwi/promise), a framework that facilitates the development of complex conversational interactions with information systems. Its use of state machine modeling concepts enables model-driven, dynamic prompt orchestration across hierarchically nested states and transitions. This improves the control of language models' behavior and thus enables their effective and efficient use. We show the applications of PROMISE in health information systems and demonstrate its ability to handle complex interactions.

Keywords: Framework · Prompt Orchestration · Language Models

1 Introduction

Natural language-based interactions are gaining importance within health information systems [5,6], showing promise in achieving key medical objectives. For example, patient treatment has been shown to benefit from medical consultations where treatment goals are discussed, patient concerns are addressed and the physician-patient relationship is strengthened by compassionate communication [7]. This entails interactions involving several successive, alternating and possibly nested conversation threads, all of which are typically infused with persuasion and empathy. Consequently, if a system is to have a similar treatment benefit between consultations, it must allow such complex conversational interactions for the collection, processing and provision of information.

While the recent advent of more powerful language models (LM) promises novel and advanced interactions, more progress must be made in supporting LM

© The Author(s), under exclusive license to Springer Nature Switzerland AG 2024
S. Islam and A. Sturm (Eds.): CAiSE 2024, LNBIP 520, pp. 157–165, 2024.
https://doi.org/10.1007/978-3-031-61000-4_18

application development [3]. Training LMs from scratch to serve a specific purpose is resource-intensive, often impractical, and fine-tuning demands meticulous data preparation, making fast, iterative experimentation difficult.

Prompt engineerng provides an efficient method for behavior control [4,9] by carefully designed prompts. However, this alone cannot ensure consistent LM behavior in complex interactions, although many prompting techniques have been developed [1,8]. Overly detailed prompts that cover the entire interaction risk confusing sequences or levels, and overly broad prompts risk missing expected responses. We therefore follow the idea of segmenting complex interactions into a sequence of more specific tasks which was shown to enhance control and predictability while harnessing LM capabilities [2].

PROMISE (Prompt-Orchestrating Model-driven Interaction State Engineering) [10] is a framework designed to facilitate the development of complex conversational interactions with LMs, which employs an extended state model to meet diverse interaction requirements, ensuring effective LM utilization. This paper outlines the motivation, presents the PROMISE interaction model, demonstrates its applicability as a preliminary validation, and concludes with key insights.

2   Motivation

The assistant-patient interaction shown in Fig. 1 exemplifies the need to achieve multiple goals wihin one single interaction. It is initiated due to a patient's failure to complete a therapy activity (swimming). The first goal of this interaction is to obtain a reason for the patient's omission (light grey) and the second goal is to arrange adaptations in order to increase the patient's adherence (dark grey).

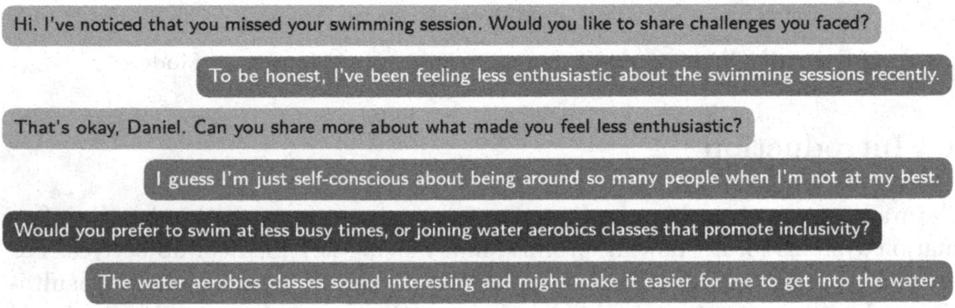

Hi. I've noticed that you missed your swimming session. Would you like to share challenges you faced?

To be honest, I've been feeling less enthusiastic about the swimming sessions recently.

That's okay, Daniel. Can you share more about what made you feel less enthusiastic?

I guess I'm just self-conscious about being around so many people when I'm not at my best.

Would you prefer to swim at less busy times, or joining water aerobics classes that promote inclusivity?

The water aerobics classes sound interesting and might make it easier for me to get into the water.

Fig. 1. Multi-State Interaction: First (Light Gray) & Second (Dark) State (Color figure online)

To support the suggestion of adaptations once a reason for omision is provided by the patient, the reason must be extracted. For example, the following JSON object should be extracted from the first four utterances shown in Fig. 1.

```
{"activity": "swimming session", "reason": "self-conscious about
    being around people when not at best"}
```

Using the extracted reason, appropriate adaptations such as

```
["choose less busy times to swim at the public pool.","water
    aerobics classes with more inclusive atmosphere."]
```

can be retrieved from a medical knowledge base, presented to the patient, and the interaction ends when they made their choice.

While the utterances produced by the assistant demonstrate the benefit of using an LM to generate them, challenges arise when controlling an LM with a single prompt: Following multiple goals requires the ability to consistently distinguish interaction phases, and to appropriately transition between phases according to specified characteristics of the conversation. The integration with knowledge bases requires the ability to comprehensively extract information from specific conversation segments, and to inject information into others. Furthermore, patients can ask additional questions or indicate that they no longer wish to interact at any time, which the system must handle appropriately. Overall, the assistant should use open-ended questions and empathetic dialog to create a supportive environment while incorporating targeted persuasion strategies.

With PROMISE, we are addressing these challenges by supporting the use of simpler, more precise and more reliable prompts, while providing the means to transparently orchestrate these prompts dynamically during an interaction.

3   PROMISE Interaction Model

Figure 2 shows a simple daily check-in interaction between patients and a health information system, which we use as an introductory example to explain the extended state model used in PROMISE.

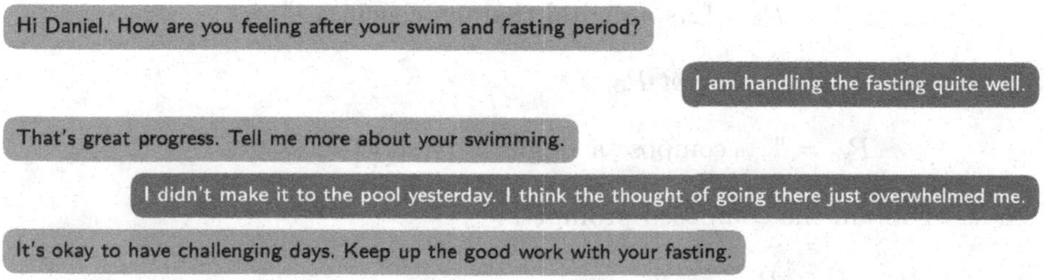

> Hi Daniel. How are you feeling after your swim and fasting period?
>
> I am handling the fasting quite well.
>
> That's great progress. Tell me more about your swimming.
>
> I didn't make it to the pool yesterday. I think the thought of going there just overwhelmed me.
>
> It's okay to have challenging days. Keep up the good work with your fasting.

Fig. 2. Single-State Interaction: System (Gray) & User (Blue) (Color figure online)

PROMISE supports including patient data from their electronic health record (EHR) to have a personalized conversation, e.g., by addressing the patient by their name and asking about their perceived progress regarding their therapy activities. PROMISE also supports empathetic dialog and the use of persuassion strategies. Notably, it provides a means of ending an interaction based on defined conditions during the conversation. In this case, the interaction is designed to end when there is enough information about the patient's adherence and well-being.

Finally, the end of the interaction is designed to summarize the conversation in a specific form, such as a JSON object as shown in the previous Sect. 2.

Figure 3 shows the state machine model of this interaction. It consists of a single state in the middle, an initial node on the left, and a final node on the right. Transitions lead from the initial node to the state, and from the state to the final node. Transitions optionally depend on triggers and guards, and actions are executed when followed.

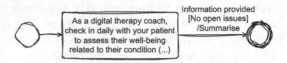

Fig. 3. Single-State Model

The state is annotated with the *state prompt* "As a digital therapy coach, ..." which will be used to control the LM while the interaction is in that state. The outgoing transition that leads to the final node is annotated with prompts indicated by "Information provided", "No open issues", and "Summarise". These prompts control the LM when evaluating the conversation concerning transition triggers, guards, and actions. As shown next, PROMISE transparently composes more complex prompts from simple prompts attached to states and transitions.

When the interaction is started, the initial node is used to identify its first state. In this state, PROMISE will create a *composed prompt* P_c by concatenating the state prompt P_s

$$P_s = \text{"As a digital therapy coach,} \ldots \text{"}$$

with the *state opening prompt* P_{so}

$$P_{so} = \text{"} \ldots \text{compose a single, very short message} \ldots$$

such as to obtain the composed prompt P_c

$$P_c = P_s + P_{so}$$
$$= \text{"As a digital therapy coach,} \ldots \text{compose a single,} \ldots \text{"}$$

The state opening prompt is an optional extension of the state prompt to be used if the state is set to start the conversation, as is the case in this example. Any prompt can be enriched with placeholders that are filled at runtime. For example, the placeholder {patient} in the state prompt "As a digital therapy coach, ... Meet {patient}." will be replaced with patient data from the EHR.

The composed prompt P_c is then used to instruct the LM. In the conversation above, the LM completion returned the utterance "Hi Daniel. How are you feeling today after your ..." which opens the conversation with the patient.

Upon every utterance from the patient, such as the first utterance, "I'm doing quite well ...", all outgoing transitions are checked before the LM is used to generate a response to the patient. First, the list of *state utterances* U_s^t, which represents the conversation held in this state so far, is extended with the incoming *user utterance* u_u as follows.

$$U_s^{t+1} = U_s^t + u_u$$
$$= [\text{"Hi Daniel. How are you ... ", "I'm doing quite well ... "}]$$

Then, to check a transition, its *trigger prompt* P_t and *guard prompt* P_g are used to obtain decisions from the LM about whether or not the transition should be followed, and the *action prompt* P_a is used to execute the action if it is followed. All these prompts may contain placeholders or consist of code instead of prompts. For example, in the case of a transition trigger, the composed prompt

$$P_c = P_t + U_s^{t+1}$$
$$= \text{"Examine the conversation ... , decide if ... patient provided ... "}$$
$$+ [\text{"Hi Daniel. How are you ... ", "I'm doing quite well ... "}]$$

is created to let the LM decide whether the conversation so far contains indications that the patient provided the expected information about their adherence and well-being. While the first patient response talks about fasting, no swimming information has been mentioned so far. Consequently, this transition trigger does not pass, and the interaction stays in the current state.

Multiple decisions may be attached to a single transition. In our example, a second decision serves as a transition guard, and instructs the LM to decide whether there are no open issues mentioned by the patient that should prevent the current interaction from being concluded unexpectedly.

If the interaction remains in the current state, the state prompt and utterances collected so far are included in the newly composed prompt

$$P_c = P_s + U_s^{t+1}$$
$$= \text{"As a digital therapy coach, ... "}$$
$$+ [\text{"Hi Daniel. How are you ... ", "I'm doing quite well ... "}]$$

which is used to obtain the subsequent response to the patient from the LM, appending to the state utterances. As seen in the example interaction above, the conversation therefore stays in the same state as long as the expected information is incomplete. If all information is provided, the conversation moves to the subsequent state attached to the transition. In this example, the subsequent state is a final state, where the interaction ends with a goodbye message.

Transitions may include multiple actions that contain a prompt or code. In our example, the action is a prompt with which the composed prompt

$$P_c = P_a + U_s$$
$$= \text{"Summarize the conversation ... in JSON format."}$$
$$+ [\text{"Hi Daniel. How ... ", ... , " ... again tomorrow."}]$$

is created and used to instruct the LM to summarise the information provided by the patient for the attending physician's review. The generated summary is stored in interaction storage and thus made available either to any other state, transition decision or action, or to any other information system component, such as the physician's dashboard.

Figure 4 shows the state machine modeling the conversational interaction shown in Fig. 1. It includes three novelties compared to the previous simple interaction: 1) there are multiple states following up on each other, 2) special-purpose states are involved, and 3) there is an outer state containing a sequence of inner states.

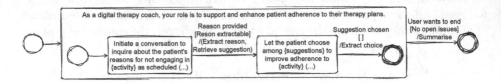

Fig. 4. Multi-State Model

First, the ability to create state sequences follows from the ability to make transitions. In this example, the interaction starts with a state assessing the patient's reasoning for missing the swimming activity. When the patient gives a sufficient reason, the interaction transitions to the next state in which options are presented. Once the patient has chosen one of these options, the interaction transitions to the final node. Any state may have arbitrarily many outgoing transitions — each triggered and guarded by decisions and accompanied by actions — that each point to a state, thus supporting different interaction flows. This supports the creation of a directed and also cyclic graph of states.

Second, PROMISE includes a library of special-purpose states that address recurring requirements. For example, an *Activity Gap Inquiry State* obtains the patient's reasons for missing the activity. To instantiate, developers simply provide the activity that was missed. Similarly, a *Single Choice State* assumes a list of choices to be made available to the patient. Such states encapsulate pre-defined prompts and transitions, effectively reducing development efforts. The library also contains states, decisions and actions that support retrieval augmented generation, e.g. for querying documents, databases or other knowledge bases and merging query results into state and transition prompts.

The third novelty relates to PROMISE's ability to support nested conversations by specifying state machines which may behave at different levels — seemingly simultaneously. In our example, the patient may indicate they want to pause or stop interacting at any state of the inner interaction. With PROMISE, an outer state follows the complete conversation within all inner states as it maintains its own utterances covering all its inner states. Therefore, each transition attached to an outer state reacts to a more extensive interaction segment when making decisions or performing actions.

Moreover, if an outer state has its own state prompt, this prompt is automatically appended to the state prompts of all its inner states. In the current example, the role prompt "As a digital therapy coach, ..." is attached to the outer state, and therefore it does not need to be repeated among all inner states. This enables developers to specify partial conversational behaviors that affect more expansive segments, e.g., to apply particular persuasion strategies.

4   Validation

This section demonstrates the PROMISE framework's practical applicability by showcasing the feasibility of bringing complex interactions to reality. Figure 5 is a simplified version of a multi-layered coaching conversation. Utterances of a simulated patient are colored in light grey, and coaching utterances are colored in dark grey. The transparent transitions between the different states make the interaction seamless for the physician.

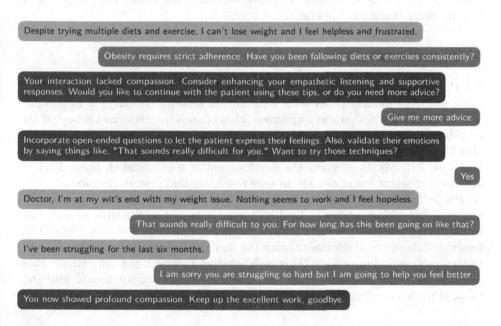

Fig. 5. Multi-Layered Interaction: Simulation (Light Gray) & Coaching (Dark) (Color figure online)

Figure 6 shows a state machine specifying this conversational interaction. The inner machine contains a state in which the simulation takes place, from which a transition triggered by a demonstration of compassion leads to a debriefing state where the physician's achievement is acknowledged. An outer state will trigger an intervention if a lack of compassion is detected in this inner machine.

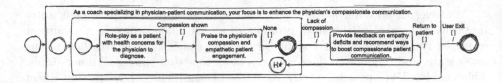

Fig. 6. Model for Medical Consultation Coach

As a result, the interaction transitions from the outer state to the feedback state, calling out and giving advice. This feedback state has a transition pointing back to the outer state containing the simulation. Notably, this transition points to a history node $H*$. This means that the interaction is automatically picked up at the state that was last active when the conversation left the outer state.

Such a cyclic alignment of states and transitions, combined with nested states and history nodes, effectively supports the design of complex conversational interactions such as multi-layered conversations. This could not be provided reliably using single prompts only.

5   Conclusion

PROMISE addresses the gap in developing complex conversational interactions using language models (LM) with information systems. It offers a framework that simplifies the design and implementation of such interactions through state modeling, enhancing LM predictability and leveraging their capabilities for complex interactions. Due to the expressiveness of the underlying state modeling language, PROMISE supports the development of sophisticated, layered interactions that adapt transparently to user responses and system decisions.

PROMISE has been effectively applied and tested in various projects, tackling challenges from improving health literacy in young adults with hearing loss to improving patient treatment adherence and tax morale. Notably, PROMISE fosters collaborative development, allowing domain experts to engage deeply with the interaction design process. This collaborative approach not only streamlines development but also ensures that the resulting interactions are meaningful and tailored to specific domain needs.

References

1. Fernando, C., Banarse, D., Michalewski, H., Osindero, S., Rocktäschel, T.: Promptbreeder: Self-referential self-improvement via prompt evolution (2023). arXiv:2309.16797
2. Helland, S., Gavagnin, E., de Spindler, A.: Divide et impera: multi-transformer architectures for complex NLP-tasks. In: Proceedings of of Swiss Text Analytics Conference (2022) (in press)
3. Kaddour, J., Harris, J., Mozes, M., Bradley, H., Raileanu, R., McHardy, R.: Challenges and applications of large language models (2023). arXiv:2307.10169

4. Korzynski, P., Mazurek, G., Krzypkowska, P., Kurasinski, A.: Artificial intelligence prompt engineering as a new digital competence: analysis of generative AI technologies such as ChatGPT. Entrepreneurial Bus. Econ. Rev. **11**(3), 25–37 (2023)
5. Peng, C., et al.: A study of generative large language model for medical research and healthcare. NPJ Digital Med. **6**(1), 210 (2023)
6. Song, H., et al.: Evaluating the performance of different large language models on health consultation and patient education in urolithiasis. J. Med. Syst. **47**(1), 125 (2023)
7. Stephens, E., et al.: Complex conversations in a healthcare setting: experiences from an interprofessional workshop on clinician-patient communication skills. BMC Med. Educ. **21**(1), 343 (2021)
8. Wei, J., et al.: Chain-of-thought prompting elicits reasoning in large language models. In: Proceedings of Conference on Neural Information Processing Systems (2022)
9. White, J., et al.: A prompt pattern catalog to enhance prompt engineering with ChatGPT (2023). arXiv:2302.11382
10. Wu, W., et al.: Promise: A framework for developing complex conversational interactions (technical report) (2024). arXiv:2312.03699

Author Index

S. Islam and A. Sturm (Eds.): CAiSE 2024, LNBIP 520, pp. 167–168, 2024.
https://doi.org/10.1007/978-3-031-61000-4

Printed in the United States
by Baker & Taylor Publisher Services

Printed in the United States
by Baker & Taylor Publisher Services